IMPACT
PREACHING

IMPACT
PREACHING

A CASE FOR
THE **ONE-POINT**
EXPOSITORY
SERMON

JIM L. **WILSON**, R. GREGG **WATSON**,
MICHAEL **KUYKENDALL**, & DAVID **JOHNSON**

LEXHAM PRESS

Impact Preaching: A Case for the One-Point Expository Sermon
© 2018 by Jim L. Wilson, Gregg Watson, R. Michael Kuykendall, and David Johnson

Lexham Press, 1313 Commercial St., Bellingham, WA 98225
LexhamPress.com

First edition by Weaver Book Company.

Print ISBN 9781683592105
Digital ISBN 9781683592112

Cover design: Frank Gutbrod
Interior Design: Nicholas Richardson

*To the Faculty
and
Students
at Gateway Seminary*

Contents

Foreword

The student sat in front of his homiletics professor and asked, "Prof, how many points should a sermon have?" To which the professor responded immediately: "At least one."

The correct answer is "exactly one." While sermons can and should offer multiple insights about the particular biblical text being preached, there should be only one core idea, lest the sermon wander off in multiple directions. We can have many so-called points in our messages, but there should be one point that forms the basis around which the entire sermon is grown.

Whether you call it the proposition or thesis, the Big Idea as Haddon Robinson coined it, the Take Home Truth à la Donald Sunukjian, or some other term, the wise expositor understands that there needs to be a single driving idea that is the essential principle taught by the text and becomes the foundation of the sermon. This gives unity to the entire message.

The goal of the expositor should be to construct a message in such a way that all its features support a single main idea, and that requires discipline on the part of the preacher. We are tempted to throw in lots of interesting asides and travel some fascinating side roads, but those detours can too easily shift our listeners away from the key biblical truth that we are trying to help them understand.

In *Impact Preaching*, Jim Wilson and a team of scholars remind us of that key truth and then provide a treasure-chest of insights about approaching various biblical genres and creating one-point sermons that faithfully proclaim those texts. Preachers will find an array of sermonic tools to aid them in understanding and using the one-point expository preaching model, from the Old Testament prophets to the book of Revelation.

Of particular value, Wilson and his co-authors focus their attention on the preaching of biblical narrative. This is an area where many preachers struggle because the "three points and a poem" model learned in many a homiletics classroom simply doesn't do justice to the great biblical narratives of both Old and New Testaments. The authors guide their readers through the process of understanding a biblical narrative and then shaping it into a powerful, effective sermon.

As Harold Bryson has observed, "A sermon needs to have a point before it has points. The points need to relate to the point." Wilson and his colleagues have produced a useful and practical book that helps us make the point with power.

MICHAEL DUDUIT, PhD
Executive Editor, *Preaching* magazine
Dean, Clamp Divinity School, Anderson University
Anderson, South Carolina

Preface

On March 14, 2013, I presented a convocation address to the faculty and students of Golden Gate Baptist Theological Seminary (now called Gateway Seminary of the Southern Baptist Convention) on the subject "Expository Preaching: What Is the Point?" It was my first public attempt at making a case for the one-point expository sermon.

I thought my yearlong research on the subject would conclude when I delivered the address. It did not. That surprised me. However, what surprised me even more was the change the academic research would have on my preaching.

While my primary work as Professor of Leadership Formation involves teaching leadership and preaching seminars to Doctor of Ministry candidates, I do preach almost as much as when I was a full-time senior pastor. As I applied what I was learning, I began to notice a change. Something was different—my preaching was having a greater impact than before.

That change motivated me to dig deeper.

I had the opportunity to publish my thoughts in chapter 7 of *Pastoral Ministry in the Real World: Loving, Teaching, and Leading God's People*, but I knew that the treatment was incomplete—a single chapter and a few sample sermons was not enough to make a case. I approached those who would become my co-authors about working with me to advance the concept. Being aware of what I do not know, I turned to hermeneutics professors to work beside me. Jim Weaver quickly accepted my proposal to expand chapter 7 of *Pastoral Ministry* into a stand-alone book.

The pages that follow are the result of a collaboration of colleagues. The biblical scholars who co-authored the book with me contributed the first draft of the chapters in part two.[1] We worked together as I rewrote the material and added sample sermons. They graciously allowed me to edit their words to maintain a consistent voice through the book and gave appropriate feedback on how I could improve the sample sermons in the chapter. We conducted an in-house peer review, allowing all co-authors to suggest improvements on each other's works. We also gave early copies to Gateway DMin candidates and MDiv students to provide feedback and make suggestions for improvement. With the help of these members of the Gateway community, I present this case for the one-point expository sermon.

I pray that this book will help you preach God's Word with the exact meaning and full impact of the text intact.

JIM L. WILSON
Hemet, CA
May 13, 2017

---

1. Gregg Watson is my co-author for chapters 4, 5, 6, 7, and 8. Michael Kuykendall is my co-author for chapters 9 and 11. David Johnson is my co-author for chapter 10.

Acknowledgments

Thank you to Dr. D. Michael Martin, Vice President of Academic Services, for creating a collegial environment where cross-disciplinary collaboration is possible.

Thank you to our colleagues, Dr. J. T. Reed, Dr. Steve Long, and Joe Slunaker, who contributed sermons as examples of one-point expository preaching.

Thank you to my research assistants, Dr. Ben Pate and Dr. Derick Wilson for their research, feedback, and copyediting.

Thank you to our colleague Dr. Paul Kelly and to the DMin candidates, MDiv students, and DMin office staff who read early versions of the manuscript and provided helpful feedback.

Understanding
Impact Preaching

──────────────────{ C H A P T E R   1 }──────────────────

Impact Preaching

S ermons are a bridge between *then* and *now*. Paul's admonition to
Timothy "to preach the word; be ready in season and out of season; reprove, rebuke, and exhort, with complete patience and teaching"
(2 Tim. 4:2 ESV) had a dual orientation: Timothy was to preach a message anchored in the past, but also to people living in his time. Twenty-
first-century preachers experience that same challenge.

THEN AND NOW

This nimble shifting between *then* and *now* is central to the preacher's
task. Donald Sunukjian writes, "Specifically, the preacher's task is two-
fold: to present the true and exact meaning of the biblical text ('Look at
what God is saying. . .') in a manner that is relevant to the contemporary
listener ('. . . to us')."[1]

In Sunukjian's construct, the meaning comes from the *then* domain;
the choices of the communication processes and the communication itself comes from the *now* domain, which is formed by what is "relevant
to the contemporary listener." While this approach is reasonable, perhaps even representing the majority view, there is an alternative worth
considering. Instead of selecting the communication medium solely from
the *now* domain, preachers can also include information from the *then*
domain to help shape the form of their sermons. Certainly, relevance to
the audience (*now* domain) is an important consideration, but it does
not have to be the only one. The literary form of the text (*then* domain)
should also influence the sermonic form.[2]

---

1. Sunukjian, *Invitation to Biblical Preaching*, 9.
2. Rowell and Goetz, *Preaching with Spiritual Passion*, 37: "I believe the sermonic
form should take its cue from textual form."

As an overall approach, the form of the expository sermon can address both the *then* and the *now* if preachers know when to separate and when to blend the two. Extraction of meaning belongs in the *then* domain and communicating the message is in the *now* domain. However, infusing the meaning of the text into sermonic form should use information from the *then* and *now* domains.

DEFINITION OF EXPOSITORY PREACHING

According to Haddon Robinson, "Expository preaching is the communication of a biblical concept derived from and transmitted through a historical, grammatical, and literary study of a passage in its context, which the Holy Spirit first applies to the personality and experience of the preacher, then through the preacher, applies to the hearer."[3] Robinson's definition clarifies how preachers approach their texts and audiences. They approach the text to discover meaning that will flow through them to their congregations in a three-phase communication process: (1) extract meaning from the text, (2) submit to the work of the Holy Spirit as he applies the text to the preacher and then the congregation, and (3) communicate that meaning to the listeners.

MEANING

Extraction of meaning belongs in the *then* domain. The text does not mean one thing to one generation and another thing to another. It does not mean one thing in this cultural setting and another in that one. Gordon Fee and Douglas Stuart say, "*A text cannot mean what it never meant*. Or to put it in a positive way, the true meaning of the biblical text for us is what God originally intended it to mean when it was first spoken."[4] It can only mean what it meant.

Expository preaching begins with the text. Other approaches may begin with a predetermined meaning before approaching the text, but expository preaching does not seek to impose meaning, it demands

---

3. Robinson, *Biblical Preaching*, 21.

4. Fee and Stuart, *How to Read the Bible for All Its Worth*, 30 (emphasis in the original). See also Carson, *Exegetical Fallacies*, 129. Carson argues that those who promote polysemy (the viewpoint that a text has multiple meanings and must be interpreted subjectively) are inconsistent because they expect readers to understand the meaning of their writings and the meaning they intend to convey.

that preachers locate the intent of the author. Sidney Greidanus says, "Respect for the Word of God requires that one do justice to the intent of the text."[5] Brian Chapell states the preacher's task is "to discern what the original writers meant."[6] Alan Jacobs says looking for the authorial intent is "more useful," and Robert Stein calls it the "basic goal."[7]

APPLICATION

The meaning comes from the *then* domain, but the application rests with the interpreter living in the *now* domain. Osborne sees application as a contextualization, whose key "is to seek a fusion of the horizons of both the biblical text and the modern situation."[8] The fusion process takes more than human effort to accomplish. Notice in his definition of expository preaching, Robinson stresses application is the work of the Holy Spirit through the preacher.

BIBLICAL FORM'S RELATIONSHIP TO SERMON FORM

Robinson's definition includes the need to study the genre, literary devices, and structural devices of the passage in developing the expository sermon. (We use the phrase "literary form" in this book to include all of these things.) The primary reason for paying attention to literary form is that it "yields essential clues for rightly interpreting the author's intended meaning of a passage." [9] It is difficult, if not impossible, to interpret a text without considering its literary form. Form affects meaning; it is not an inert container simply holding a proposition in place. Osborne says,

---

5. Greidanus, *Sola Scriptura*, 172.

6. Chapell, *Christ-Centered Preaching*, 77.

7. Jacobs, *Theology of Reading*, 16. Stein, *Interpreting the Bible*, 9.

8. Osborne, *Hermeneutical Spiral*, 426. See also Stein, *Interpreting the Bible*, 44. Stein draws this same distinction but uses a different word than application or contextualization; he speaks of meaning and significance. While a text can have only one meaning, it can be significant in different ways in different settings to different people. After determining the meaning, preachers are then free to find its significance and to preach it contextually to their people.

9. Vogel, *Biblical Genres*, 170–71: "Two observations pertaining to Robinson's definition are in order. First, literary study of a passage is an essential part of the hermeneutic Robinson endorses. Thus, an exegetical method applying this hermeneutic must take account of literary genres and features. Second, not only is the hermeneutic used to guide the interpretation of the text by the preacher in his study, but it also controls the explanation of the text by the preacher in his pulpit."

"Meaning is genre-dependent."[10] The genre controls the rules interpreters use to discover meaning in the text. The chosen literary form will nuance meaning at the least and at the most shape it. Thomas Long writes:

> Texts are not packages containing ideas; they are means of communication. When we ask ourselves what a text means, we are not searching for the idea of the text. We are trying to discover its total impact upon a reader—and everything about a text works together to create that impact. We may casually speak of the form and the content of a text as if they were two separate realities, but if "content" is used as a synonym for "meaning," the form must be seen as a vital part of the content.[11]

How vital is their relationship? Form and meaning are inseparable.[12] They are conjoined twins who share the same heart.

Studying the literary form can help preachers know what the meaning is, and how to communicate the meaning.[13] Jeffrey Arthurs says, "I contend that exegeting the text's literary features helps equip preachers to reproduce the text's rhetorical impact in their sermons. Paying attention to how the text communicates helps preachers know how to recommunicate it."[14] Just as the literary form is vital in understanding the meaning, the sermon form is vital in transmitting the meaning with its full rhetorical impact intact. Expository preachers must allow the text to shape the

---

10 Osborne, *Hermeneutical Spiral*, 26.

11. Long, *Preaching and the Literary Forms of the Bible*, 12–13. This point of view is not just one held by Biblical interpreters. In the Arts, many view form and content as "inseparable." See Pickering, *Theatre*, 34: "It has long been a generally accepted critical opinion that form and content are, ultimately, inseparable. That is to say, somehow the form in which a work of art is cast has as much to do with its emotional, or subjective, and intellectual, or objective 'meaning' as any other aspect of the work."

12. For an example of how form and meaning are inseparable, see Bartlett, *The Shape of Scriptural Authority*, 66: "Even the simplest metaphor derives its power in part from the fact that what it says cannot be said in any other way." See also Vanhoozer, *Drama of Doctrine*, 290.

13. Vogel, *Biblical Genres*, 169: "Indeed, although there are possible excesses involved in genre studies, conservative interpreters and expositors recognize that, rightly wed to a high view of biblical inspiration, such studies are valid and fruitful."

14. Arthurs, "Old Testament Narratives," 73–74.

sermon, getting clues from literary form, informed by the intent of the author.[15]

WHAT ARE THE POINTS?

VERSE-BY-VERSE

Some biblical literary forms, such as the Epistles, lend themselves to the expositional approach of read, explain, illustrate, and apply. A widespread variation of this approach is verse-by-verse preaching, which will generate as many points as time allows.[16] Origen used a similar approach in the third century, as did John Chrysostom in the fourth century, and many other preachers through the Middle Ages.[17] The strength of this method is that everything is covered and it does not require selecting an expository unit, or shaping the sermon by a predetermined number of points. However, it is difficult to defend this method as the only expository form since there is no correlation between the chapter and verse numbers and authorial intent. The current chapter divisions were not in place until the early thirteenth century, put there by the Archbishop of Canterbury, Stephen Langton; Hugo did not subdivide the chapters until 1248, and Stephanus did not add verses until 1551.[18] Therefore, the form created by verses should not necessarily dictate the final form of a sermon.

One weakness of this approach is it tends to become a running commentary, or a grammar lesson, instead of expressing and applying the

---

15. Stott, *Between Two Worlds,* 229. Stott calls this the "golden rule for sermon outlines." He says "each text must be allowed to supply its own structure." See also Vogel, *Biblical Genres,* 189, and Waltke, *An Old Testament Theology,* 55.

16. Blackwood, *Preaching from the Bible,* 39. While acknowledging it is a good form in the hands of a gifted preacher, Blackwood also says "it would be a pity if verse-by-verse explanation were the only type of expository preaching."

17. Edwards, *History of Preaching,* 40. Stitzinger, "History of Expository Preaching," 44.

18 Dahan, "Genres, Forms, and Various Methods," 207. Bullinger, *How to Enjoy the Bible,* 34. Carr, *Introduction,* 19. The Masoretes divided the Old Testament into unnumbered verses over three hundred years, beginning in the seventh century, and their work is still seen in the Hebrew Bible. Although similar in many respects, the divisions used in Christianity are traced to Robert Estienne—better known as Stephanus. See McKnight, *Blue Parakeet,* 45. For more information on the ancient divisions of the Hebrew text, see Tov, *Textual Criticism,* 4–8.

point(s) of a text selection. Chappell calls the type of sermons that
emerge from this approach "pre-sermons" because of their lack of
relevant application.[19] Another weakness is the tendency expositional preachers have of preaching narrative passages the same way they
preach the Epistles. As a result, it is possible to confuse plot movements
with points (chap. 2). Biblical narratives include plot dynamics that
propel the story toward a focused theological truth. The plot dynamics
are movements, not points. The point is the final resolution, and the
movements are the twists and turns of the story that carry the listener to the point (chap. 2).[20] Greidanus explains typical Old Testament
narrative as action with a beginning and ending. The action begins
with a conflict in a specific setting and context. It climaxes at a point of
great intensity, before it begins to unravel and is resolved, resulting in a
communicated outcome. The action ends, concluding the story.[21] The
theological truth emerges at the resolution of the conflict. Again, the
resolution is the point, not the plot dynamics that transport the listeners
to the resolution.

Synoptic pronouncement stories are a good example of how a narrative
passage makes a single point (chap. 8). Usually, Jesus told these stories in
response to an observation he made or a question posed to him. The
function of the narrative is to communicate a focused truth to his hearers.

This is not to say that all narrative passages make only a single point,
only that as a rule, it is wise to look for a single point instead of assuming that the complexity of plot dynamics automatically dictates multiple
points exist in the narrative.[22]

THREE-POINT SERMONS

A new sermon form emerged after Pope Innocent III gave the Franciscans
permission to preach in 1210. Their sermon form mimicked the shape of
a tree. The three branches (sermon subpoints) grow out of three boughs

---

19 Chappell, *Christ-Centered Preaching*, 55.

20. Hunter, *Interpreting the Parables*, 11. Hunter gives four rules of story, the final of
which is the rule of "end stress." That is, the point of the story is usually at the end.

21. Greidanus, *The Modern Preacher and the Ancient Text*, 204.

22. Osborne, *Hermeneutical Spiral*, 221. Osborne states a preference using multiple
points in a didactic sermon, but treating the shifts in action in a narrative passage as
movements, rather than points.

(sermon points), which emerge from the trunk (the text). This new approach emphasized dividing and subdividing the text into smaller thematic units. The goal was to understand the whole by dividing it into parts. They spiced their exegesis with illustrations to drive home their points.[23]

The Oxford Convention affirmed the division of the text into three parts and that each should have three significant words. Charles Smyth explains the perceived wisdom of their assertion when he writes, "Single things said are soon forgotten. Too many confuse. Arrangement in threes binds them together, and a threefold cord is not swiftly broken."[24]

The three-point sermon structure that emerged during the Middle Ages survived the Reformation, so that preachers from both the Catholic and Protestant traditions used it as standard fare. However, they were not identical in form to the medieval sermon structures. Influenced by Scholasticism, they included a proposition and a logical flow to the sermon structure, but they maintained the propensity toward subdividing into thirds.[25]

Again, the Epistles lend themselves to this three-point, propositional sermonic form. It is often the case that the writer makes a claim and then weaves a logical, multi-point argument to buttress the assertion. In these cases, expository preachers should select the text and do their exegetical work looking for points that naturally emerge from the text.

---

23. Dieter, "Arbor Picta," *Quarterly Journal of Speech* 51, 123–44. Also, see Larsen, *Anatomy of Preaching*, 54. Larsen uses the tree metaphor as a model for the modern-day, multi-point sermon. Edwards, *History of Preaching*, 216–17. Larsen, *Company of the Preachers*, 122.

24. Smyth, *Art of Preaching*, 48–49. Smyth bolsters his contention with the claims from anthropology, the arts, and personal observation. Anthropologists know of tribal people who only number things to three, and then say, "A great number." Plays are usually in three acts, and a person can only see three or four things at a time. See also Stott, *Between Two Worlds*, 34. Stott comments that Smyth's explanation of the three-point sermon is a "rigid structure of the medieval 'sermon scheme.'"

25. Bayley, *French Pulpit Oratory*, 108–11. Latourette, *A History of Christianity*, vol. 1, 496–98. Scholasticism was not limited to theological studies, but did result in an understanding of the connection to faith and reason. It rekindled an interest in the contribution of the ancients, including Aristotle, in matters of faith and rhetoric. Edwards, *History of Preaching*, 223.

What Is the Point?

Other biblical literary forms require preachers to ask, "What is the point?" rather than, "What are the points?" These forms represent genres (or literary structures) that typically have a single primary point. Among them are narrative (chaps. 4, 5, 8), parallelism (chap. 6), proverb (chap. 7), and parable (chap. 9).

By itself, the narrative genre comprises almost half of the Bible. When including the others, it is safe to say single-point literary forms comprise the majority of the Bible,[26] which makes the search for a single point appropriate for expository preachers who use literary analysis as part of their sermon preparation process. Because of the sheer volume of single-point literary forms, there is a need for the one-point expository sermon.

Sermon Structure Should Mirror the Text Structure

Just as biblical genre is not an inert vessel, neither is sermon form. If the goal is to keep the meaning and impact of the text intact through all hermeneutical and homiletical processes, then the sermon form should mirror the structure of the text.[27]

However, there is a tendency to shape the sermon according to the preacher's predilections. For instance, Craig Blomberg's sermon, "Pray and Persevere," based upon Luke 18:1–8, is a three-point sermon, even though he sees the text as having a single point with two lessons. He says that he wrote it with three points to make it a fuller, richer, and clearer sermon, and because he has a "predilection for three points!"[28] If a text has only one point so should the sermon. As previously stated, choosing the medium of communication is a *then* and *now* task. Certainly, elements from the *now*, such as a preacher's predilections and congregational

---

26. Greidanus, *The Modern Preacher and the Ancient Text*, 355. I'm not attempting to draw strict lines here. It is possible to use a one-point narrative approach for a didactic text, a point that Greidanus makes.

27. Akin, "The Work of Exposition: Structuring the Message," 142: "Our structuring of the text and locating its seams will naturally and helpfully impact the structuring of our message. Whether we refer to them as points, movements, or segments, we will honor the natural seams and divisions we discover in the text when we relocate them in the body of our message."

28. Blomberg, *Preaching the Parables*, 169–77. I do not mean to imply that Blomberg's sermon distorted the meaning of this text. I cite this as an illustration of a decision that preachers face as they sculpt the form of their sermons.

norms, are germane in selecting sermonic form, but so are the elements from the *then* domain.[29] While it is possible to preach a multi-point sermon based upon a text with a single point without altering the meaning, it may also result in distorting the conveyed meaning and/or its impact. If a text has a single point, so should the sermon, or the sermon risks altering the meaning and/or impact of the text.

Preachers who are looking for three points are likely to find them. It would be easy to see Matthew 7:7 in thirds: (1) "*ask,* and it will be given to you," (2) "*seek,* and you will find," (3) "*knock* and it will be opened to you." The form of this verse includes parallelism; therefore, *ask, seek,* and *knock* function as synonyms, not three modes of praying. However, the tripartite sermon structure can imply that there are three separate actions involved in praying.

Taken as a separate point, seeking or knocking could lead the hearer to the conclusion that the petitioner should actively attempt to bring about the desired resolution through human activity. In this case, prayer becomes a secondary solution to the problem, human activity being the primary—God just helps the petitioner who is seeking for a solution. While this idea is consistent with Benjamin Franklin's philosophy, that "God helps them that helps themselves,"[30] it counters the context of Matthew 7:7, which encourages those who pray to do so with "an expectant attitude,"[31] because God is dependable and loving. He cares for his people and he will answer their prayers. The emphasis is on God who provides, not on the energy the petitioner puts into the act of praying.

In this case, ignoring the context and the organic unity of the synonymous parallelism used in Matthew 7:7 and imposing a three-point structure shifts the emphasis away from expecting that God will answer to an entirely different message: pray and do your part in answering the prayer. This example no doubt takes the meaning from the *then,* but it

---

29. I have refrained from making a case for the one-point sermon structure from the *now* domain, so as not to detract from my argument that the literary form of the text should influence the form of the sermon. For an example of those that make the other argument, see Stanley and Jones, *Communicating for a Change,* and Craddock, *As One without Authority,* 55.

30. Benjamin Franklin, *Poor Richard's Almanac,* 82. Although popularized by Franklin, Algernon Sidney originated the phrase in 1698 in his *Discourses Concerning Government,* section 23. It was also the moral of Aesops's story, *Hercules and the Wagoner.*

31. Blomberg, *Matthew,* 129.

untethers the message from the textual form. While being a co-worker with God is a biblical concept (1 Cor. 3:9), it does not emerge from this text. An expository sermon must extract meaning from its text.

Preachers who gravitate toward the common three-point proposition-al sermon, without regard to the understanding of structure derived from the form, limit themselves. Stott uses stronger language; he says they con-fine themselves in a "strait-jacket." Craddock refers to it as "impaling" the gospel "on the frame of Aristotelian logic."[32]

The notion that a preacher can proclaim the meaning of an immutable text with an interchangeable sermon chassis has the feel of homiletical Gnosticism—one being sacred, the other not.[33] There is an organic unity between form and meaning; they affect one another,[34] and should stay unified throughout the sermon writing and preaching event. Craddock calls the separation of the two "fatal for preaching."[35] Stott says, "Each text must be allowed to supply its own structure."[36] The inspiration of the Holy Spirit, and the intent of the author, forever link the form and meaning together, he speaks of the "form of the content."[37]

---

32. Stott, *Between Two Worlds*, 230. Craddock, *As One without Authority*, 38. Equally, there is a valid argument that those who lean toward a one-point structure also limit themselves if they do not look for sermon points in genres that typically have multiple points.

33. By interchangeable chassis, I mean any predetermined form that a preacher uses to shape the sermon. In my view, the form of the text should dictate the form of the sermon. See Allen, *Determining the Form*, 4. Allen cites Browne to support a view that the sermon should grow out of the biblical form: "In *Ministry of the Word,* Browne argues that the gospel should not be reduced to a standard structural formula (such as three propositions or interpretation followed by application). Instead, the sermon must authentically and artistically grow out of the character of the person preaching and relate to the form of revelation represented in the biblical text being preached." However, in his book, Allen illustrates eight different sermon forms using the same text (1 Kings 19:1–15a). This can also happen with those who align themselves with the New Homiletic. See Lowry, *The Homiletical Plot*, 12–13. Lowry argues that every sermon can have a plot and can be a narrative. His interchangeable sermon chassis has five movements, not three points and a poem, or an expositional approach of interpretation followed by an application.

34. Larsen, *Anatomy of Preaching*, 63. Even though Larsen argues for a multi-point sermon form, which does not align with my assertion, he does say "substance and form affect one another."

35. Craddock, *As One without Authority*, 5.

36. Stott, *Between Two Worlds*, 229.

37. Long, *The Witness of Preaching*, 13, 24. Long argues that the biblical writers are not just concerned with what they said, but how they were saying it. Genre therefore is part of authorial intent. I link it with the message and affirm it is inspired by the Holy Spirit.

If the biblical author, under the inspiration of the Holy Spirit, used a genre that makes a single point, the meaning extracted from the text is dependent on that textual form. Sunukjian writes, "The sermon outline may indent or symbolize a bit differently than the passage or truth outline. It may slightly change the author's structure (but never his meaning!)."[38] Then, can changing the structure (as dictated by the literary genre and context) change the meaning?

"THE MEDIUM IS THE MESSAGE"

Communication theorist Marshall McLuhan coined the phrase "the medium is the message" to describe the effects communication media have on a message. He contended that the way communicators say something is as important as what they are saying. Actually, he argues that the medium is more important. "The content or message of any particular medium has about as much importance as the stenciling on the casing of an atomic bomb."[39] In a macro sense, as in the introduction of the Roman alphabet, Gutenberg press, or electronic media into culture, he argued that media shaped the cultural environment to such an extent that the medium is more important than the words the alphabet formed, the printing press printed, or the electronic media broadcasted.

Each technological innovation changed how people processed information and what they did with their time. The Roman alphabet, not the words it formed, reshaped thinking from pictures to words, from spatial to linear.[40] It made changes as far as the east is from the west. Philosophers might point to Aristotle and Confucius to highlight the differences between the cultures, McLuhan would indicate that the difference began with the Western adoption of the Roman letters, instead of something like the logographic Chinese characters.[41]

The printing press made orality antiquated and flattened time. After the mid-fifteenth century, readers could easily spend their leisure time in isolation interacting with thinkers from another time and place, instead

---

38. Sunukjian, *Invitation to Biblical Preaching*, 39.

39. McLuhan and Zingrone, *Essential McLuhan*, 238.

40. While Egyptian hieroglyphics and Phoenician cuneiform made this shift centuries before the Roman alphabet, McLuhan's argument focused on the Roman alphabet.

41. McLuhan, *Understanding Media*, 121. McLuhan and Zingrone, *Essential McLuhan*, 122.

of exchanging their heritage stories in their community. This resulted in less tribalism and more individualism.[42] McLuhan would argue that it was not the words that the press printed that made post-mid-fifteenth century generations more individualistic, but that the introduction of the printing press itself caused the transformation.

The electronic media formed a global village that blurs the lines between here and there. The world came into the living room in McLuhan's day and into the palm of users' hands today. While it shrinks the world into a tiny screen, it also expands the users' world. It creates a cultural fusion where the east and west constantly churn and blend resulting in fewer distinctions, less privacy, and more awareness.[43] McLuhan argued that it was not the words that producers broadcasted that ushered in these changes, but the electronic media itself.

Most of the time, when McLuhan used the phrase "the medium is the message" he was referring to this macro sense of how media shapes its environment and does more to influence people than the words spoken, read, or heard. However, he does make an important distinction between hot and cold mediums.[44] Some communication mediums, such as the narrative form, invoke a higher level of participation from the audience. It is a cool medium requiring the use of multiple senses and mental capacities. Other communication mediums are hot, requiring only a single sense. A photo projected on a screen is a hot medium (requiring only the visual sense).

Imposing a three-point deductive sermon structure upon a one-point inductive biblical narrative shifts the communication medium from cold to hot, resulting in lower audience involvement. This movement, taking a literary cold medium and shifting it to an oratory hot medium, has the possibility of altering the impact of its meaning, if not the meaning itself. The author of an inductive narrative intended the listeners to immerse themselves in the story and discover the truth as the tension in the story resolves. Instead, with the three-point, deductive sermon structure,

---

42. McLuhan, *Understanding Media*, 122.

43. Ibid., 53–55.

44. Ibid., 39: "Hot media are, therefore, low in participation, and cool media are high in participation or completion by the audience." In other words, *hot* media equals single sense requiring lower participation; *cold* media equals multiple senses requiring higher participation.

the storyline no longer requires their involvement, just their attention to the expert, who will explain its significance and make an application for them.

Remember, the biblical authors wrote their words for listeners not readers. Prior to Gutenberg, the text was not widely available and the people would gather to listen to it. They did so after rebuilding the walls of Jerusalem (Neh. 8:5–6) and during Domitian's reign (Rev. 1:3).[45]

On a micro sense, shifting the temperature of the communication medium from cool to hot may alter the impact of the message and obscure the intended meaning, but on a macro sense, it can change the way the listeners come to regard the Bible. In the same way the introduction of the Roman alphabet, printing press, and electronic media affected Western culture, altering the literary genre from a single point focus to a multipoint sermonic form can shift the way listeners view the Bible. The medium is the message.

Sermons based on narrative passages that tilt away from the story to propositions-for-living communicate something besides their content. They shape the congregations' view of the Bible. Long says, "Idea-centered sermons are prone to communicate, over time, that the Christian faith itself can be boiled down to a set of concepts to which people are supposed to give assent. The gospel thus gets presented as a list of propositions, and sermons become didactic devices for explaining these truths and how each of them logically connects to the others."[46] A steady diet of propositional preaching of narrative passages can result in people viewing the Bible as an answer book for life's problems, or an owner's manual for the Christian life, or a textbook for a Christian education. While the Bible may be useful in those pursuits, its purpose is greater. The Bible is not a collection of propositions for Christians to understand and apply. It is God's story to be experienced. The Bible does not just contain narratives. It is narrative. Even the Epistles have a narrative foundation. Greidanus writes, "A vibrant story lies just beneath the surface of many an epistle text."[47]

---

45. Ἀναγινώσκων (anaginōskōn) is a word that denotes reading aloud. In Revelation 1:3, John blessed the one that would read his words aloud to God's people.

46. Long, *Witness of Preaching*, 101–102.

47. Greidanus, *The Modern Preacher and the Ancient Text*, 335. See also Goldingay, *Old Testament Theology*, 31. In an explanatory footnote to the sentence, he says that "the

Long continues, "The first-order work of the biblical writers was to 'reveal the enactment of God's purposes in history.'"[48] More times than not, expository sermons will reveal something about God and the way he works in redemptive history.[49] If preachers align their sermons with authorial intent, the majority—if not all—of their sermons will be theo-centric, and will encourage the listeners to respond in faith to God as revealed in the sermon. The literary form will provide clues to how many points the sermon will have, and in some cases, the structure of the sermon can come from the movements within the text.[50]

ONE-POINT SERMON FORMS

According to Chapell, "As preachers mature, they will discover that rhetorical 'moves,' homiletical 'plots,' concept-rich 'images,' thoughtful transitions, implied ideas, and other measures, can often substitute for the formal statement of points in their outlines."[51] Typically, one-point sermons are inductive in nature and use movements to progress their listeners through the sermon. In the case of preaching through a biblical narrative, movements often come from plot dynamics of the text itself. In other cases, the preacher provides the movements for the sermon structure. Long argues, "Even though the possibility of matching sermonic movement to text movement is clearest when the biblical text is a narrative, non-narrative texts possess their own inner movements that can also serve as the patterns for sermons."[52]

Whatever form a sermon takes, the sermon must make a difference. A multi-point sermon's strength is the multiple options it provides for information and inspiration; if one of the points does not apply, there is a chance the next one will. Not so for the one-point sermon, it delivers a

---

biblical gospel is not a collection of timeless statements such as God is love. It is a narrative about things God has done." Goldingay elaborates, "The narrative form of the Gospels makes this point evident, but a 'narrative bedrock' also underlies the non-narrative form of Paul's writings."

48. Long, *Preaching and the Literary Forms of the Bible*, 70.

49. Vogel, *Biblical Genres*, 185: "The intention of biblical stories is to teach us about God and His ways. They capture and express timeless truth concerning God and the human condition in relation to Him."

50. Taylor, "Shaping Sermons," 140.

51. Chapell, *Christ-Centered Preaching*, 134.

52. Long, *Literary Forms*, 131.

single point, and if it is not strong and well delivered, the hearers leave with little benefit. The one-point sermon must have atomic impact. It must be powerful and it must be clear. The strength of a one-point sermon is that it does not force any point to compete with another for the audience's attention. Instead of the pressure to develop a point in a third of the time allotted for the sermon, preachers can devote all their time to develop the single point to make a clear, atomic-sized impact.

This book focuses on the one-point expository sermon. Not because we de-value the familiar verse-by-verse or the three-point sermon's approaches to preaching, but because some texts are better suited for the less familiar one-point sermon form. Because we hold a high view of Scripture, we want our sermons to convey the impact found in the author's original intent.

The remainder of the first part of the book will help preachers who tend to preach verse-by-verse or three-point sermons explore key issues of the one-point expository sermon. It includes a chapter that explains the differences between points and movements, another on developing a transformative point based upon the transformative truth in the text.

The second part of the book demonstrates which of the Bible's different literary forms lend themselves to the one-point expository sermon, and includes some sample sermons.

FOR FURTHER REFLECTION

- Do your sermons lean more in the *then* or the *now* direction? How can you bring more balance to your approach?
- Does the form of the biblical passage influence the form of your sermon? If not, how can you change this in the future?
- While you were reading, did you think of a sermon you have preached with a structure that was not appropriate for the form of the text? Take a minute to pull it from your sermon file and see how you would rewrite it to allow the text to shape the sermon.
- What are the strengths and weaknesses of introducing a new preaching approach to a congregation?

How Movements Function
in a Narrative

Movements are not the same as points. Movements carry the listener between the points of a multi-point sermon and to the point of a one-point sermon.[1] Movements transport listeners to the destination, keeping them interested along the way.[2] The point(s) is (are) the theological truth preachers want the listeners to understand and put into practice. In this chapter, you will spend some time seeing how points relate to one another in different variations of multi-point sermons, and gain greater understanding of how a multi-point sermon flows. These things will likely be familiar to most readers, who have listened to and/or preached many multi-point sermons. We will then move from the familiar multi-point sermon to the largely unfamiliar one-point sermon. This approach will provide a point of reference to explore the unfamiliar—the one-point sermon structure and how the flow moves through the plot dynamics of the text to the single point.

---

1. In multi-point sermons, movements also occur between different phases of the sermon. Bugg, *Preaching from the Inside Out*, 97: "Transitions are important parts of a sermon. They are bridges over which we carry people from one movement to another. One breakdown in the preparation of sermons is awkward transition. This is particularly evident in the move from the introduction to the main part of the sermon and from the main part to its conclusion."

2. Allen, *Determining the Form*, 9: "Movement is essential for keeping the hearers interested in what is being said and open to the transforming power of the gospel. Every sermon, regardless of its form, has a beginning, a middle, and an end. The relationship to the unified focus is different in each of these phases of the sermon. The beginning in some way hints at the claim that is to be offered. The middle unpacks and develops the claim in a way that draws hearers into a deeper understanding of the text, doctrine, or issue being discussed. And the end, in different ways, seals the claim in the hearts and minds of the hearers and hopefully influences their behavior."

POINTS

In multi-point sermons, the points divide a concept into contrasting, equal, or progressive parts. By their nature, two-point sermons tend to divide; three-point sermons tend to combine.

Two-Point Sermons

Two-point sermons work best to compare and contrast two opposing ideas and challenge the listener in choosing the best alternative. Two points divide ideas to highlight the "big idea" in the sermon.[3] Below is an example of a two-point sermon outline that contrasts two choices for who/what to love.

Title: What's Love Got to Do with It?
Text: Hebrews 13:1-5
Thesis: Christians should use things and love people, not the other way around.
  I. Have a proper attitude toward people (13:1-4)
     a. Be hospitable toward strangers
     b. Care for prisoners
     c. Respect the marriage relationship
  II. Have a proper attitude toward things (13:5)
     a. Do not love money (also 1 Tim. 6:10)
     b. Be content with what you have
     c. Depend on God to care for your financial needs

In this sermon outline, the two-point structure allows for a contrast between a proper attitude toward people (love people) and a proper attitude toward things (use things), resulting in helping listeners distinguish between what they should love and what they should use. The big idea of loving people and using things emerges from the movement created by contrasting one idea with the other.

---

3. To better understand the "big idea," see Robinson, *Biblical Preaching*, 33–47. I agree with Robinson that every sermon should have a big idea. However, what I mean by one-point expository sermon is different from what Robinson meant by big idea.

FIGURE 1: TWO-POINT SERMONS COMPARE AND CONTRAST

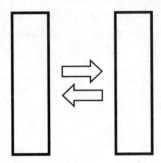

THREE-POINT SERMONS

Three-point sermons tend to bring ideas together by showing the smaller components of the whole, or a cascading list (ascending or descending) of interrelated ideas. [4] They are helpful in dividing the big idea into bite-sized pieces to understand, or showing incremental steps in accomplishing the sermon's goal.

THREE COMPONENTS

This sermon outline illustrates how a three-point sermon can divide the big idea into three separate points to help explain it:

> Title: Temptation
> Text: 1 John 2:16
> Thesis: Satan uses three primary tools to tempt people to sin.
> I. Lust of the Flesh
>   a. Satan tempted Adam and Eve with the lust of the flesh (Gen. 3:6: *good for food*)
>   b. Satan tempted Jesus with the lust of the flesh (Matt. 4:3: *turn the stones to bread*)
> II. Lust of the Eyes
>   a. Satan temped Adam and Eve with the lust of the eyes (Gen. 3:6: *a delight to the eyes*)

---

4. Four-point sermons fit into this category also; however, once preachers go beyond four points, they risk turning a sermon into a listing of related ideas, a string of pearls if you will, instead of a cohesive thought package.

      b. Satan tempted Jesus with the lust of the eyes (Matt. 4:9: *the splendor of the kingdoms of the world*)

III. Pride of Life

      a. Satan tempted Adam and Eve with the pride of life (Gen. 3:6: *was desirable to make one wise*)

      b. Satan tempted Jesus with the pride of life (Matt. 4:6: *the angels will rescue him*)

Preachers using this approach to the text could insert a third subpoint for each main point, or use a fresh sermon illustration for how Satan continues to use the same tactics today.[5]

FIGURE 2: THREE-POINT SERMONS CAN SHOW THREE PARTS TO A WHOLE

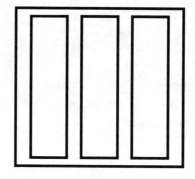

THREE RELATED IDEAS

A three-point sermon can combine three related ideas into a to-do list. This sermon outline, based on the book of Philippians, gives listeners a checklist of things they can do to contribute to a joyful atmosphere in their church.

Title: Cultivating Joy in the Church
Text: Philippians

---

5. See my (Wilson) Fresh Sermon Illustrations at www.freshsermonillustrations.net, which provides sermon illustrations based on current events, movies, and books. The illustrations are available online, in printed form, and electronically through WordSearch, Accordance, and Logos Software programs.

Thesis: Each member of the church can contribute to a joyful church
   atmosphere.
   I.   Avoid grumbling or disputing (2:14)
   II. Avoid selfish ambitions (3:17–19)
   III. Stay connected in spite of disagreements (4:2)

While not claiming to be an exhaustive list, this three-point sermon
outline extracts principles from the text that will contribute to making
a church a more joyful place. Each of the points is a valid stand-alone
thought, but presenting them together strengthens the case for the thesis.

Another example is the following sermon outline that combines related ideas as mentioned by Paul in his first letter to Timothy:

Title: Last Day Perils
Text: 1 Timothy 4:1–11
Thesis: Christians can become ineffective in their Christian walk
   and should avoid the pitfalls inherent in the last days.
   I.   Avoid the danger of being deceived (4:1–5)
   II. Avoid the danger of following silly myths (4:6–7)
   III. Avoid the danger of living undisciplined lives (4:8–10)

While there is interplay between the points in a three-point sermon,
each point can stand-alone and have value apart from the others. For instance, avoiding "being deceived," relates to the other two points because
they are all dangers to avoid but one is not dependent upon the others to
have impact on the hearer.

FIGURE 3: THREE-POINT SERMONS CAN BE THREE RELATED IDEAS

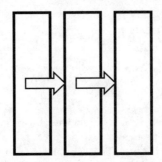

THREE INCREMENTAL STEPS

The sermon outline below shows how the points in a three-point sermon can build upon one another in an escalating fashion:

> Title: The Judgment of God
> Text: Zephaniah 3:9–17
> Thesis: God's mercy is central in his judgment.
> I. God's judgment fosters humility (3:9–12)
> II. God's judgment promotes righteousness (3:13)
> III. God's judgment results in praise (3:14–17)

This outline has a logical progression. Humility is a step toward righteousness, which leads to praise. The points are dependent upon one another, even building on each other, yet each one is a significant thought by itself.

FIGURE 4: THREE-POINT SERMONS CAN HAVE ONE POINT THAT LEADS TO ANOTHER

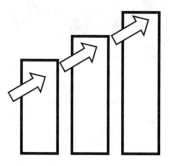

In each of these multi-point sermons, the other points in the outline influence each individual point. In the two-point sermon, they move back and forth between each other to show similarities and contrasts, ultimately leaving the listener with the responsibility of choosing between the two choices. In the three-point sermons, the movement between the points is to help the listener understand the main idea better by understanding the component parts of the idea. As the sermon progresses, moving from one point to another, the commonalities they share inform each other. Since the points are similar in nature, it makes logical sense to group them together to help the listener understand each of them better. Alternatively, in the case of the incremental steps outline, understanding the first point is foundational as the sermon progresses moving to the next two points. In all of these cases, the points work together to form an *organic unity* as the sermon moves from one point to the next, teaching the big idea of the selected text.[6]

ONE-POINT SERMONS

What happens with one-point sermons? They have no other points to move from or move to. Unlike multi-point sermons, the sermon movement in one-point sermons does not come from comparison, contrast, or interacting with other points.

Since a point cannot interact with itself, the movement of a one-point sermon comes from the plot dynamics in the text. This can be an advantage if the preacher desires to keep points from competing with each other.[7] However, it can also create an obstacle for preachers accustomed to always having interacting points. Overcoming the obstacle begins with understanding how movement occurs in plot structures.

FIGURE 5: ONE-POINT SERMON MOVEMENTS COME FROM THE PLOT DYNAMICS IN THE TEXT

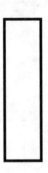

---

6. O. Wesley Allen Jr., *Determining the Form,* 4: "Sermonic form and content should be organically related."

7. Al Fasol, *Preaching Evangelistically,* 117: "Notice the body of the sermon" ['What Do You Mean by Sin, and What Do You Mean by the Cross?'] is built on movement rather than points. If the sermon had been preached in two points, the thought pattern would have run the risk of being separated or divided. With the narrative style of the sermon, the same exegetical information that is often brought out in a rhetorical, point-by-point style is brought out without breaking the flow or movement of the sermon."

In its most basic form, sermonic plot includes the introduction of tension at the beginning[8] (movement 1), the ultimate resolution of the tension at the end (movement 4), with failed attempts to resolve the tension in between (movements 2 and 3). While there are variations, these four movements are helpful to understand how to keep a one-point sermon moving from the beginning to the end.[9]

FIRST MOVEMENT INTRODUCES THE PROBLEM

The first movement captures the audience's attention by introducing the problem that the Scripture passage addresses. It becomes the "before picture" that the fourth movement will ultimately address.

FIGURE 6: THE FIRST MOVEMENT INTRODUCES THE PROBLEM

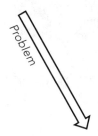

---

8 Fant, *God as Author*, 99: "Instead of the classical notion of tying and untying a knot, the knot is rather *untied* and *retied*. Instead of action rising and falling, the action instead *falls*, as one might fall off a cliff and feel anxiety, and then rises as the climax rebounds toward a resolution." In effect, the plot pyramid is inverted for sermons—the first movement is a downward stroke instead of an upward one. In Lowry's homiletical plot loop (*Homiletical Plot*), the first of his five movements is downward, as is my first of four movements in the "W," which I explain in the next section of this chapter.

9. There are multiple ways of explaining and illustrating plot. School teachers often use a plot pyramid (see http://www.readwritethink.org/classroom-resources/student-interactives/plot-diagram-30040.html for an example). The plot pyramid takes into account Characters, Setting, Conflict, Rising Action, Turning Point, Falling Action, Resolution, and Theme.

Snyder, *Save the Cat*, 70. Screenplay writers have intricate multi-scene formulas using more than a dozen "beats," including Opening Image, Theme Stated, Set-up, Catalyst, Debate, Break into Two, B Story, Fun and Games, Midpoint, Bad Guys Close In, All is Lost, Dark Night of the Soul, Break into Three, Finale, and Final Image.

Because sermons deal with narrative episodes, not full-blown narratives like novels, dramas, or screen plays, simpler breakdowns like the "W" included in this chapter are helpful. I have found the four-movement "W," as explained in this chapter, useful when I am teaching to illustrate the way tension builds and releases in narrative episodes.

Fourth Movement Resolves the Tension

The fourth movement provides the biblical solution to the problem that the first movement introduced. It is a call for action based upon the biblical truth that emerges during the exploration. This movement takes the listener from the immediate problem to the ultimate answer.

FIGURE 7: THE FOURTH MOVEMENT TAKES THE LISTENER FROM THE IMMEDIATE PROBLEM TO THE ULTIMATE SOLUTION

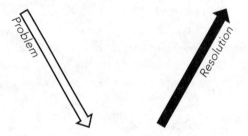

Second and Third Movements Intensify the Tension

In between the first and fourth movements are failed attempts to resolve the problem and the tension it creates. The second and third movements serve to intensify the tension by showing how there are obstacles to finding a solution to the problem.[10]

FIGURE 8: THE SECOND AND THIRD MOVEMENTS INTENSIFY THE TENSION

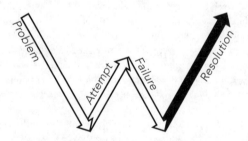

---

10. For clarity's sake, I tend to label multiple second and third movements contained in the same sermon 2b, 3b, 2c, 3c, etc.

WHERE IS THE POINT?

The single transformative point of the sermon (see chap. 3) occurs between the third and fourth movements. The preacher encourages listeners to respond to God's character, as revealed in the sermon, to trust in him with a faith response, which brings resolution.

FIGURE 9: THE SINGLE TRANSFORMATIVE POINT OF A ONE-POINT SERMON COMES BETWEEN THE THIRD AND FOURTH MOVEMENTS

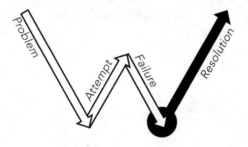

BIBLICAL PLOT DYNAMICS

Movements propel the message forward along the plot structures, usually using the conflict or tension inherent in the structure of the text.[11] Biblical writers used this basic plot structure often when writing narrative passages. The plot of the book of Ruth has four major movements:

1. Complication (1:3–22)
2. Solution (2:1–23)
3. Complication that prevents implementing the solution immediately (3:1–18)
4. Resolution (4:1–17)[12]

---

11. Buttrick, *Homiletic*, 23: "In speaking of 'moves,' we are deliberately changing terminology. For years, preachers have talked of making points in sermons. . . . Instead, we are going to speak of moves, of making moves in a movement of language."

12. Block, *Judges, Ruth*, 616. This outline is adapted from Block's diagram he provides to explain the plot. He also commented on the literary aspects of the book: "We have already noted that from a literary perspective the book of Ruth is one of the most delightful pieces ever produced in the history of literature. The narrator is a master at painting word pictures; skillfully employing the techniques of suspense, dialogue, characterization, repetition, reticence, ambiguity, wordplays, and inclusios; and creatively adapting ancient traditions to produce this moving work of art. But it is the tightly knit and carefully controlled plot of this composition that is especially impressive."

In the case of the book of Ruth, the ultimate solution was present in the second movement, but the third movement delayed resolution with the information that Boaz was a near kinsman. He was not the nearest kinsman and would not be her kinsman redeemer without first offering the opportunity to the relative that was closest to her husband. The ultimate resolution came as Boaz received permission to proceed and did so.[13]

Another example of this plot dynamic at work in the Bible is the events surrounding the Passion Week from Matthew's Gospel:

> ↓ Jesus informs the disciples that death is imminent for him (20:17–18)

> ↑ The people greet him as a king (21:8–11)

> ↓ Jesus dies on the cross (27:45–46)

> ↑ Jesus raises from the grave (28:5–6)[14]

Narratives incorporate plot structure into the story. One way to preach a one-point sermon is to follow the movements in the text. However, this is easier to say than to do. Preachers who are accustomed to writing sermons by moving between points can have difficulty when they exegete a passage of Scripture from a literary form like narrative that makes a single point, which is usually located at the end of the story. The natural tendency would be to see the movements along the plot structures as points.

Remember, movements are the journey, while the point is the destination. No one would confuse the transition statement between points in a three-point sermon as a theological truth to consider and apply to life; however, there are times that preachers confuse movements in a narrative with points.

---

13. See the sermon in chapter 5, "Under His Wings," based on Ruth 3:7–9.

14. The crowds greeting Jesus as king could have influenced the disciples to believe that Jesus might have been mistaken about his death prediction and fed their misunderstanding of the kind of Messiah Jesus would be, which made the fulfillment of his death even more disheartening. With the resurrection, Matthew emphasizes that the rule of Jesus the Messiah was not political in nature.

To see how plot movements transport listeners to the point, consider Jonah's story.

Jonah's Story

The foul stench of Nineveh's wickedness meandered into heaven and turned God's stomach. Therefore, God ordered Jonah, a prophet of the Lord, to go to Nineveh, a foreign land, and proclaim his judgment against it. Jonah did not like the assignment.

Jonah ran to Joppa and headed for Tarshish. As he put it, he was running from the presence of the Lord.

He boarded a ship in Joppa headed toward Tarshish, a Phoenician city on the southern coast of Spain—the opposite direction from Nineveh. God instructed Jonah to go to the far east. In his rebellion, he chose to do the exact opposite and go to the distant west.

He could run, but he could not hide. God was where Jonah ran.

The all powerful, all knowing God whom Jonah described as the "LORD God of heaven who made the sea and the dry land" (1:9) hurled a great wind on the sea that caused a great storm. Great enough, that the crew believed there was a good chance that the ship would be lost. To lighten the load, they jettisoned the cargo. To rescue the ship, they fell on their knees and started praying to their gods. The captain of the ship awoke Jonah and asked him to do the same.

Meanwhile, the crew cast lots to see who was to blame for the lost cargo and their imminent doom. The lot fell on Jonah.

Standing on the deck of a ship headed toward Tarshish, Jonah and the entire ship were in danger of sinking, because Jonah, a prophet of the Lord, rebelled against God's instructions to go to Nineveh and preach against their sin. The sailors questioned Jonah until he confessed.

As the storm threatened to tear the ship apart, Jonah told the sailors that he was the problem. Though Jonah was honest with the sailors, he was not particularly helpful. The sailors asked, "What should we do to you that the sea may become calm for us?" Jonah told them to throw him overboard. If Jonah knew that he was the cause of the problem and that the solution was for him to get off the boat, why didn't he just jump into the water himself? Was he trying to take the ship down with him? Or was he trying to get the sailors on the ship to join him in his struggle against God?

That is what happened. Instead of throwing Jonah overboard, the sailors attempted to out row God. Like a B-grade movie, the men on the ship rowed "desperately," trying to get the ship to shore so Jonah would not be lost.

I wonder what Jonah was thinking as he watched his new friends try to out row God's wind? How did he feel when he saw other people suffering for his sin?

Jonah rebelled against God, and innocent people lost their cargo and feared for the safety of their ship because of his sin. Finally, exhausted by the struggle, the sailors laid down the oars, picked up the prophet, and threw him overboard. As the sea received the runaway prophet, the storm calmed and the men who were battling against God came to fear him and offer sacrifices to him.

Jonah appeared to be a dismal failure. He tried to outrun God and conspired with his shipmates to try to out row him too. Neither worked. Finally, those onboard the ship tossed him overboard into the storm-tossed sea. It appeared that it was over for Jonah, but it was not.

The Lord appointed a big fish to rescue Jonah (1:17). Jonah probably did not view the fish as God's grace, but it was. The fish was not punishment; it was a biological submarine prepared by God to sustain Jonah's life.

God miraculously cared for Jonah. Even when he tried to outrun God and conspired with others to try to out row God, he remained in the palm of God's hand. And while he was in the belly of the fish, Jonah rested, along with all of God's creation, in the palm of his hand (Ps. 95:4).

Jonah prayed.

He begins his prayer by blaming God for his troubles (2:3–4). Wait a minute. Wasn't Jonah trying to run from the presence of God? Then why was he upset when he thought he was out of God's sight? Didn't he tell the sailors to throw him overboard? Then why did he blame God for ending up in the sea?

Jonah moves from blaming God to complaining about his problems (2: 5-6a). It could not be much worse for Jonah. He was at the "roots of the mountains," a poetic way of referring to the bottom of the ocean.

Then there was a dramatic turn-around in Jonah's attitude (2: 6b–9). He remembered the Lord and his salvation.

The God who "hurled the wind" and "appointed the fish" commanded the fish to vomit him on the shore, and it did. Jonah stood on the dry land, cleaned himself up, and began walking to Nineveh, where God told him to go in the first place.

In Nineveh, Jonah was a reluctant missionary, who preached in a half-hearted manner. Nineveh was a large city—it would take three days to walk through it—but Jonah only spent a single day preaching. He was a minimalist, doing the very least he could to get by. Not only did Jonah cover only a small portion of the city, but also his message was short—only five Hebrew words (3:3–4).

Jonah's message, even if they understood it (Assyrians did not speak Hebrew), offered no hope: "Yet forty days and Nineveh will be overthrown," he said.

The only joy in his message was his hope that it was true. He relished the thought of the punishment of his enemies in Nineveh.

He did not want to go. He tried to outrun God and conspired with others to try to out row him. After three days at the bottom of the ocean, Jonah finally agreed to go. Jonah's attitude stunk. His work ethic was sick and his message brief, but God still used him as he uses others with questionable motives (Phil. 1:15–18).

However, the people of Nineveh believed and repented. They put on sackcloth (the sign of mourning) and began fasting (a sign of commitment). They took care of their own spiritual condition and called on others to do the same.

Like a row of dominoes falling—one pushing down the next—repentance spread. When the word came to the king, he decreed compliance with God's will (3:7–8). He issued a proclamation calling the nation to repentance and prayer; he acted more like a prophet than a politician would. And the people followed.

What do you expect Jonah's reaction was to Nineveh's repentance? Did he join the people of Nineveh in repentance and marinate in God's grace? No, he got angry (4:1).

Does it surprise you that Jonah became angry? Jonah affirmed that his loving God is gracious and compassionate (4:2)—nothing wrong with his understanding of God. Also, notice how he misapplied his accurate theology. Jonah said, in essence, he would rather be dead than witness God pouring his grace on people he despised. Like others in Scripture (Luke 15:29–30; Matt. 20:12; Luke 7:39), he was not happy seeing other people experience God's grace.

Then God made a leafy plant to grow that spread its leaves over Jonah's head to shelter him from the heat. Comfortable under the shade that God graciously provided, he waited and hoped to see an apocalyptic destruction of the city—a fulfillment of his five-word prophecy.

As Jonah waited, God, who hurled the great wind, appointed a great fish, and caused a large leafy plant to grow, prepared a small worm to destroy the plant and sent a scorching wind to beat the prophet down into submission. Jonah became angry because he had lost the plant—he was angry enough to die.

"So the Lord said, 'You cared about the plant, which you did not labor over and did not grow. It appeared in a night and perished in a night. Should I not care about the great city of Nineveh, which has more than 120,000 people who cannot distinguish between their right and their left, as well as many animals?'" (4:10–11).

While the story includes information about a wicked people repenting and encountering God's grace, it is not a story about "How to Bring Revival."[15] The things Jonah did, disobey God, attempt to run from his presence, involve others in his rebellion, blame God for his problems, preach in a half-hearted way, and get angry at God when he showed mercy to the people, are not actions that bring about revival. They are movements in a narrative, not points for a sermon.[16]

The movements in the story transport the reader to the story's climax (4:10–11), which reveals something about God's character. From Jonah's

15. Of course, no reasonable person would make a case that these movements are a listing of how to bring revival. It is self-evident that they are not. That is why I am using this story as an example. Likely all readers will agree that the movements are not points in this story. My hope is that it will illustrate that movements are not points in any story.

16. By using Jonah's story as an example for plot movments, I do not mean to suggest that preachers should cover all these movements in a single sermon, or that the entire book has only a single point.

story, we learn that God's grace flows in the direction of his choosing. Sometimes it is to us and people like us. Sometimes it is to others who are not like us at all. We must be open to be conduits of grace to those who speak different languages, live in different cultures, and are of different generations. We must not run from God's redemptive purposes; we must cooperate with him even if it means sacrificing our preferences.

Just as preachers can confuse movements for points in narratives, they can confuse structural devices with main points in Hebrew poetry (chap. 6). Each literary form has its challenges, which we will address in Part 2 of this book.

VARIATIONS OF SERMON STRUCTURES FOR NARRATIVES

One way to preach the narratives is to follow the plot dynamics to the point. But that is not the only way.

WEAVER SERMON

Preachers will often do their biblical exegesis, and then show how the text applies to contemporary life with a true-to-life story, either from a fresh illustration or from their own experience. (J. T. Reed does this in his sermon "Living the Resurrection" in chap. 6.) The weaver sermon places the matching movements together to bring both stories to a climax at the same time. (I do this in my sermon "In His Time" in chap. 8.) In reality, there are not just two stories—the listeners intuitively weave their stories into the sermon to add a third strand.

WHO DONE IT?

This type of one-point sermon gets its name from the slang used by many to refer to murder mysteries. In this approach, preachers upset the equilibrium in the first movement of the sermon, and then use a series of second and third movements to eliminate unworkable solutions, until they present the final resolution at the end.[17] In this case, the diagram of the sermon would look more like a zigzag, \/\/\/\/\/\/\/, or teeth in a saw blade, than a *W*; there are multiple second and third movements. Through a process of elimination, they arrive at their point. (My sermons

---

17. For clarity's sake, I tend to label multiple second and third movements contained in the same sermon 2b, 3b, 2c, 3c, etc.

"Why Did He Do It" in chap. 8 and "Celebrate!" in chap. 9 are examples of this approach.)

SERIAL PREACHING

In this approach, the sermon ends on a cliffhanger, by closing the sermon on the third movement, and beginning the next week with a recap, then going straight to the fourth movement. After closing out the previous week's sermon, the preacher delivers the next three movements. Here is an example of a conclusion I used in a sermon based on Jonah 1:10–16:

Things don't look so bright for Jonah, our young hero. As his ship-mates are praising the Lord, he is sinking deeper and deeper into his destiny. What will happen to Jonah? Has God turned his back on his wayward prophet? You'll have to come back next week to find out.

Last week, Jonah learned that he couldn't outrun God, this week he discovered that even with the help of others, he couldn't out row him either. Jonah was caught up in a battle of wills, and discovered that his was weak, but God's will is sovereign.

What about you? Do you find yourself struggling against God's will for your life? Are other people suffering because of your sin? Are you ready to turn back to God, or will you wait for others to come and throw you overboard?[18]

Notice that this conclusion comes after this downward movement in Jonah's story:

⬇ Jonah's shipmates throw him overboard.

The next sermon begins with this upward movement:

⬆ God appoints a great fish to preserve Jonah's life.

---

18. Wilson, *How to Write Narrative Sermons*, 113–14.

This approach works well in a series of protracted meetings or a retreat setting. It might not be as effective when there are seven days between the sermons.

FOR FURTHER REFLECTION

- Look back over your last six weeks of sermons. Do the sermons all have the same structure? Did the structure naturally emerge from the text, or did you impose a favorite structure on the text?
- During your Bible reading, look for the "W" movements in the text. See if they start to jump off the page as you read.
- If you tend to preach only three-point sermons, look for opportunities to write a two-point sermon that compares and contrasts points in a passage.
- Select a narrative passage and try the "cliffhanger" approach in your next retreat setting. Observe the response and conversation to see if the listeners are "getting it."
- Changing the structure of your sermons may make you and those who hear you preach uncomfortable. Be ready for some push back and be prepared to explain why you are working to allow the shape of the text to influence the shape of your sermons.
- Look for movements as you read through narrative passages during your quiet time.

CHAPTER 3

Transformation: Preaching That Changes Lives

Preaching involves *teaching people the Bible so they can encounter God and live transformed lives.* For this to take place, the listeners will need to do more than understand biblical teachings. They will need to integrate them into their lives. This requires preachers to identify the transformative truth in the text and develop a transformative point based upon the truth.

TEACHING THE BIBLE

No doubt, preaching includes teaching the Bible. Because the Bible is God's inerrant word, preachers must preach it with boldness and clarity. If they do, it will build listeners' faith (Rom. 10:17), which will give them life direction (1 Cor. 5:7).

While their sermons need to be relevant, preachers do not need to make the Bible relevant. In "Five Temptations of the Pulpit," A. C. Craig writes, "I offer one last temptation of the preacher. It is the temptation to try to make the Bible relevant, to make it come alive. This particular temptation used to be the sole province of the liberal theological tradition. But in the past few years, it has gained a number of victims in the evangelical community."[1] If Craig is right, then the shift will have consequences. When preachers no longer trust the Bible to be relevant, their sermons become a mixture of biblical advice and pop-psychology. This reduces the sermon's authority to the equivalence of any self-help book displayed at a checkout counter.

---

1. Craig, "Five Temptations of the Pulpit," 155.

Homileticians and preachers who take the sufficiency of the Scriptures seriously take issue with any suggestion that preachers need to make the Bible relevant. The idea makes as much sense as trying to make water wet. Dietrich Bonhoeffer said, "Do not try to make the Bible relevant. Its relevance is axiomatic."[2]

The Bible does not need a makeover, a contemporary update to make it relevant to a contemporary audience. Preachers must preach the Word—we can never do better than the text.

Perhaps not all who use the phrase "make the Bible relevant" are questioning its sufficiency (though likely some are). Maybe they are using inexact language to communicate the need to make sermons relevant. Howard Hendricks wrote, "I work hard to make the Bible relevant, alive, exciting."[3] However, a former student of Hendricks credits him with saying, "People tell me they want to make the Bible relevant. Nonsense. The Bible's already relevant. You're the one that's irrelevant!"[4] This is a pithy way to make the point that the Bible is relevant.

Karl Barth wrote, "Preaching is the attempt enjoined upon the church to serve God's own Word, through one who is called thereto, by expounding a biblical text in human words and making it relevant to contemporaries, in intimation of what they have to hear from God himself."[5]

While some who doubt the sufficiency of Scripture might point to Barth's quote to support their position, likely Barth did not mean to imply that the Bible is irrelevant. Barth debunked nineteenth-century liberalism with his emphasis on God's revelation of himself through the Scripture,[6] and asserted "preaching must be exposition of Scripture."[7] Barth encouraged sermons to be thoroughly biblical. He said, "If a sermon is biblical, it will not be boring. Holy Scripture is in fact so interesting and has so much that is new and exciting to tell us that listeners cannot even think about dropping off to sleep."[8]

---

2. Metaxas, *Bonhoeffer*, 261.
3. Hendricks, "What Makes Christian Education Distinct," 24.
4. Denny Burk, "The Death of a Mentor, Howard Hendricks (1924–2013)."
5. Barth, *Homiletics*, 44.
6. Godsey, "Barth and Bonhoeffer."
7. Barth, *Homiletics*, 49.
8. Ibid., 80.

The Bible is relevant. Preachers can never do better than the text, but because they are teaching people, they need to make sure their sermons are relevant to their audiences.

Teaching the People

Preaching is teaching *the people* the truth of the Scripture, it is not teaching the Scripture. This is not mere semantics. It is a valid distinction with a significant difference. Likely this idea is at the heart of Barth's use of the phrase "making it relevant." It is equivalent to "make it comprehensible."[9] In other words, speak in an understandable, relevant way to your audience. Teach in such a way that the people can understand.

Therefore, the key question is not whether the Bible is relevant—it is relevant. The real question is, Is my sermon relevant?[10] There is a difference between speaking truth and people actually hearing what the preacher says. Because the Bible is an ancient text, preachers must communicate scriptural truth to a contemporary audience in a relevant way—they have to make their sermon relevant, bridging the gap between ancient and modern times. To teach the people well, preachers must overcome some communication barriers.

Communicating through the Noise

Just as loud noises can drown out a speaker's voice, psychological noise can keep people from hearing. They will not benefit from the sermon's content if it is over their heads or insults their intelligence. In addition, if speakers offend the listeners with cultural insensitivities, they will shut down and stop listening. Relevance, varied education levels, and cultural differences are not the only communication barriers that hamper good communication. Other barriers include preferences, misunderstandings, learning styles, personality types, and distractions.[11] These work against

---

9. Barth, *Church Dogmatics*, I/1, 61.

10. Briscoe, "Filling the Sermon with Interest," 67: "There's no problem with the Scriptures. They're relevant. But I have to do my part to make the sermon as relevant as the Scriptures, because I want people to leave saying, 'I see!' and not 'So what?'"

11. Knowles, Holton, and Swanson, *Adult Learner*, 150–54. Hirsh and Kise, *Type and Spirituality*, 22. Different personality types concentrate on different things in devotion to God. Sensorial Thinkers (STs): "applying spirituality to practical needs"; Sensorial Feelers (SFs): "showing devotion in tangible ways"; Intuitive Feelers (NFs): "inspiring others to stick to their ideals"; Intuitive Thinkers (NTs): "defining the truth and acting on it."

clear communication. For these and other reasons, preachers prepare sermons for specific audiences and take care to communicate the biblical message to their audiences in a relevant, comprehensible way.

For preaching to be transformative, the message must break through the noise, but that is not enough. It must also be consistent with what God is saying to his people.

THE PREACHER IS NOT THE ONLY SPEAKER

The preacher's words are not the only thing the listener encounters during the sermon. Multiple lines of communication exist.

God speaks through preachers, but he also speaks to preachers. They heard from God as they prayed for their congregation and interacted with them during the week. They heard from God as they prepared the sermon and studied his Word. They also hear from God while preaching it.

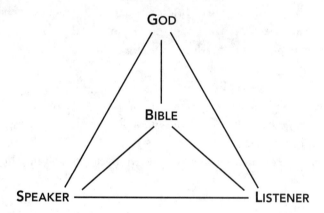

FIGURE 10: LINES OF COMMUNICATION

Certainly, the line of communication from the speaker to the listener is significant, but there are others. God also has direct access to the listener. Listeners heard from God as they prepared their hearts for worship, practiced spiritual disciplines, and interacted with others during the week. During the sermon, God speaks to them as they pray and read the text.

Listeners also have a voice. While the preachers are preaching, listeners give them indirect and direct feedback during the worship service, along with feedback throughout the week.

Beyond the words spoken, the ethos of the speaker, the physical environment, the worship service, and other worship elements speak to those in attendance. The words spoken in the sermon are just one of the many lines of communication. However, they are words that have grown out of God's Holy Scripture, shaped by interaction with God and his people. God uses them to change lives.

CLEARING THE FOG

Noise is not the only communication barrier. *Fog* is another.[12] It is one thing for preachers to understand a biblical truth, but another to communicate it in a clear, understandable, relevant way.[13] If there is fog in the pulpit, there will never be clarity in the pew. This is the argument that homileticians use to emphasize the importance of a thesis statement—preachers must know what they want listeners to understand and must be able to state it in a single sentence. It is the same argument I am using for the necessity of creating a clear transformative point based upon transformative truth without equivocation or nuance.[14] Preachers must know what they want their listeners to do and they must call them to do it. The transformative point is clear, direct, and life changing.

PREACHING FOR TRANSFORMATION

Preaching involves *teaching people the Bible so they can encounter God and live transformed lives.* While it is good for people to understand biblical truth, it is better when they apply it to their lives. It is better still when that applied truth transforms their lives. Preaching should be transformative.[15]

---

12. Lamb, *Dynamics of Biblical Preaching*, 67: "I'm afraid that sometimes there is indeed a fair amount of fog in the pulpit. Some preachers leave their hearers less clear after the sermon than they were before it."

13. Bugg, *Preaching from the Inside Out,* 79: "The true test of the form of a sermon is clarity, not cleverness. Our chief purpose in preaching is to make the message clear."

14. Mohler, "As One with Authority," 93: "Sadly, many preachers today are also artisans of nuance. They will hint at what a text might be about, but leave a seed of doubt as to whether the text is actually about anything at all. These modern day spinners of elasticity and masters of equivocation speak a dozen possible interpretations of a text without coming to any firm conclusions. Even worse, they label as 'dogmatic' anyone who claims to have a sure and certain understanding of a text of Scripture."

15. Edwards, *Elements of Homiletic*, 63. Some writers make the point that transformation

Preachers cannot transform their congregations, and people cannot transform themselves. God is the agent of transformation. Transformation is impossible outside of the empowering work of God. Paul wrote, "I appeal to you therefore, brothers, by the mercies of God, to present your bodies as a living sacrifice, holy and acceptable to God, which is your spiritual worship. Do not be conformed to this world, but be transformed by the renewal of your mind, that by testing you may discern what is the will of God, what is good and acceptable and perfect" (Rom. 12:1–2 ESV).

Paul used the word translated "transformed" twice in his writings (Rom. 12:2 and 2 Cor. 3:18).[16] Both times it denotes a work that happens inside the believer that occurs by an outside force with the person's consent.[17] In the Romans passage, the transformation results in knowing, and by extension living God's will. In the Corinthians passage, it results in reflecting Christ's likeness.[18] In both instances, the verb is in the passive voice, meaning that an outside force, in this case God, is doing the transformative work.

There is something that God does—he transforms. However, there is also something his people must do—they must renew their minds, present themselves to God, and resist forces that conform them to the world.[19]

---

comes from God and his Word, not from preaching. See Keller, *Preaching: Communicating Faith in an Age of Skepticism*, 5: "No church should expect that all of the life transformation that comes from the Word of God (John 17:17, cf. Col. 3:16–17 and Eph. 5:18–20) comes strictly through preaching." Willimon, "Transforming Word," 327: "The goal of preaching is sometimes said to be transformation. But we can get that wrong. The word of God transforms, the Spirit transforms, Christ transforms, not the preacher's rhetoric." While their point is well taken, that God and his Word are the means of transformation, good preaching—transformative preaching—is not merely man speaking, but God speaking through the preacher and his Word.

16. Mark uses the divine passive with this same verb to describe Jesus' transfiguration in Mark 9:2.

17. Behm, "Μορφοω," 758. Mounce, *Romans*, 232–33: "We must 'let ourselves be transformed.'"

18. Bruce, *Romans*, 224: "The same verb (*metamorphoō*) is rendered 'transfigured' in the transfiguration narratives of Matthew 17:1–2 and Mark 9:2. The only other place where it occurs in the New Testament is 2 Corinthians 3:18, of believers being 'changed' into the likeness of Christ 'from one degree of glory to another' by the operation of 'the Lord who is the Spirit'—a passage which is a helpful commentary on the present one."

19. Morris, *Romans*, 435: "There can be little doubt that the two verbs are not synonyms and that there is a basic difference between outward conformity and inward transformation."

Inasmuch as gospel preaching encourages people to think (renewing of the mind), submit to God (present themselves as a living sacrifice), and act righteously (not being conformed to the world), it facilitates transformation. God uses the "foolishness of preaching" (1 Cor. 1:21) to transform lives.[20] That is why we say that preaching involves *teaching the people the Bible so they can experience life transformation.*[21]

Life Application Is Necessary for Transformation to Occur

The present tense of the verb (*metamorphoō*) indicates that transformation is a continual pursuit, not a solitary event.[22] Transformation is a process. It does not occur instantly; rather, it happens over time. With a steady diet of listening to God's story, God's people can experience his transformative power.

Ultimately, transformation is the goal of preaching. The primary thing pastors can do to aid in the transformation of their people is to stay out of the way of the text and let it do its transformative work.

Developing the Transformative Point

Writing the transformative point is a two-step process that begins with an exegesis of the text in order to discover the transformative truth (what the biblical author is revealing about God, his nature, his attributes, or his glory in the passage of Scripture). Since the Bible is a book about God, he—not humanity—is the focus of the body of the sermon. This is different from moralistic preaching that looks for signs of virtue in the

---

20. Cranfield, *Romans,* 2:597: "The earnest appeal, based on the gospel, to those who are already believers to live consistently with the gospel they have received." Mounce, *Romans,* 230: "Only the Christian faith, rooted as it is in a supernatural act that took place in history (the incarnation, life, death, and resurrection of Jesus Christ), has the ultimate moral authority as well as the effective power to transform human life according to the divine intention." Jackman, "Preaching That Connects, Part 2," 193: "The motivation, therefore, is a deep-seated desire to conform the thinking and behavior of the people to the faith of the Bible." Fallon, "The Bible Preaches on the Bible," 301: "Preaching transforms lives in the Bible. Preaching today that teaches and proclaims the gospel in such a way that is heard and understood can similarly change lives."

21. Earley, *Pastoral Leadership Is . . . ,* 147: "Effective preaching evokes *change* in the hearer. It is more than giving information. It is a means of *transformation.*" See also Chapell, *Christ-Centered Preaching,* 57.

22. Mounce, *Romans,* 232.

Bible characters and then calls on the listeners to emulate them.[23] Bible characters have no virtue (Rom. 3:10) apart from their faith response to God (Rom. 1:17). It is also different from how-to preaching that turns the Bible into a self-help book.[24]

The next step is to determine what response the audience should take to the mind-renewing, transformative truth as revealed in the text. The transformative point will call the audience to submit to God and resist the world-conforming forces. Transformation happens at the intersection of trusting in God and obeying him. God's people must respond by putting their faith in him and putting their faith into practice (Matt. 7:23–27).[25]

Encountering God, as revealed in the text, allows the audience to "behold his glory" (2 Cor. 3:18) and "renew their minds" (Rom. 12:2). This reveals God's good, pleasing, and perfect will (Rom. 12:2). (This is the sermon's transformative truth.) The listeners' faith response is to do the will of God, by not continuing with their sin-shaped, "conformed to the world" actions (Rom. 12:2). Instead, they offer faith-actions as a sacrifice to God (this is the sermon's transformative point), so they can please him (Rom. 12:1) and ultimately experience transformation into his image (2 Cor. 3:18).[26]

The second and third movements in the dramatic arc (see chap. 2),[27] which we labeled "attempt" and "failure" respectively, often mirror typical sin-shaped "conformed to the world" actions in response to the

---

23. Greidanus, "Preaching in the Gospels," 332–33: "Often this switch from Jesus to other characters is made for the best of reasons: relevance. One Sunday the sermon may be about Mary and her submission to the Lord and the congregation is encouraged to imitate her godly attitude. The next Sunday the sermon may be about Judas and his betrayal of Christ and the congregation is warned never to betray Christ like Judas did. However, this kind of example preaching is basically moralistic and subverts the gospel when it turns the Christocentric gospel message into an anthropocentric sermon."

24. Chapell, *Christ-Centered Preaching*, 221.

25. Hunt, *Redeemed!* 155: "The most familiar biblical expressions for the believer's response are *repentance* and *faith*. Faith is the basic term, but faith always implies repentance." (See Acts 20:21.) Moo, *Romans*, 1150: "The essence of successful Christian living is the *renewing* of our minds so that we might be able to *approve what God's will is*— that is, to recognize and put into practice God's will for every situation we face."

26. Mounce, *Romans*, 232–23: "Paul taught that believers, as they behold the glory of the Lord, are being 'transformed' into his likeness."

27. For clarity's sake, I tend to label multiple second and third movements contained in the same sermon 2b, 3b, 2c, 3c, etc.

"problem" presented in the first movement. The transformative point, usually located at the transition between the third and fourth movements, ushers in the desired resolution in the fourth movement.

The following table shows the transformative truths and transformative points from the sermons contained in this book. Column 4 shows the transformative truth revealed in the sermon; column 5 is the transformative point, based upon that truth.

TABLE 1: TRANSFORMATIVE SERMON POINTS

Title	Text	Location in Book	Transformative Truth *What does God reveal about himself in this Scripture?*	Transformative Point *What is our faith response to God, as revealed in this Scripture?*
"Dangerous Choices"	Daniel 3:15b	Chapter 4	God is dependable. He will accomplish his will and will never forsake his children.	When you face a choice with uncertain outcomes, trust in God. Maybe he will save you from the fire, maybe he won't. What I know for sure, is that if he doesn't, he will be with you through the fire and on the other side.
"Impacting Eternity"	Genesis 41:34–42	Chapter 4	God is sovereign and is in control of history. He uses grace in the moment and for his eternal purposes.	Believers must forgive those who've hurt us. Don't think that you extend grace just to benefit people in the moment; it impacts eternity. It is God's great plan for you.

"Under His Wings"	Ruth 3:7–9	Chapter 4	God is all powerful and merciful. He wants his children to be merciful to one another.	Because of God's sovereignty, you must ignore your own self-interest and choose to show God's steadfast love to vulnerable people.
"You are the Man!"	2 Samuel 12:1–6	Chapter 5	God is faithful to forgive sin when we confess our sins.	Today, I'm asking you to examine your sins, and to confess them to God and ask him for forgiveness. I'm not saying that all consequences for your actions will disappear, just that God stands ready to offer you grace, if you confess your sins.
"Contrasting Choices"	Psalm 1:1–6	Chapter 6	God nourishes his children with his instruction and empowers them to live according to it.	Today, I want to encourage you to do the right thing, not the easy thing. Immerse yourself in God's instruction, and then live your life according to it.
"Do You Love or Do You Hate Your Child?"	Proverbs 13:24	Chapter 7	God's love is shown through his discipline.	Therefore, if you really want to love your children, you must do more than simply provide for their physical needs, you must love them enough to discipline them, just as God disciplines you out of his love for you.

"Powerful Living"	Proverbs 31:1–9	Chapter 7	God establishes authorities and requires them to serve his purposes.	You must use your advantages to serve others and the cause of justice.
"In His Time"	Luke 1:13	Chapter 8	God is eternally faithful. But that does not mean he follows our timetable.	Because he is faithful, God can be trusted, even while you wait on his response to your need.
"Why Did He Do It?"	Matthew 27:11–26	Chapter 8	God loves his fallen creation enough to send his son to die for our sins.	Love made salvation possible. Believe in Jesus today and make salvation personal.
"Celebrate!"	Luke 15:3–24	Chapter 9	God's grace flows to the undeserving.	Because God is gracious, extend God's grace to others, and celebrate it in your own life, and theirs.
"The Reward for Faithfulness"	Matthew 25:14–30	Chapter 9	God is worthy of our worship and requires that we serve him wholeheartedly.	God does not exist to make your life easier. You exist to serve and worship him and the greatest reward you can ever receive is to have the honor of having more responsibility, and the greatest thing you can ever do in life, is to fulfill the potential that God has given you.
"Living the Resurrection"	1 Corinthians 15:1–34	Chapter 10	Jesus rose from the dead, defeating death, hell, and the grave.	Because Christ rose from the dead, you should influence others with the gospel; don't allow them to influence you.

"Hope in Uncertain Times"	Revelation 5:8–14	Chapter 11	The resurrection makes new life possible.	You can place your trust in the Lion from the tribe of Judah, who is the slaughtered Lamb that lives.

A faith-action response grows out of the transformative truth. A transformative point is a personal, memorable, and concrete statement of the preferred response a listener should make to God's nature, attributes, or glory as revealed in the text (the transformative truth).

PERSONAL

It is personal. That is why it uses the second-person pronoun "you." All listeners will need to know that it is not enough if "we" as a congregation take the action. It is not a collective response. It is an individual, personal response.

MEMORABLE

The transformative point must be memorable, even if it is not bumper-sticker memorable. If you review the list of those in the table above, you will notice that I do not try to make a slogan out of the point, but I do not see anything wrong with the transformative point sounding like a slogan if doing so is consistent with the preacher's personality.[28]

By memorable, I mean that if the server at lunch asks, "What was the sermon about?" his customers would be able to answer, "The pastor said that since God is gracious, we should be willing to forgive people who wrong us."

CONCRETE

The transformative point must be clear, but it also must call for action. In the example above, the transformative truth is God is gracious. The transformative point is that we should forgive those who wrong us. It is clear, but to make it concrete, it is helpful for preachers to "shape the

---

28. Ericson, *The Rhetoric of the Pulpit*, xiv–v: "You are a particular person addressing a particular group of listeners on a particular text. . . . So, trust yourself. Be yourself. Make the sermon your own."

path" for applying the transformative truth. [29] The same leadership principles that apply for vision casting apply to calling for personal life transformation. Preachers must not preach in generalities, but must call the people to make a specific response.[30]

FOR FURTHER REFLECTION

- How can the criterion of "preaching is to teach people the Bible so they can encounter God and live transformed lives" influence the sermons you write and preach?
- Look at the sermons you have preached in the last six months. Did you preach to facilitate transformation, or did you merely impart information?
- Find five people who know you well, hear you preach often, and love you enough to answer this question: "Have my last three sermons been relevant to your life?"
- Do you have a transformative truth and a transformative point for your sermons? Develop both for your next sermon and see how it changes the way you approach the sermon.
- Evaluate the transformative truth and transformative point of your next three sermons by asking these questions: Was it personal? Was it memorable? Was it concrete?

29. Heath and Heath, *Switch*, 180.
30. For example, see Wilson, *Pastoral Ministry in the Real World*, 169–84.

PART 2

Developing High Impact Sermons

Old Testament Narrative Episodes

READING THE TEXT: WHAT DOES IT SAY AND HOW DOES IT SAY IT?

Much of the Old Testament is narrative—a collection of the stories of God's people.[1] What we read were once face-to-face stories fathers told their children or worship leaders told their congregations. They are intimate communication.

Stories entertain. However, that is not their only function. Great stories shape culture. All types of stories—pure fiction, historical fiction, and historic narrative—all shape culture. Not only do stories shape culture, they also become a cultural repository that reinforces the beliefs, values, and laws of a culture. They are storehouses of cultural traditions and values—they are a community's collective memory—having a homeostatic effect that sustains a culture's ethos for future generations.

Interwoven into these narratives are other types of literature—poetry, legal material, allegories, and parables—that add depth and functional purpose. In legal texts, the writers provide explicit directions for God's people to follow. When Hebrew poetry is in a narrative, it often recasts significant events in Israel's history in an epic form. It uses poetic language to give emphasis to aspects of an event in the narrative the poem echoes.[2]

Allegories and parables illustrate and emphasize the moral or theological ideas the narrator is communicating. Each component works within its larger narrative frameworks with organic unity. It is the whole, with its

---

1. Fee and Stuart, *How to Read the Bible for All Its Worth*, 89, places the number at 40 percent.

2. Compare Judges 4 (the story of Deborah and Barak) with Judges 5 (the poetic rehearsal of the same story).

individual parts woven together into a meaningful tapestry, that reveals God's will to his people.

The stories are more than a mixture of narrative with other types of literature. They have a plot that serves as the skeleton, and all other elements are like its muscle and sinew.[3] The plot of the story moves the characters through the events of a story from a beginning to a final scene. The plot provides the narrative with the ability to communicate its meaning. To find the narrative's point, the reader must follow the plot to the point (meaning) of the story, while being careful not to confuse movements with points (chap. 2).

Transition words like "meanwhile," "then," and "however" signal movements—twists and turns in the plot. They serve to alert readers that the writers are introducing new scenes or characters, or that there is a shift in topic or focus to follow. For instance, Jonah 1 has several of these shifts of focus. Yahweh delivers his word to Jonah to go to the people of Nineveh and denounce them because of their evil. This is the first shift in focus, and it is obvious. God has commanded Jonah to get up, go to Nineveh, and denounce the people. And, while he does get up, he does not go to Nineveh; he flees toward Tarshish. That is, as far away from where God had told him to go as possible. The translators of HCSB use the word "however" in the 1:1–3 passage to communicate this disjunction:[4]

> The word of the LORD came to Jonah son of Amittai:
> "Get up!
> Go to the great city of Nineveh

---

3 In the last couple of decades, analysis of the literary features of Hebrew narrative has become more prevalent. The following works give helpful overviews not only of plot, but in describing how it functions in both the interpretation of Biblical Hebrew Narrative and in preaching and teaching it: Fewell and Gunn, "Narrative, Hebrew," 4:1023–27; Eskanazi, "Torah as Narrative, and Narrative as Torah," 11–30; Amit and Bauer, "Narrative Literature," 4:223–25; Greidanus, *The Modern Preacher and the Ancient Text*, 188–227; Wilson, *How to Write Narrative Sermons*, 3–10.

4. The block diagrams in this chapter are organized around the independent clauses, since that is where the topic or focus of the narrative portion is presented and carried forward. The subordinated clauses are arranged in relationship to the independent clauses they modify. The block diagram provides a graphic display of the structure and organization of the passage.

> and
> > preach against it,
> > > because their wickedness has confronted Me."
> > > > *However,*
> Jonah got up to flee to Tarshish from the LORD's presence.
> He went down to Joppa
> > and
> found a ship going to Tarshish.
> He paid the fare
> > and
> went down into it
> > to go with them to Tarshish, from the LORD's presence.

Notice how effective this word choice is in communicating Jonah's disobedience. While "but" would communicate the idea well (as in the NIV and ESV), the word "however" is more explicit in this context.[5] Even at this early stage in the story, it communicates a significant turn in the plot so that from the outset the reader notices Jonah's folly.[6]

Several other things are worth noting before addressing the other topic-switching devices. *Direct speech* is often more revealing of the nature of a plot than any other element. The reader gets insight into the feelings or motivations of the narrator through speech. Often a narrator reveals his own feelings about the characters or events (in Jonah, a commissioning from God) in the story. This serves to sway the feelings or attitudes of his readers. In this case, the speech alone communicates God's expressed will to Jonah, while the initiation of the narrative in verse 3 characterizes both the prophet and his actions in a negative way.

Further, the narrator uses *motive clauses* to supplement the impact, first of God's speech, and then of Jonah's actions. The express reason Yahweh is sending Jonah to Nineveh is "because their wickedness has

---

5 Tucker, *Jonah*, 11–18. Technically, while verses 1 and 2 are a part of the plot, they serve as an introductory scene-setting device—everything that happens in this chapter, and indeed the rest of the book is in response to Yahweh's commissioning of Jonah. The actual narrative does not begin until verse 3, where Jonah arises "to flee . . . from the presence of Yahweh" (Gregg Watson's translation).

6 Notice also that there is a distinct change of subject here. The logical subject in verses 1–2 is Yahweh; the express subject in verse 3 is Jonah.

confronted (literally, "come up before") me." Then, in verse 3, the motive for Jonah's flight is expressed by "to go with them to Tarshish from
Yahweh's presence."

Verses 4–5 create two distinct shifts. The first is from Jonah's nap in
the belly of the ship to the setting outside his seemingly warm and cozy
nest; the second is to reintroduce Yahweh as the major character in the
story.

> *Then*
> the LORD hurled a violent wind on the sea,
> > and
> > > such a violent storm arose on the sea
> > that
> the ship threatened to break apart.
> The sailors were afraid,
> > and
> each cried out to his god.
> They threw the ship's cargo into the sea
> > to lighten the load.
> > *Meanwhile,*
> Jonah had gone down to the lowest part of the vessel
> > and
> had stretched out and fallen into a deep sleep.

Notice the change of subject from Jonah in verse 3 to Yahweh in verse
4. The word "then" accommodates the switch—not only in subject, but
also in the topic or focus. The narrative moves away from Jonah and his
motives for fleeing to Yahweh's response. Though it is brief, it is enough
to communicate to the reader that Yahweh is not at all happy with Jonah's
decision. This leads to another slight change in both subject and focus—
from Yahweh's displeasure to the sailors' fear.

There are two more shifts: one ending verse 5, and the second beginning verse 6. The word "meanwhile" indicates a shift in verse 5, which is
obvious by an abrupt switch in subject from the sailors back to Jonah. In
effect, the narrator has taken the reader on a circular route from Yahweh
(commissioning) to Jonah (fleeing and sleeping) to Yahweh (hurling a
storm) to the sailors (fearing and hurling cargo) to Jonah (sleeping while

fleeing). Jonah is apparently completely unaware of the upheaval going on around him. He is the only character introduced so far who remains ignorant of the circumstances his actions have created, which could be a plot device that foreshadows Jonah's ignorance of God's gracious behavior (Jonah 4).

The last shift occurs between verses 5 and 6. It is apparent by a simple and somewhat abrupt switch in subject. While Jonah sleeps, the head sailor approaches, wakes him, and in understandable bewilderment says three things: "what are you doing sound asleep," "get up and call on your God," and with fading hope, "perhaps he will bear us in mind and we won't perish." In other words, "Wake up and pray, fool, or we die!" It is worth noting here that, according to verse 10, the sailors already knew what Jonah was up to because "he had told them," apparently when he boarded the ship.

To recap the movement of the plot to this point and beyond, the story begins when Yahweh extends a call to Jonah. The complications on the Mediterranean Sea have their origin in Jonah's flight from Yahweh's commission. He went down to Joppa, hired a ship, and then went down into its cargo hold to go to sleep. When Yahweh hurled a storm (Jonah was asleep), the sailors became afraid and tried to save the ship. The captain confronted him with his apparent apathy and asked him to pray. In the meantime, the sailors began casting lots to determine who caused the peril. When the lot indicated Jonah was the guilty party, they questioned him about his origin, identity, and ethnicity. When he told them, they were horrified, even though they already had this information. Because the sea was getting rougher, they asked how they might calm the sea. Jonah's simple solution, which was to have them throw him into the sea, added to their terror. Rather than do so, they attempted to return to the shore. When they realized the futility of trying to land the ship, they decided to throw Jonah overboard as he had instructed. However, in doing so, they cried out to Yahweh. While throwing Jonah overboard, they threw themselves on God's mercy.

Notice how the author has steadily increased the tension of the account: the sailors become increasingly fearful as they first attempt to discover the cause of their predicament, and then, faced with the necessity of possibly killing Jonah, are thrown into an internal conflict. At the same time, the increasing intensity of the storm serves the same purpose. With so much danger in the air, the reader anticipates the resolution to the matter, leading to the resolution to the conflict in chapter 1—with the hurling[7] of Jonah into the sea, the storm ceased. And, in a rather surprising, and ironic twist, the sailors acted as any faithful Israelite would: they feared Yahweh, they sacrificed to Yahweh, and they made vows, presumably in the name of Yahweh.[8]

Notice how the narrator built tension within the plot of chapter 1. The broad outline provided by the plot does not require the reader to invest in the story, but through the strategic and tactical use of these elements, the plot moves forward. The plot moves the story along, while the other elements create a pause in the action to add new information, thus informing both the plot and the reader of the nature of the immediate circumstances, and creating a more interesting story line through which the author communicates the major themes and theological emphases.

In general, other Old Testament narratives operate in much the same way. Even though the stories span many centuries, the basic characteristics of storytelling in the Old Testament remain remarkably consistent. Reading the text, identifying the plot of a narrative, and determining how the original author fleshed it out is how you discover the main point of a story. To find the point (meaning), follow the plot.

GRASPING THE HISTORICAL CONTEXT: IDENTIFYING WHAT THE TEXT MEANT

Though the literary context is a key component for interpreting the Old Testament, several important historical aspects of the text impact its meaning.

First, the overarching perspective on the Bible that pervades what has been (and will be) said here is that this is God's Word to his people. The inspiration of its writers took place in a particular time, for a particular people, for a particular purpose. In other words, the Holy Spirit acted in history to communicate his will and his truth to his people. It is therefore that message to those people through those writers in that language that was inspired. These inspired stories present a timeless repository

---

7. This is the same word used when Yahweh hurls the wind into the sea, and when the sailors hurl the cargo from the ship into the sea.

8. Their response foreshadows the response of the Ninevites in Jonah 3:6–9.

of truth from which God's people are to understand how to live, serve, and work as God's people. It is historic in that God entered history to communicate, and it is timeless in that its message applies to all people of all times.

Second, because the events took place in ancient times, using an ancient language that reflects cultural influences that seem far different from what is common in modern times, it takes some work to understand what motivated an author to choose the people and events that comprise his narratives. For instance, in the story of Jonah, he receives a commission from God, walks from his home in Gath-hepher (this is an assumption, as the author has not told us where Jonah began his adventure) to Joppa, finds a ship, pays its fare, and so on. What was significant about Joppa that Jonah would choose it as his point of departure? What were boats and ships like during his time? What was casting lots? And, along those lines, what was the religious background of the sailors? While absolute answers to these questions may be elusive, locating the events recorded in the narratives in space and time, and identifying the cultural, social, and religious perspectives brings the stories to life.

Old Testament narratives contain both a literary and a historical dimension. It is important to realize that a biblical narrative is both historical and literary in nature. The desire to communicate important historical events combines with an artistic impulse that is primarily theological in nature.[9] It is in the combination of the literary and theological, and the attendant and inevitable overlap between the two that enables the careful interpreter to discern the timeless theological emphases that exist in the text. It is the theology—the understanding of how the Creator relates to humanity, how humanity relates to its Creator, and how God and humanity relate to the created world—that makes the Word of God eternally relevant to the community of faith.

Sermon Samples from Old Testament Narratives

At the end of each chapter in part 2, you will find sermon manuscripts of one-point expository sermons that keep the meaning and the impact of

---

9. Longman III, "Literary Approaches," 91–192; Silva, "God, Language, and Scripture," 193–280; Long, "The Art of Biblical History," 281–429; Provan, Long, and Longman, *A Biblical History of Israel*, 3–104.

the text intact through the hermeneutical and homiletical processes. The manuscripts are not transcriptions of every word spoken when preached; rather, they are a concise summary of the sermon.[10] Many of the chapters will have a single sermon to illustrate the chapter; a few will have a couple of sermons. But this first chapter has three sermons to reinforce the principles you have read so far in hopes that the principles will come to life in the sermons.

One of the three sermons is from the Hebrew Torah; the other two are from the Writings. The first two select a single episode in a larger story, the third sermon illustrates how to preach an entire story—in this case, an entire book of the Bible, in one sermon. In the chapter that follows, there will also be a sample sermon from another Old Testament narrative from the Hebrew Bible's Former Prophets.

In the sermon "Dangerous Choices," I demonstrate that our best option is to trust in God, regardless of the immediate price we will pay for following him.[11] I have an ongoing pastoral concern that people often seek to know God's will just as an option to choose from, not because they have a commitment to abandon their will to his. This sermon underscores the need to find and follow God's will, not just discover it.

Just as God was still in charge when his people were in exile, he is still in charge today. We serve a God that can rescue us, but we must have a commitment to follow him, even if he does not deliver us. As you read, notice the movements of the sermon:

⬇ King Nebuchadnezzar requires everyone to bow before his statue

    ⬆ Three Hebrew children refuse because they know God can deliver them, but do not know if he will

---

10. In some cases, I (Wilson) made changes in the sermon manuscript after I preached it to make needed improvements. I also edited and made changes in sermons preached by our colleagues (with their permission of course). In addition, my colleagues occasionally encouraged me to make some changes in one of the manuscripts to improve it and I followed their advice.

11. Unless otherwise noted, Wilson is the author of the sermon samples throughout the book.

⬇ King Nebuchadnezzar has them thrown into the furnace that is seven times hotter than normal

⬆ God delivers them

Dangerous Choices

Daniel 3:15b

But if you don't worship [the statue I made], you will immediately be thrown into a furnace of blazing fire—and who is the god who can rescue you from my power?

In a tribute to his greatness, Nebuchadnezzar built a 90-foot gold-plated statue. He required all the people regardless of their religion, nationality, or ethnicity to worship his statue when they heard the call to worship played on the various instruments.

The people complied with his demands. When the call to worship came, they bowed before the statue and paid homage (Dan. 5:7). Well, almost everyone did. Shadrach, Meshach, and Abednego refused to bow—not out of disrespect to the king, but out of devotion to their God.

The Chaldeans noticed the three men standing in the sea of compliant worshipers and reported what they saw to the king. The king was furious. No one defied this king and lived! When he led the Babylonian troops into battle against Egypt, he left destruction in his wake. When Jehoiakim refused to pay tribute money, he sacked Judah and brought King Jehoiakim into captivity with his people. Now three of the Jewish captives dared to defy his order and would not worship the graven image.

Nebuchadnezzar questioned the Hebrew men, reiterating the consequences they would suffer if they did not comply with his demands. "But if you don't worship it, you will immediately be thrown into a furnace of blazing fire—and who is the god who can rescue you from my power?" (Dan. 3:15b).

Shadrach, Meshach, and Abednego found themselves at a crossroads. Not every decision changes everything. Choosing coffee or tea has few consequences. Attending the late service or the early one likely does not make a difference. However, this was not that kind of a choice. If they did not bow down, they would face the violent anger of a controlling king. If they did bow down, they would be breaking one of the Ten Commandments: "Do not have other gods besides me" (Exod. 20:3). In the process, they would deny who they were at their very core—monotheists who exclusively worshiped the one true God. It was a dangerous choice regardless of what they did. They could anger the king or they could anger God.

The three Hebrew children came from a long line of compromisers. The Jewish people had a history of compromising their exclusive devotion to God. They had done so at the very time that Moses descended from the mountain with the Ten Commandments (Exod. 32:2–6). They worshiped Baal during the time of the judges (Judg. 2:11–12) and the kings (2 Kings 1:2–3). They worshiped idols many times in Israel's history (2 Kings 16:10–16; 17:32–33; 17:41).

The choice the three Hebrew children faced was clear. They could compromise, just as their people had done at other times, and live. Or they could defy King Nebuchadnezzar and face the heat in the furnace.

They stood at a crossroad. Shadrach, Meshach, and Abednego had every reason to believe that Nebuchadnezzar would carry out his threats.

He had the means: There was a furnace handy—likely the very one that the smelters used to purify the gold that adorned the graven image.

He had the reputation: Nebuchadnezzar was a ruthless military man. When he was the crown prince of Babylon, he led his nation's army at the Battle of Carchemish with a scorched earth policy. With the decisive victory came the spoils. He gained control over what King Neco of Egypt previously dominated (2 Kings 24:7).

When he learned of his father's death in 605 BC, Nebuchadnezzar returned home to assume the full power of his father's throne. It was during this time that all the kings of Syria began paying tribute to Nebuchadnezzar. He dominated the region, and everyone paid. Even Jehoiakim, king of Judah, submitted to Nebuchadnezzar for a season (2 Kings 24:1), but after the three years he rebelled even though Jeremiah warned him to continue to submit (Jer. 27:4–11). Nebuchadnezzar could not allow this open rebellion, so Babylon invaded Judah, plundered the temple, captured the king, and led him away in chains (2 Chron. 36:6–7). Nebuchadnezzar was ruthless. When people did not do what he told them to do, they paid—often they paid with their lives. The three Hebrew children knew their very presence in Babylon was a direct result of King Jehoiakim defying Nebuchadnezzar. If a king could not get away with defiance, neither could they.

I do not know if they knew about Nebuchadnezzar killing Zedekiah and Ahab, two other captives, by roasting them in the fire (Jer. 29:22). But I am certain they did not doubt for a moment that Nebuchadnezzar was not bluffing; he would throw them into the furnace, just as he said.

For those who have heard this story before, please do not discount the inherent peril of this moment just because you know how the story ends. The three men were certain about the consequence of their defiance—Nebuchadnezzar would throw them into the furnace. They were certain about what they would do—they would not bow down. Their only uncertainty was whether God would intervene.

Shadrach, Meshach, and Abednego replied to the king, "If the God we serve exists, then he can rescue us from the furnace of blazing fire, and he can rescue us from the power of you, the king. But even if he does not rescue us, we want you as king to know that we will not serve your gods or worship the gold statue you set up" (Dan. 3:17–18).

Notice the important distinction they made. There was no doubt in their minds that God could save them, they just did not know if he would save them. The space between *could* and *would* is where faith matures and character develops.

Faith that God can do something is important. We serve a God that can! God could save them from the fire and rescue them from peril. God could save them through the fire and walk with them in the midst of their troubles. And God could save them in spite of the fire and greet them on the other side in heaven, a place he has prepared for them.

Faith that God would do something is irrelevant. Each of these possible outcomes required the same response: faithfulness.

God does not always intervene in tight spots. Sometimes innocent people suffer. Sometimes persecutors behead Christians who will not renounce their faith. Usually being faithful costs a person something. Sometimes it costs everything.

Those who feel that God exists to enrich their lives will accuse God of being cold, calloused, and uncaring when he does not intervene. Because they do not understand all of God's purposes, they do not have a point of view to explain what he is doing. Job said, "Even if he kills me, I will hope in him. I will still defend my ways before him" (Job 13:15), but he never knew that his faithfulness during times of suffering was a winning argument God made to Satan about why people serve God. If Job knew, God's purpose would not have been served. He did not know why God was allowing what was happening to him; he just knew that he trusted in God.

What about you? When you find yourself in these situations, will you do a cost-benefit analysis and choose what appears to benefit you the most? Or will you remain faithful regardless of the immediate cost? James 4:4b says, "Don't you know that friendship with the world is hostility toward God? So whoever wants to be a friend of the world becomes the enemy of God."

Nebuchadnezzar carried through on his threats and gave orders to make the fire seven times hotter and had his most valiant men throw the Hebrew children into the fire (Dan. 3:20–22). The furnace was so hot that the king's men perished, but not the victims of his wrath. They were fine.

In verse 25, the king learns of the men's fate from his high official, "Look! I see four men, not tied, walking around in the fire unharmed; and the fourth looks like a son of the gods" (Dan. 3:25).

In that moment, Nebuchadnezzar learned the answer to the question he asked in Daniel 3:15. The Lord God Almighty was able to rescue his servants from the king's hands. There was no doubt that day who was worthy of worship, and it was not the lifeless god that was decorated with the gold smelted in the furnace. The living God rescued his people in the furnace.

When you face a choice with uncertain outcomes, trust in God. Maybe he will save you from the fire, maybe he won't. What I know for sure, is that if he doesn't, he will be with you through the fire and on the other side.

God's people may have been in captivity, but God was not.

Nebuchadnezzar may have pillaged the Jerusalem temple, but he did not knock God off his throne. He is the Lord God Almighty and he does not bow to anyone, and neither do his servants.

The three Hebrew children faced a dangerous choice in their lives. Because they were faithful, everyone in Babylon knew there is a God, and that he is not a mere 90 feet tall.

REFLECTIONS ON THE SERMON

As I wrote this sermon, my starting point was the thought that most of those in the audience who were familiar with it would see it as a child's Sunday school story. I thought their familiarity would be an obstacle for them to get the full impact of the text. I wanted them to appreciate and experience the three Hebrew children's predicament.

I made the homiletical choice to weave the historical background information into the body of the sermon while using the narrative plot as the sermon's structure instead of separating the background information from the body of the sermon. Likely most of those hearing the sermon did not have the information about the ruthlessness of the king, and for them to know the situation the three Hebrew children were in, they needed the information. Because there was a large volume of background information, I feared I would lose the audience if I front-loaded it as an information dump in the introduction. Instead, I provided it just in time parallel with the plot.

This choice I made in writing the sermon required that I follow my manuscript more closely than I typically do, because the background information was critical to increase the tension; it worked in tandem with the plot line.

I foreshadowed the transformative point with the section that began with the following: "Notice the important distinction they made. There was no doubt in their minds that God could save them; they just did not know if he would save them. The space between *could* and *would* is where faith matures and character develops." I felt it was important to do some teaching about the relationship of faith and obedience. Though I did not cite Bonhoeffer in the sermon, I had his concept of cheap grace in mind and the importance of obeying even when we lack faith as I developed this section. Even though I had yet to state the transformative point, I began applying it early on.

This sermon was not about escaping the fire (a moralistic interpretative approach)—it was about using your life to make the name of God famous in all circumstances, knowing that God is with us. It was about how God uses our lives to glorify himself.

* * *

The text for the next sermon, "Impacting Eternity," is from a narrative episode from Genesis. The sermon follows the plot line of Joseph's story and shows God's greater purpose in Joseph's choice to forgive. This plot has multiple twists and turns due to multiple second and third movements as explained in chapter 2.

⬇ Famine strikes the land.

⬆ Joseph's brothers go to Egypt to get grain.

⬇ Joseph pretended not to believe them, accused them of being spies, and threw them into jail. (The brothers do not know that the man they are dealing with is their brother whom they sold into slavery, but Joseph knows who they are. The reader does not know whether Joseph's actions are revengeful or not. They do not know until the story resolves and Joseph forgives.)

⬆ Three days later Joseph releases them, allows them to take grain home, and requires they bring their younger brother with them next time as proof that their story was true.

⬇ Food runs out again.

⬆ All of the brothers, including the youngest, return to Egypt and attend a feast with Joseph. They return home with additional grain.

⬇ As they passed beyond the city, Joseph's stewards stopped

them and accused them of stealing from Joseph. They searched their belongings and found Joseph's cup in the younger brother's bag. Joseph threatens to throw Benjamin into jail and not release him unless the father returns.

↑ Judah offers to take Benjamin's place.

↓ In an emotional moment, Joseph reveals that he is their brother that they sold to the slave traders. His brothers face the reality of their situation.

↑ Joseph does not take revenge, but forgives.

As you read the sermon, pay special attention to when I break from telling the story to reading from the narrative. Usually, I do so when there is a significant movement in the narrative. It is my way of putting the focus on the text, not the sermon.

Impacting Eternity

Genesis 41:34–42

"Let Pharaoh do this: Let him appoint overseers over the land and take a fifth [of the harvest] of the land of Egypt during the seven years of abundance. Let them gather all the [excess] food during these good years that are coming. Under Pharaoh's authority, store the grain in the cities, so they may preserve [it] as food. The food will be a reserve for the land during the seven years of famine that will take place in the land of Egypt. Then the country will not be wiped out by the famine." The proposal pleased Pharaoh and all his servants, and he said to them, "Can we find anyone like this, a man who has God's spirit in him?" So Pharaoh said to Joseph, "Since God has made all this known to you, there is no one as discerning and wise as you are. You will be over my house, and all my people will obey your commands. Only I, as king, will be greater than you." Pharaoh also said to Joseph, "See, I am placing you over all

the land of Egypt." Pharaoh removed his signet ring from his hand and put it on Joseph's hand, clothed him with fine linen garments, and placed a gold chain around his neck.

The events unraveled just as Joseph said they would. Seven years of famine followed seven years of abundance. During the years of plenty, Joseph had two sons, and oversaw the storage of grain for the famine. Genesis 41:55 says, "So when all the land of Egypt was famished, the people cried out to Pharaoh for bread; and Pharaoh said to all the Egyptians, 'Go to Joseph; whatever he says to you, you shall do'" (NASB).

Verse 55 says it vividly: Joseph had absolute power. As the famine progressed, people from everywhere came to Egypt to get food. One of the groups of visitors who knelt before Joseph asking for help was Joseph's brothers. Just as Joseph had dreamed when he was a child, his brothers bowed down before him. Joseph recognized them, but they did not recognize him. They told Joseph they were ten of twelve sons from the land of Canaan wanting to buy food. According to the brothers, their youngest brother was still at home, and the other brother was dead. Joseph pretended not to believe their story, accused them of being spies, and threw them into jail for three days. Was Joseph taking revenge?

When three days passed, Joseph released all but one of them and told them to take some grain home with them but to return with their youngest brother to prove their story and show they were who they said they were.

The brothers spoke to one another in their language, not knowing that Joseph could understand them. They grieved over what they had done to Joseph years ago, believing that God was punishing them for that sin. When Joseph heard them, he went into another room and wept.

Joseph returned and sent the brothers away with the grain they bought with a special package inside the bag—the money they'd given for the grain. When the brothers arrived home, they told their father what happened and told him they had to take Benjamin back with them to verify their story and redeem Simeon. Here's his reply: "But Jacob said, 'My son shall not go down with you; for his brother is dead, and he alone is left. If harm should befall him on the journey you are taking, then you will bring my gray hair down to Sheol in sorrow'" (Gen. 42:38 NASB).

But when the food ran out, Israel had a change of mind and sent gifts with Benjamin. When they stood before Joseph, he instructed his servants to prepare a feast and invite the brothers to his house for dinner. When he saw Benjamin with his brothers, he went into a private room and wept again.

After dinner, the steward filled their sacks with grain and the money they brought, but that's not all. He also put Joseph's cup in Benjamin's sack. The trap was set and Joseph was ready to spring it. Genesis 44:4–5 says, "They had just gone out of the city, and were not far off, when Joseph said to his house steward, 'Up, follow the men; and when you overtake them, say to them, '"Why have you repaid evil for good? Is not this the one from which my lord drinks, and which he indeed uses for divination? You have done wrong in doing this"'" (NASB).

Why was Joseph doing this? Was he being spiteful and exacting revenge? This was a perfect opportunity for Joseph to take vengeance on his brothers for throwing him in a pit, threatening to kill him, and then selling him to slave traders. This is a turning point in the story. Will Joseph rise above his pain to remain focused on his assignment of preserving life? Or will he forgo his purpose so he can exact revenge for the pain his brothers inflicted on him when he was young?

While these actions appear vengeful, they are not. Joseph was leveraging his father's love for Benjamin to force him to travel to Egypt. However, Joseph could not have anticipated what happened next. When the brothers returned, Judah made a passionate plea to imprison him and let the other brothers, especially Benjamin, go free. Please remember the name Judah. It will be very important in about ten minutes that you remember who made this offer. Judah made it clear that if his father suffered any more sorrow that it would kill him.

Let's rejoin the text to see what happens next: "Then Joseph could no longer control himself before all his attendants and he cried out, 'Have everyone leave my presence!' So there was no one with Joseph when he made himself known to his brothers. And he wept so loudly that the Egyptians heard him, and Pharaoh's household heard about it" (45:1–2 NIV).

Joseph said to his brothers, "I am Joseph! Is my father still living?" But his brothers were not able to answer him, because they were terrified at his presence.

> Then Joseph said to his brothers, "Come close to me." When they had done so, he said, "I am your brother Joseph, the one you sold into Egypt! And now, do not be distressed and do not be angry with yourselves for selling me here, because it was to save lives that God sent me ahead of you. For two years now there has been famine in the land, and for the next five years there will not be plowing and reaping. But God sent me ahead of you to preserve for you a remnant on earth and to save your lives by a great deliverance. So then, it was not you who sent me here, but God. He made me father to Pharaoh, lord of his entire household and ruler of all Egypt. Now hurry back to my father and say to him, "This is what your son Joseph says: God has made me lord of all Egypt. Come down to me; don't delay. You shall live in the region of Goshen and be near me you, your children and grandchildren, your flocks and herds, and all you have. I will provide for you there, because five years of famine are still to come. Otherwise you and your household and all who belong to you will become destitute."
>
> "You can see for yourselves, and so can my brother Benjamin, that it is really I who am speaking to you. Tell my father about all the honor accorded me in Egypt and about everything you have seen. And bring my father down here quickly."
>
> Then he threw his arms around his brother Benjamin and wept, and Benjamin embraced him, weeping. And he kissed all his brothers and wept over them. Afterward his brothers talked with him" (Gen. 45:1–15 NIV).

Few people have suffered more injustice in life than Joseph did. His own flesh and blood—his brothers—sold him to slave traders. His brothers betrayed him. When he refused to sleep with his owner's wife, she had him thrown into prison. His owner's wife betrayed him. In prison, he helped some prison mates through some troubling times by interpreting their dreams. One of them promised to put in a good word to Pharaoh for Joseph when he got out, but he did not. Once again, someone betrayed Joseph. It would have been easy for Joseph to be vengeful and get even with everyone who had betrayed him, but he did not. Why? He understood that all of the pain he suffered was collateral damage in God's great plan to use him to preserve Israel. Genesis 45:7 says, "But God sent me ahead of you to preserve for you a remnant on earth and to save your lives by a great deliverance" (NIV). What was at stake was not just the well-being of his family. I asked you to remember a name a few minutes ago: Who was it that offered himself as a substitute for Benjamin? What tribe was Jesus descended from? Out of Judah's family lineage a Savior would be born—Joseph's decision not to sabotage God's plan for a moment of personal revenge had great impact. God had devised a way for the ancestors of Jesus to live through a terrible life-threatening famine, and it included some personal suffering on Joseph's part.

Believers must forgive those who've hurt us. Don't think that you extend grace just to benefit people in the moment; it impacts eternity. It is God's great plan for you.

The Bible says, "And be kind and compassionate to one another, forgiving one another, just as God also forgave you in Christ" (Eph. 4:32). Is there someone you need to forgive today? If so, begin that process right now by asking God for the strength to forgive. Forgiveness will benefit you. It will benefit the person who harmed you—and who knows—it may just impact eternity.

REFLECTIONS ON THE SERMON

One of the functions of this story's inclusion in the book of Genesis is to show how God's people got into Egypt in the first place. Another one is to show this pivotal scene of how one of Jesus' progenitors escaped imprisonment through Joseph's gracious act. The twists and turns throughout the Old Testament with Jesus' lineage fascinate me, so I always notice when God protects Jesus' ancestors.

People often focus on their pain instead of God's plan. Joseph's pain was collateral damage; it was not God's plan. God's plan in the moment was the protection of his chosen people through the famine—in eternity, it was for believers' eternal salvation. Judah, Jesus' human ancestor, offered to take his little brother's place, and Joseph did not let him. Jesus did more than offer to take our place; he willingly went to the cross and died for our sins.

Because God forgives us, we can forgive.

The following sermon "Under His Wings" summarizes the teachings of an entire book of the Bible. It is a macro view of God's providence and his grace as he works through the crisis in a Moabite woman to meet her physical needs. More than that, it shows how he provides for the spiritual needs of generations to follow.

I feared that the popular use in wedding ceremonies of Ruth's "wherever you go I will go" portion of the text would be the audience's primary connection with the narrative. I did not want this to compete with the primary message of the book for the audience's attention. The point of the book of Ruth is not that Ruth was willing to follow Naomi; it is about God's "covering" or protection of vulnerable people through the righteous choices and actions of his people.

As you read, mark the movements in the sermon with the upward and downward arrows.

Under His Wings

Ruth 3:7–9

After Boaz ate, drank, and was in good spirits, he went to lie down at the end of the pile of barley, and she came secretly, uncovered his feet, and lay down. At midnight, Boaz was startled, turned over, and there lying at his feet was a woman! So he asked, "Who are you?" "I am Ruth, your servant," she replied. "Take me under your wing, for you are a family redeemer."'

Because of a famine, Naomi, her two sons, and her husband Elimelech took the seven- to ten-day journey from their home in Bethlehem (which means "house of bread") to find refuge outside of the promised land in Moab. While there, Naomi's husband Elimelech died leaving her dependent on her two sons for support. The sons married and supported her for ten years, but then both of them died and Naomi had no one.

Naomi heard that the famine was over in Bethlehem so she decided to go home. She gave her daughters-in-law the choice to go back to their families. She knew she was too old to have another son, but her daughters-in-law could remarry and take care of themselves if they turned back. One of the women left, but Ruth refused, saying, "Don't plead with me to abandon you or return and not follow you. For wherever you go, I will go, and wherever you live, I will live; your people will be my people, and your God will be my God. Where you die, I will die, and there I will be buried. May the LORD punish me, and do so severely, if anything but death separates you and me" (Ruth 1:16b–17).

Ruth's selfless act stands in stark contrast to the times. This story unfolds during the times of the judges when everyone was doing what was right in their own eyes (Judg. 21:25). However, while most people were looking out for their self-interest, Ruth looked out for the interests of her mother-in-law. She did this by returning to Bethlehem with Naomi and by working to support her. The Levitical law required landowners to allow widows and other poor people to pick up what the harvesters missed (Lev. 19:9–10), so Ruth began working in the fields (Ruth 2:2) to provide for her and Naomi.

Ruth worked in Boaz's field. He provided a safe place for Ruth to glean (2:8), ordered the workers to leave her alone, invited her to drink the water and eat the food he provided for his employees (2:9; 2:14), and asked the workers to leave extra grain for her (2:16). He did all of these things because of the noble way she was treating her mother-in-law (2:11), and because he viewed her as someone under God's protection. He said to her, "May the LORD reward you for what you have done, and may you receive a full reward from the LORD God of Israel, under whose wings you have come for refuge" (2:12).

Now he finds Ruth, Naomi's Moabite daughter-in-law, at his threshing floor asking him to "spread your cloak over me" (3:9). Boaz had a choice to make.

Let's examine his choices. The threshing floor was a convenient place for workers to sleep during harvest time. It was also a location frequented by prostitutes. When the prophet Hosea wanted to highlight Israel's unfaithfulness, he compared them to threshing floor prostitutes (Hosea 9:1).

Boaz had been around prostitution for most of his life. Rahab, his mother (Matt. 1:5), was a prostitute (Josh. 2:1). Therefore, Boaz had a choice to make about whether or not to treat Ruth as a prostitute. Boaz had another option; he could fulfill the obligation of the levirate marriage and be her kinsman redeemer.

The levirate marriage (Deut. 25:5–6) was an important safety net, especially for a widow who did not have a son. You will remember that children had the responsibility to provide financially for their parents (Exod. 20:12) when they were not physically able to provide for themselves. If the widow grew old without a son to provide for her, she would be vulnerable (Isa. 1:23; 10:1–2; Jer. 7:4–16) and could face oppression from society. The levirate marriage protected people in Naomi's and Ruth's situation. If Ruth and Boaz were to marry, their first son would bear the name of Mahlon, her late husband.

When Ruth said, "Spread your cloak over me, for you are a family redeemer" (Ruth 3:9b), she was asking Boaz to fulfill the obligations of the levirate marriage in the first part of her request and for him to redeem the family land in the second part.

The phrase "spread your cloak" is especially significant when you remember Boaz's words in Ruth 2:12: "May the LORD reward you for what you have done, and may you receive a full reward from the LORD God of Israel, under whose wings you have come for refuge." The phrase was a euphemism for the two becoming one aspect of the marriage relationship, but the psalmist also used the spreading of wings as a metaphor for God's protection (Ps. 91:4).

The other provision is the kinsman redeemer (Lev. 25:25–28), who was a close relative that worked to ensure that family property stayed in the family. If it was not possible and they had to sell it outside of the family, the buyer returned the land to the original owner during the year of Jubilee. This is similar to a "right of first refusal," except that the family retains the right to buy back the land even if someone else purchases it first.

On the spot, Boaz promised to see that Ruth and Naomi were cared for. He knew she was a virtuous woman (Ruth 3:11), and he knew God had placed her under his protection. However, there was a problem; she had a kinsman whose rights came first. "Yes, it is true that I am a family redeemer, but there is a redeemer closer than I am. Stay [here] tonight, and in the morning, if he wants to redeem you, [that's] good.

Let him redeem [you]. But if he doesn't want to redeem you, as the LORD lives, I will. Now lie down until morning" (3:12–13).

Boaz was not going to take advantage of Ruth. She was a child of God, living under God's protection. Boaz viewed himself as an agent of God's loving-kindness, and he was accountable to God for his actions. He also understood that his private choices had public consequences. He was a member of a community and was accountable to members of the community for his conduct.

The next day Boaz went to the city gate and waited for the nearest kinsman to come by so he could ask him to fulfill the responsibilities of the levirate marriage and the kinsman redeemer. When he arrived, Boaz spoke to him in the presence of ten city elders and asked him to be the kinsman redeemer for Naomi and purchase Elimelech's land, which he agreed to do. However, when he asked him to perform the duties outlined in the levirate marriage and take Ruth as his wife so he could perpetuate Mahlon's name, he balked. "The redeemer replied, 'I can't redeem [it] myself, or I will ruin my [own] inheritance. Take my right of redemption, because I can't redeem it'" (4:6). With the obligations of the levirate marriage and the kinsman redeemer intertwined, he declined so that he did not jeopardize his own inheritance. This cleared the way for Boaz to redeem the land and provide an heir for Ruth's dead husband.

The actions of Naomi, Ruth, and Boaz grew out of two beliefs. First, they believed that God is sovereign and provides for his people. Ruth understood that she answered to Yahweh for the way she would treat Naomi (1:17). Naomi saw her affliction as God's hand against her (1:13), and Ruth ending up in Boaz's field as God's favor on her (2:20). Boaz viewed his field as a place of refuge for Ruth provided by God (2:12). The narrator of the story saw Ruth's conception as a gift from God (4:13).

J. Hardee Kennedy writes, "God acts in human affairs. His sovereignty of power and mercy reaches to all human beings and to the whole life of every person. His providence of wisdom and love rules, or else overrules, even in seemingly unimportant people and their unimportant affairs."[12]

---

12. Kennedy, "Ruth," 480.

Their second belief was that people are responsible to treat others graciously with God's steadfast love. While Naomi responded to her trials by becoming bitter (1:20), Ruth and Boaz made different choices.

Because of God's sovereignty, you must ignore your own self-interest and choose to show God's steadfast love to vulnerable people.

Boaz took full responsibility, married Ruth, and God gave her a son. Not just any son. The book of Ruth ends by revealing that their son is in the lineage of Jesus. Let's read the genealogy. "The neighbor women said, 'A son has been born to Naomi,' and they named him Obed. He was the father of Jesse, the father of David. Now these are the family records of Perez: Perez fathered Hezron. Hezron fathered Ram, Ram fathered Amminadab. Amminadab fathered Nahshon, Nahshon fathered Salmon. Salmon fathered Boaz, Boaz fathered Obed, Obed fathered Jesse, and Jesse fathered David" (4:17–22).

Earlier in the message, I said that if Ruth and Boaz were to marry, their first son would bear her late husband's name. Notice that is not what happened. The Scripture says, Salmon fathered Boaz, who fathered Obed (4:21). It could be, as a matter of law, that Obed was in line for both Mahlon's and Boaz's inheritance. However, it is important to note that in the genealogy, Obed is listed as Boaz's son. Why? Perhaps it is to show that while many were doing what was right in their own eyes, God used a devoted Moabite woman and a son of a prostitute who looked out for others with God's steadfast love to be in the lineage to bring a Savior into the world.

Later their descendant would do that, and so much more. "For God loved the world in this way: He gave his one and only Son, so that everyone who believes in him will not perish but have eternal life" (John 3:16).

REFLECTIONS ON THE SERMON

In this sermon, I once again made the homiletical choice to weave the background material beside the narrative's plot line. In this case, I was careful not to let the details of the levirate marriage (Deut. 25:5–6) or the kinsman redeemer bog down the plot development of the sermon. The original hearers of the book of Ruth would have known the information, but I could not assume that those in the audience would. I also knew that they needed the background to understand Boaz's response to Ruth's request. The sermon progressed with the following movements:

    ↓ Husbands died, leaving their wives in a desperate situation.

        ↑ Ruth stayed with Naomi, they returned to Bethlehem where Ruth gleaned Boaz's field. Ruth approached Boaz, asking him to "spread his cloak" over her.

    ↓ Boaz informed her that there was a nearer kinsman and he must offer the option to him.

        ↑ The nearest kinsman refused. Boaz fulfilled the obligation of the near kinsman and levirate marriage.

I made another important homiletical choice in this sermon: I used Boaz's point of view instead of Ruth's. In the past when I have preached from this book, I used Ruth's point of view, but in this case I felt Boaz's choice to allow the Scripture's teaching to inform his action was important to highlight. It was important to keep the point of view consistent throughout the sermon to avoid confusion.

Once again, my fascination with those in the lineage of Jesus surfaces, as I underscore the place that Ruth and Boaz have in the biblical genealogy and draw the parallel between Boaz's place as a kinsman redeemer and the ultimate mission of his descendant, who would be the Savior of the world.

WRITING NARRATIVE SERMONS

Since this is the first chapter in part 2, it might be helpful to cover some thoughts about how to write a sermon from narrative episodes, which will apply to Old Testament and other biblical narratives.

1. Structure the sermon with the plot in the biblical narrative. The movements in the plot will carry the sermon to its point at the end, building tension along the way.
2. Read the text multiple times in different translations. Read it aloud. Let the text grip your heart. Pray over it, ask God to reveal his truth to you.

3. As you study the text of the sermon, mark it with upward and downward arrows that correspond to the movements of the plot as explained in chapter 2 and the first part of this chapter. Let the transition words, focus shifts, and narrator interruptions influence your markings (see first part of this chapter for explanation).

4. When you discover the transformative truth in the text, go ahead and write it out. You may not include this sentence in your sermon but it is important to let it guide you as you write the rest of the sermon.

5. Now write the transformative point, following the guidelines in the previous chapter. Remember to follow the plot to find the point. (For instructions on how to word transformative points and to see examples, refer back to chap. 3.)

6. As you read, look for the homiletical bind—the problem that appears in the narrative—this will become your first movement. As you write this and other movements, go back to the text to make sure that you are accurately summarizing what happened in the story.

7. After writing the first movement, find the resolution of the story and write the fourth movement.

8. After you have these movements written, look for the way the tension builds in the story, and write the second and third movements.

9. As you put the sermon together, alternate between summarizing the text and reading the text. Look at the sermons above to see when I inserted the reading of the biblical text. I often return to a reading of the biblical text at the transition point of a movement.

10. Write the movements in such a way that you tell what the narrative says before you tell the people what the narrative means.

11. After you have finished the draft, set it aside for a day or two and come back to it with fresh eyes to revise and improve it. Continue in prayer for God's guidance as you improve the manuscript.

If you are new to preaching inductive sermons based upon narrative texts and are more accustomed to the propositional approach of giving the big idea of the sermon in the beginning, please discipline yourself to let the tension build as the narrative unfolds, and reserve the transformative point and its application to the end.

FOR FURTHER REFLECTION

- When writing a sermon on an Old Testament narrative passage, ask what would it have been like to hear this story in a gathering of family and friends. What impact would it have had on the original hearers?
- What is the significance of the people, places, events, and cultural and historical elements of the story that are unfamiliar to modern readers?
- What is the theology of the story? How does it relate to the historical context?
- Provide the historical and/or theological background information just in time instead of doing an information dump during the introduction.
- What is the literary context? How does it contribute to the meaning of the passage?
- How can you shape the structure of the sermon to align with the plot of the narrative in the text?
- As you write the sermon, make sure you refrain from telling what the narrative means until after you have told the listeners what the narrative says.

---[C H A P T E R   5]---

Narrative Episodes from the Former Prophets

The narratives contained in the Former Prophets from the Hebrew canon share many similarities with other Old Testament narratives. However, they deserve their own chapter to clarify the special handling they require because of their historical and canonical context.

This chapter does not cover the narrative sections of prophetic books like Isaiah and Jeremiah, which are primarily composed of poetic material with narrative segments interspersed throughout them. Instead, we are focusing on Joshua–2 Kings, sometimes referred to as Deuteronomistic history and/or the Former Prophets in the Hebrew canon. They are books that communicate Israel's history from a prophetic perspective and therefore have a prophetic purpose. Both the historical context and the canonical context are important to understand the authorial intent of these books.

Historical Context

Historical context refers to the historical events and characters represented in a narrative: that is, who they were, when they lived, and what their relationship was to their contemporary world. It would also include the cultural, religious, and political circumstances reflected in the narrative. The term also refers to the historic circumstances under which a text was written or compiled: that is, what need or circumstances motivated the inspired writer to write as he did and why he chose the characters, events, and ideas through which he communicated his prophetic message. Historical context is important to a correct understanding of Joshua–2 Kings and the prophetic message of its author or compiler.

CANONICAL CONTEXT

The canonical context is the location or ordering of a book, or collection of books, within the larger collection of the Old Testament. Significant differences exist between how modern translations order Old Testament books and how they are ordered in the Hebrew Bible, which was originally divided into three distinct collections: the Torah, the Prophets, and the Writings. The table below illustrates the basic differences between the two:

TABLE 2: ENGLISH AND HEBREW CANONICAL ORDER

English Order	Hebrew Order*
Historical Books	**Torah** (Torah)
Genesis, Exodus, Leviticus, Numbers, Deuteronomy (Torah), Joshua, Judges, Ruth, 1, 2 Samuel, 1, 2 Kings, 1, 2 Chronicles, Ezra, Nehemiah, Esther	Genesis, Exodus, Leviticus, Numbers, Deuteronomy
Poetic Books	**Prophets** (Neviim)
	Former Prophets
Job, Psalms, Proverbs, Ecclesiastes, Song of Songs	Joshua, Judges, 1, 2 Samuel, 1, 2 Kings
	Latter Prophets
Prophetic Books	*Major Prophets*: Isaiah, Jeremiah, Ezekiel
Isaiah, Jeremiah, Lamentations, Ezekiel, Daniel, Hosea, Joel, Amos, Obadiah, Jonah, Micah, Nahum, Habakkuk, Zephaniah, Haggai, Zechariah, Malachi	*Minor Prophets*: Hosea, Joel, Amos, Obadiah, Jonah, Micah, Nahum, Habakkuk, Zephaniah, Haggai, Zechariah, Malachi
	Writings (Kethuvim)
	Psalms, Job, Proverbs, Ruth, Song of Songs, Ecclesiastes, Lamentations, Esther, Daniel, Ezra, Nehemiah, 1, 2 Chronicles

* The order of the Hebrew books shown is the one that appears in recent versions of the *Biblia Hebraica Stuttgartensia*, but it should be noted that while all the books listed are present in other canonical traditions of the Hebrew Bible, the order varies.

Obviously, there are great differences between the two arrangements.[1] Take for instance the placement of the books Joshua–2 Kings. In the Protestant canon of the Old Testament, Joshua–2 Kings appear with a number of other books and are commonly treated as the historical books, but in the Hebrew canon these books are considered part of the prophetic canon. So rather than seeing them simply as a recounting of the history of Israel, they present history from a prophetic perspective. Or put differently, these works use important events in Israel's history to encourage change in the spiritual life of the nation.

THEMES FROM DEUTERONOMY

There is, however, more to the relationship among these books than their location in the canon. Some of the central ideas of this history emerge from the book of Deuteronomy. In other words, not only is this collection prophetic in its origin and purpose, it reflects the theological and social emphases in the book of Deuteronomy.

Old Testament scholars refer to this collection as Deuteronomistic history because of the Deuteronomic influence on these books.[2] A good

---

1. In short, the differences may be simply described as the difference between Western perspectives, in which the type of literature (historical, poetic, prophetic) was a primary concern, and Eastern perspectives, in which other, more tradition-oriented matters were of greater concern. See Sanders, "Canon: Hebrew Bible," 1:837–52; Robinson, "Canon of the Old Testament," 1:591–601; LaSor, Hubbard, and Bush, "The Concept of Canon," 598–605.

2. The literature on this topic is voluminous, and the issues involved in scholarly debate are complex. The following works will provide starting points for the explanations of its history and development. Note that the critical positions described below are not traditional, evangelical perspectives and may be objectionable to theological conservatives. In citing them, we are not aligning ourselves with all they espouse: Noth, *The Deteronomistic History*; Shepherd, "Deteronomistic History"; McKenzie, "Deuteronomistic History," 2:160–68; Knoppers, in *Eerdman's Bible Dictionary*, 341–42.

A growing number of evangelical conservatives have acknowledged that the former prophets (Joshua–2 Kings) are related to themes presented in Deuteronomy and that the books provide a message of hope and restoration to those living in the Babylonian exile. Some of these are LaSor, Hubbard, and Bush, *Old Testament Survey: The Message, Form, and Background of the Old Testament*, 131–221, esp. 131–37; Longman and Dillard, *An Introduction to the Old Testament*, 102–43, 151–89; Richter, "Deuteronomistic History," 219–30, esp. 228–30.

To read other conservative scholars who evaluate the strengths and weakeness of Deuteronomistic history and accept its value, see Arnold and Beyer, *Encountering the Old Testament*, 161–65; Howard, *An Introduction to the Old Testament Historical Books*, 88–89, definition is a theory of composition of the historical books from Joshua–2 Kings that asserts that the theological and social emphases in the book of Deuteronomy serve as the basis for the story of Israel's history from the conquest (Joshua), through the settlement (Judges), and the monarchy up to the time of the exile (Samuel–Kings).

The programmatic words of Moses in Deuteronomy are the organizing principle for the prophetic history. Such themes as the idea of covenant, centralization of worship, kingship, and prophetic ministry appear with great frequency in Joshua–2 Kings and provide a constant undercurrent to the message of its compiler(s).

As a recounting of Israel's history, the authors/compilers may have composed this collection during the exile, from various sources dating to or around the time that the events actually occurred. Some important indicators exist that they created this history during the exile. For instance, the last passage in 2 Kings 25:27–30 has Jehoiachin being pardoned and released from prison. The date for this cannot be before 550 BC; therefore, the date of authorship for the books of Kings cannot be before that date. So if Joshua–Samuel is intimately tied to Kings as asserted below, it is a simple deduction that the entire history was compiled sometime after Jehoichin's release from prison.

The authors wrote this history to address specific theological issues raised in the minds of the exiles of Judah, because of the trauma of the fall of Jerusalem. A close reading of the books of Joshua–2 Kings yields a sense that the author of this work was seeking to answer a series of questions asked by the exiles. These questions are the following:

- Why, if Judah was Yahweh's covenant people, were they in exile? Has Yahweh broken his covenant with them?
- How could anyone destroy Yahweh's holy city of Jerusalem, especially since the temple, the sole focus of Yahweh's presence on earth, lay in ruins? Had Yahweh removed his presence from them?
- Was Babylon's defeating of this people and the destruction of Jerusalem and the temple evidence that the chief Babylonian god, Marduk, was more powerful than Yahweh?

203–207; Hess, *The Old Testament: A Historical, Theological, and Critical Introduction,* 167–70, 202–204, 298–301.

- Was there any way to rectify these circumstances and find reconciliation with Yahweh?
- How could atonement for sin take place if the temple lay in ruins?

These questions emerge from a close reading of the text of Joshua–2 Kings.[3] Much of Israel's faith in the pre-exilic period hinged around two promises of God. The first concerned his choice of Jerusalem as his dwelling place, and the second one on his promises to David of an enduring dynasty.[4]

The historical realities associated with these promises created and confirmed a sense of overconfidence in them. First, the dynasty of David had endured for over three centuries, giving the people of Judah the sense that there would always be a descendant of David to occupy the throne of Israel. This certainty was based primarily on the Davidic covenant in 2 Samuel 7. Also at the heart of this overconfidence was the event that took place in 701 BC. Yahweh had strongly affirmed his choice of Jerusalem by intervening when Sennacherib, king of the Assyrian Empire, had besieged Jerusalem, and Yahweh dispersed his armies, driving them back to Mesopotamia. This was a watershed event in the history of Israel, because just twenty years previous they had witnessed the Assyrian army destroy the northern kingdom of Israel. It is little wonder that they felt nothing could harm them, not even their own unfaithfulness.

Because of events like these, Judah had a sense of impregnability that they could live much as they pleased without having to worry about the collapse of their kingdom. When that happened in 586 BC, with the Babylonian conquest and subsequent deportation of Judah's citizens, the exiled people were disillusioned and uncertain of either their future or their relationship with Yahweh.

Into this context, the Deuteronomistic historian undertook the task of addressing the reason(s) Judah was in exile. The Deuteronomistic history is, in its own way, sermonic material—a historic account of the causes

---

3. From this point forward, we will refer to these works as the Deuteronomistic history and its author(s) as the Deuteronomistic historian(s). While we do not embrace the critical view of Deuternomistic history, we do align ourselves with other conservatives who see a relationship between Deuteronomy and the Former Prophets. We affirm that the writer(s), inspired by the Holy Spirit, told the historical events for prophetic purposes.

4. Longman and Dillard, *Introduction to the Old Testament*, 181.

that led Israel into exile. The intent is more than condemnation; it also seeks to point the way to reconciliation with Yahweh so that the people can find their way back to a proper relationship with God.

The principles of restoration drew on the principles of the book of Deuteronomy as the theological and social basis for this change of position. As an example of this, note the emphasis of Deuteronomy 30:1–10:

> When all these things happen to you—the blessings and curses I have set before you—and you come to your senses while you are in all the nations where the LORD your God has driven you, and you and your children return to the LORD your God and obey him with all your heart and all your soul by doing everything I am commanding you today, then he will restore your fortunes, have compassion on you, and gather you again from all the peoples where the LORD your God has scattered you. Even if your exiles are at the farthest horizon, he will gather you and bring you back from there. The LORD your God will bring you into the land your fathers possessed, and you will take possession of it. He will cause you to prosper and multiply you more than he did your fathers. The LORD your God will circumcise your heart and the hearts of your descendants, and you will love him with all your heart and all your soul so that you will live. The LORD your God will put all these curses on your enemies who hate and persecute you. Then you will again obey him and follow all his commands I am commanding you today. The LORD your God will make you prosper abundantly in all the work of your hands, your offspring, the offspring of your livestock, and the produce of your land. Indeed, the LORD will again delight in your prosperity, as he delighted in that of your fathers, when you obey the LORD your God by keeping his commands and statutes that are written in this book of the law and return to him with all your heart and all your soul.

Notice how this passage from Deuteronomy is ready-made for the very circumstances the Deuteronomistic historian was addressing. Both the reasons for the exile, which accord fully with the curses in Deuteronomy 28, and the means of reconciliation are present in this one passage.

Beyond this theological basis, there are social aspects in Deuteronomy from which the historian draws significantly. These include the expectations for kings (17:14–20), judges (16: 18–20), and prophets (18:14–22), just to name a few. All of these offices appear prominently in this history. The book of Deuteronomy features a prominent discussion about God choosing a "place he chooses to have his name to dwell" (12:5, 11, 14, 18, 21, 26; 14:23, 24:25; 15:20; 16:2, 6, 7, 11, 15, 16; 17:8, 10; 18:6; 26:2; 31:11), a very distinctive reference to the temple. The Deuteronomistic historian places the building of the temple as a place where Yahweh's name would dwell (1 Kings 8:22–30) in a preeminent position within his history.

Another important characteristic of the Deuteronomistic history is its focus on a cycle of sin, judgment, and reconciliation. The cycle is a consistent literary pattern that occurs throughout the Deuteronomistic history, particularly the book of Judges, but also in a less explicit fashion in Samuel and Kings. The cycle generally follows this pattern:

1. A sin is committed, usually idolatry but sometimes adultery (e.g., 2 Sam. 11–12).
2. The sin is followed by some expression of divine anger, normally something like "and once again the anger of Yahweh burned against Israel."
3. Some expression of that wrath in the form of judgment follows, which always expresses itself in terms of the curses listed in Deuteronomy 28, most usually some conflict with an enemy.
4. There is some act by the people that indicates they are suffering. Most often in Judges this is described as "groaning" or "crying out," but in Samuel and Kings there is usually some kind of confession.
5. In response, Yahweh provides some mitigation of his punishment. In Judges, he raises up a judge to deliver the people. In Samuel and Kings, God usually responds to intercession or direct repentance from an individual.
6. Finally, God restores Israel or an individual. In Judges, the people have peace for a specified number of years until they once again worship idols, starting the cycle anew. In Samuel and Kings, the pattern is typically forgiveness of sin and a pronounced

restoration of the relationship between God and the sinner. As mentioned, the book ends with the release of the exiled Davidic King Jehoiachin.

By using this strategy, the Deuteronomistic historian is able to address the consequences of Israel's sin. It is interesting to note that this cyclical pattern is in a historical continuum. That is, there is a progressive aspect to the use of this cycle that really makes the term inadequate to describe it. A better way to describe this is as a downward spiral.[5] A cycle represents a stagnant process that does not progress; it simply recurs. With the idea of a downward spiral, it is possible to see the cycle described above as a recapitulation of a pattern of behavior that while growing progressively worse is leading historically to a resolution. The end of the process is going to answer for the last time the question of Israel's relationship to the land (they lose it forever), while leaving in question their status as the people of Yahweh.

There are four more specific answers to the questions posed by the exiles (see above):

1. Why, if Judah was Yahweh's covenant people, were they in exile? Has Yahweh broken his covenant with them?

As for the first question, the answer is no. Yahweh was maintaining his part of the covenant by carrying out the punishment written in the

---

5. Longman and Dillard, *Introduction to the Old Testament*, 182: "The writer of Kings sets out to explain the exile and the destruction of Judah in a way that would rescue the faith of the people in the face of such questions. A quick reading of the book gives the impression that Kings is overall not an upbeat history, but rather it records a downward spiral. Why should this be so? In part at least, it is because the writer is telling Israel that the exile was not the result of a failure on God's part, but that God had acted to confirm his holiness by judging the nation for its transgressions. The exile did not show that Yahweh lacked power—just the opposite: it was the proof that he was ruling over history and that the armies of Babylon were simply doing his bidding. The Deuteronomic history is largely a history of the nation's failure to keep its covenant with God. 'From the day their ancestors came out of Egypt until this day' (2 Kings 21:15), the people had provoked God through disobedience until he decreed disaster for them."

covenant whereby Israel's breaking of the covenant would lead to their defeat and exile (Deut. 4:25–30; 30:1–10; 1 Kings 8:22–61).

2. How could anyone destroy the holy city of Yahweh, Jerusalem, especially since the temple, the sole focus of Yahweh's presence on earth, lay in ruins? Had Yahweh removed his presence from them?

The answer to the second question is yes. Yahweh had removed his protective presence from them because of their sin.

3. Was Babylon's defeating of this people and the destruction of Jerusalem and the temple evidence that the chief Babylonian god, Marduk, was more powerful that Yahweh?

No is the answer to the third question. Because Yahweh had simply used the Babylonians to punish Israel, there would come a time when Babylon would pay for their wickedness.

4. Was there any way to rectify these circumstances and find reconciliation with Yahweh? How could any sin be atoned for if the temple lay in ruins?

Finally, the answer to the fourth question is yes, but it would involve a new commitment of faith on the part of the people. In addition, it would involve a new understanding of the role the covenant played in their lives: they would have to repent of their sins, turn back to Yahweh, and experience forgiveness, even without the temple and the sacrificial system.

AUTHORSHIP

In the current debate, there are two approaches to the question of authorship of Deuteronomistic history: the critical view that does not affirm Mosaic authorship of Deuteronomy, and the more conservative view that affirms Mosaic authorship.

Our position, the more conservative one, affirms Mosaic authorship and takes seriously the literary and theological relationship between Deuteronomy and the books of Joshua–2 Kings. Scholars in this camp would assert, however, that Deuteronomy was composed by Moses, and by virtue of this and its relationship to Exodus and the rest of the Pentateuch, carried a great deal of authority.[6]

They would also acknowledge that the book did undergo some editing and expansion (e.g., the notice of Moses' death in Deut. 34). However, rather than understanding the book as a product of later schools of prophets, there was a tremendous amount of influence from Deuteronomy on the prophets who lived later.[7]

For whatever reason, the book appears to have been lost for a time and then recovered during Josiah's reforms in 621 BC. His reaction upon hearing it read indicates that he understood immediately why it was significant. Further, Deuteronomy appears to have greatly influenced Jeremiah, and it is possible that he had some influence on those who told Israel's history from the conquest to the exile, in the form of the books Joshua–2 Kings.

---

6. See Longman and Dillard, *Introduction to the Old Testament*, 102–43, 151–89; and LaSor, Hubbard, and Bush, *Old Testament Survey*, 131–221, cited above. Other more detailed discussions from this perspective can be found in Howard, *An Introduction to the Old Testament Historical Books*, 179–82; McConville and Millan, *Time and Place in Deuteronomy*, 140–41; McConville, *Law and Theology in Deuteronomy*, 154–59; and Satterthwaite and McConville, *Exploring the Old Testament*, vol. 2, *The Histories*, 199–218.

7 The critical perspective addresses the authorship question differently. In their view, Deuteronomy shares a great deal in common with the books of Joshua–2 Kings, Jeremiah, and other exilic prophets, and we know that Kings was completed sometime during the exile, because it gives details of things that occurred during that period. The line of reasoning for their perspective is generally as described below:

Many presuppose that the book discovered by Hilkiah while cleaning up the temple (2 Kings 22) was some form of the book of Deuteronomy. Most critical scholars hold that what was found was in fact a literary creation by prophets and priests of Josiah's time intended to provide a Mosaic base of authority for the reforms that Josiah was seeking to carry out in Judah.

Second, because of this understanding, and the belief that Deuteronomy was written around the time of Josiah's reforms, some have asserted that Deuteronomy does not belong to the Pentateuch because it is much later than the J and E sources. Also, it provides the theological basis for Joshua–2 Kings, and thus serves as the theological basis for the history recorded in those books, creations of the period immediately preceding the exile and following into it.

Finally, the prophetic nature of Deuteronomy is very close in vocabulary and style to a great deal of Jeremiah, Zephaniah, and Habakkuk, who were prophets associated with the exile, giving stronger ties to the exile as the period for the Deuteronomic history.

This perspective includes (1) a deep appreciation for and understanding of the book of Deuteronomy; (2) that there was an extended process that involved the collection, selection, and arrangement of ancient accounts of the conquest, settlement, united and divided monarchic periods, and the exile; (3) the editorial work of selecting and arranging the Deuteronomistic history.

Preaching the Narratives from the Former Prophets

Below are a few suggestions for writing sermons from the Former Prophets:

1. Ask the usual questions: What is the historical context of the story and characters? How does this episode fit with the other episodes around it? How does it inform the message of this book? Refer to the previous chapters for these types of questions.
2. How are the broader concerns of the Deuteronomistic historian communicated in this episode? How does he address the needs of his audience?
3. Remember, the Deuteronomistic history is crisis literature, addressing the people of Israel in the crisis of exile. How would those in exile feel as they heard this narrative? What hope would it bring?
4. It might be a good idea to read the book of Deuteronomy if you are planning to preach a series from the Former Prophets. This will keep the teachings of the book fresh in your mind.
5. Because the writers were teaching principles from Deuteronomy, take time to consider if there is a teaching in Deuteronomy that this narrative illustrates. If so, you should consider including a quotation from Deuteronomy to undergird the transformative point of the sermon.
6. With these concerns in mind, how does the message of the episode address a need in the lives of a contemporary audience?

Sermon Sample from the Former Prophets

The following sermon is from a familiar text. Those in exile who heard the story would have related to David's hopeless situation. He committed a sin that by his own admission deserved death—there was no hope for him. In exile, there was no temple and no sacrificial system for the people's sin. As they heard the story, they would find great encouragement in the grace David experienced in spite of the consequences for the sin.

You Are the Man!

2 Samuel 12:1–6

So the LORD sent Nathan to David. When he arrived, he said to him: "There were two men in a certain city, one rich and the other poor. The rich man had very large flocks and herds, but the poor man had nothing except one small ewe lamb that he had bought. He raised her, and she grew up with him and with his children. From his meager food she would eat, from his cup she would drink, and in his arms she would sleep. She was like a daughter to him. Now a traveler came to the rich man, but the rich man could not bring himself to take one of his own sheep or cattle to prepare for the traveler who had come to him. Instead, he took the poor man's lamb and prepared it for his guest."

David was infuriated with the man and said to Nathan: "As the LORD lives, the man who did this deserves to die! Because he has done this thing and shown no pity, he must pay four lambs for that lamb."

It was the time of year when kings led their troops to war, but David remained home. While walking around the palace roof, he spotted a beautiful woman taking a bath. Instead of turning his head and walking away, he stayed and watched.

Later, he consummated his sin with her; as a result, she became pregnant. In a cover up attempt, he brought her husband back from the front lines of battle so it would appear that the child belonged to him.

Uriah, her husband, was one of thirty elite officers in David's army, probably a mercenary who accepted Hebrew citizenship and converted to their faith. If Bathsheba was taking a bath in her own home when David spotted her, his home was adjacent to the king's palace, which was probably a decent neighborhood. Some scholars believe that Bathsheba was the granddaughter of David's chief advisor, and her father was one of the thirty elite officers.[8]

David offered Uriah some time off after receiving a briefing about the battle, but Uriah refused to go home and be with his wife. Instead, he slept in the same place with all the king's servants. When David asked him why, Uriah said, "The ark and Israel and Judah are staying in temporary shelters, and my lord Joab and the servants of my lord are camping in the open field. Shall I then go to my house to eat and drink and to lie with my wife? By your life and the life of your soul, I will not do this thing" (2 Sam. 11:11 NIV).

David wrote a message for Uriah to give to his commander Joab, which was in essence, Uriah's death sentence. David schemed to put Uriah in a dangerous forward position and then have Joab withdraw the supporting troops, leaving Uriah vulnerable. David's plan worked. I do not know if Uriah ever knew David betrayed him, but I do know that he died doing his duty. He died the way he lived—with integrity.

Something I cannot say about his wife or his king. Nothing can excuse their behavior. A man after God's own heart like David should have known better. Why wasn't he out to war with the other kings? Why didn't he turn away when Bathsheba first caught his eye? Why did he commit adultery and later murder?

Second Samuel 11:27 sums up the whole sordid affair: it "was evil in the sight of the LORD" (NASB). Up until this point in David's life, he has been a real spiritual hero, but now, because of this event, this grave sin footnotes any statement about his character. He started well, but he didn't finish well.

When Nathan the prophet sought advice from the king about what should happen to a wealthy man who served a neighbor's pet lamb as dinner for a traveler, David was incensed and immediately recognized that the man deserved to die.

Have you ever noticed how easy it is to be arbitrary with judgment against others? We can usually see, with crystal clarity, the sins and faults in others and judgment usually makes perfect sense. David was right, this man "deserves to die!" Romans 6:23 says, "For the wages

8. Young, "Uriah," 848–50.

of sin is death." There are plenty of Scriptures that make us want to stoke the fires of hell for sinners the likes of this man. And certainly, God judges sin. Matthew 3:12 says, "His winnowing fork is in his hand, and he will clear his threshing floor, gathering his wheat into the barn and burning up the chaff with unquenchable fire" (NIV). Judgment is sure. Solomon wrote, "God will judge both the righteous man and the wicked man, for a time for every matter and for every deed is there" (Eccl. 3:17 NASB).

In verse 6, David continues with his judgment, "And he must make restitution for the lamb fourfold, because he did this thing and had no compassion" (2 Sam. 12:6 NASB). David does more than pass judgment on this man, he requires him to make restitution—to try to make the crooked way straight, as the Scripture prescribed in Exodus 22:1.

While David passed judgment on the rich shepherd, his own sin was lurking in the background. He'd committed a great sin against God, one which was far greater than killing an animal—he'd killed a man after committing adultery with the man's wife.

Then, Nathan spoke the sobering words in verse 7: "You are the man!"

Just as David finished communicating the prescribed judgment, Nathan delivered a blow to David's mid-section: he is the man. David was not pronouncing a death sentence on one of his subjects; he was condemning himself to death.

In 2 Samuel 12:7–12, Nathan rebukes David for his sin:

Nathan then said to David, "You are the man! Thus says the LORD God of Israel, 'It is I who anointed you king over Israel and it is I who delivered you from the hand of Saul. I also gave you your master's house and your master's wives into your care, and I gave you the house of Israel and Judah; and if that had been too little, I would have added to you many more things like these! Why have you despised the word of the LORD by doing evil in His sight? You have struck down Uriah the Hittite with the sword, have taken his wife to be your wife, and have killed him with the sword of the sons of Ammon. Now therefore, the sword shall never depart from your house, because you have despised Me and have taken the wife of Uriah the

Hittite to be your wife.' Thus says the LORD, 'Behold, I will raise
up evil against you from your own household; I will even take
your wives before your eyes, and give them to your compan-
ion, and he shall lie with your wives in broad daylight. Indeed
you did it secretly, but I will do this thing before all Israel, and
under the sun'" (NASB).

After this conversation with Nathan, the weight of his sin sunk in. People often blame others for their mistakes. That's what Adam did. "The man replied, 'The woman you gave to be with me—she gave me some fruit from the tree, and I ate'" (Gen. 3:12).

Others try to justify their sin with excuses like Saul did. "But I did obey the LORD!" Saul answered. "I went on the mission the LORD gave me: I brought back King Agag of Amalek, and I completely destroyed the Amalekites. The troops took sheep, goats and cattle from the plunder—the best of what was set apart for destruction—to sacrifice to the LORD your God at Gilgal" (1 Sam. 15:20–21).

However, Samuel wasn't convinced. "Then Samuel said: 'Does the LORD take pleasure in burnt offerings and sacrifices as much as in obeying the LORD? Look: to obey is better than sacrifice, to pay attention is better than the fat of rams'" (1 Sam. 15:22 NASB).

Saul intentionally disobeyed God's command. He thought he could get away with his disobedience if he offered a sacrifice from the spoils of his rebellion. It did not work. Samuel called him out for his sin and said that his rebellion was the moral equivalence of witchcraft (1 Sam. 15:23). It was because of this sin that God removed his blessing from Saul and eventually placed it upon David.

But now, David, a man after God's own heart, had committed a terrible sin. Nathan confronted King David just as Samuel had confronted King Saul. David stood before the prophet with no defense. He had already pronounced the judgment—there was no sacrifice that could atone for his sin; he was without hope.

Have you ever felt that way? Have you ever felt hopeless? The original audience of this story knew what hopelessness felt like. They were in exile. Jerusalem and the temple were in ruins. The sacrificial system—their means of atoning for their sins—was gone. They were without hope.

How will David respond in his hopeless situation? Will he try to walk the judgment back? Will he try to shift blame to others?

What will happen to David? Will he suffer the death penalty he prescribed? Will Nathan give him a pass because of his powerful position?

Second Samuel 12:13 gives the answer. Let's read it. "David responded to Nathan, 'I have sinned against the LORD.' Then Nathan replied to David, 'The LORD has taken away your sin; you will not die.'"

There was no pass for David. He suffered the consequences for his sin.

David suffered the loss of his newborn son (2 Sam. 12:18), just as Nathan predicted (1 Sam. 12:9–12). The death of this son was the first of four premature deaths of David's sons. There was also the death of Amnon, who raped his daughter Tamar (1 Sam. 13:1–29), the death of Absalom (1 Sam. 18:14–15), who openly had sex with David's wives (2 Sam. 16:20–22), and Adonijah, whose brother Solomon ordered him killed (1 Kings 2:23–25).

David suffered public humiliation for his adultery and a fourfold payment for the murder he committed. He suffered the consequences for his sin, but not the penalty.

By his own admission, he deserved to die. However, God forgave him and spared his life.

There was hope for David. And there is hope for you. God specializes in bringing hope to the hopeless.

Today, I'm asking you to examine your sins, and to confess them to God and ask him for forgiveness. I'm not saying that all consequences for your actions will disappear, just that God stands ready to offer you grace, if you confess your sins.

First John 1:9 says, "If we confess our sins, he is faithful and righteous to forgive us our sins and to cleanse us from all unrighteousness."

REFLECTIONS ON THE SERMON

The sermon illustrates two perspectives about the consequences of sin found in Deuteronomy: (1) that people suffer personal consequences (Deut. 24:16), (2) as do their families (Deut. 5:9). However, sin does not have the final word. Grace does.

In the sermon, I alternated between summarizing the story and reading the text, following the narrative plot of the passage.

↓ David commits adultery, Bathsheba gets pregnant, and David has Uriah killed.

↑ David rightly passes judgment when Nathan asks for his advice.

↓ Nathan tells him that "he is the man," and David suffers the consequences for his sin.

↑ David receives God's forgiveness.

I also introduced how others responded in similar situations to provide depth and contrast to David's choice. In the overarching Old Testament narrative, King Saul is a tragic figure, who failed to reach his potential as a "head and shoulders above the rest" leader. King David, on the other hand, was the least likely of his brothers to become a leader, yet he became the greatest king of Israel. Because of the way the biblical narrative tends to contrast the two, I thought it would be helpful to show the contrast in how David handled his sin as opposed to how Saul handled his.

The transformative point shows that though our choices have consequences, God is a merciful God who can and will forgive us our sins. The key is to confess them.

While not every member of the audience the day I preached this sermon felt as hopeless as David, and those in exile did, I know there was at least one that might have. After the service, a young woman spoke to me about her desire to leave her occupation (the oldest profession) and her desire to break the power of drugs in her life. She heard a word of hope that day, which if applied, will change everything for her.

FOR FURTHER REFLECTION

- As with other narrative episodes, be sure to consider the historical context of the story and characters. How does this episode fit with the other episodes around it? How does it inform the message of this book?
- Consider including a quote from Deuteronomy in your sermons from the Former Prophets to underscore the point that emerges from the passage.

- Knowing that Deuteronomistic history is crisis literature (it addresses the people of Israel in the crisis of exile), how does the passage you've selected address the needs of the original audience?
- With these concerns in mind, how does the message of the episode address a need in the lives of your contemporary audience?
- Ask the question: "How would those in exile have experienced this point?" For instance, during the exile the people questioned how their sins could be atoned for since they no longer had a temple or sacrifices. What impact would Samuel's words to Saul in 1 Samuel 15:22 have had upon them? Would they have been encouraged by learning that God wanted obedience, which was something they could still do in exile, not sacrifice (something they could no longer do)? If you have written a sermon on that text, please pull it from your sermon file. What changes in the sermon should you make based on this insight to keep the impact of the text intact?

Poetry

Hebrew poems, like narratives, typically have a single main point. However, just as it is easy to confuse movements with multiple points in narratives (chap. 2), it is easy to confuse structural devices with multiple points in poetry.

Contextualizing Hebrew Poetry

Poetry appears virtually everywhere in the Old Testament.[1] The biblical writers often use poetry as an effective and memorable way to drive home a point with unmistakable emotional impact. Sometimes epic poems are set beside important events in a narrative to mark their historic significance (Judg. 5; Exod. 15). Other times, confessional statements composed for memorializing important theological themes are embedded in a narrative to mark them within a given tradition (Gen. 12:1–3; Exod. 34:6–7).[2] The key question is what distinguishes Hebrew poetry from narrative as a distinct literary form?[3]

---

1. While the total count in English versions varies, there are approximately eighty poems embedded in books traditionally considered primarily composed of narrative (Genesis–Nehemiah). We should include Jonah 2:1–9 as well, since it is the one book among the prophets of the English canon that is comprised mostly of narrative.

2. The argument can be made that some of the poems embedded in narrative are far older than the narratives in which they appear. See, for instance, Block, *Judges, Ruth*, 211–318. On the antiquity of Exodus 15, see Carpenter, "Songs of Praise for Deliverance at the Sea" (15:1–21).

3. There is an ongoing debate about whether there is a true distinction between Hebrew narrative and Hebrew poetry, for many of the traits that can be identified in one are present in the other. See Kugel, *The Idea of Biblical Poetry*. For instance, he insists that, because some examples do not have elements generally considered characteristic of Hebrew poetry, there is little left to distinguish it from Hebrew narrative. This position is overstated. As will be shown, the use of certain literary features are far more prominent and used with greater emphasis and effect than is true of narrative.

At the risk of oversimplification, the following broad characterizations apply to Hebrew poetry: thematic arrangement, parallelism, imagery, terseness, literary devices, and meter.

Thematic Arrangement

While narratives trace events in a linear fashion, a poem arranges its content around a central theme or themes. Remember that most poetic passages in the Old Testament do not connect directly to immediate historic events. This is particularly true of the book of Psalms; though some psalms (like Ps. 51) do connect to past events, most do not. Nonetheless, biblical writers tended to create their poetry to explore a single theme, even when connected to a historical event.

Parallelism

Parallelism refers to the correspondence between the consecutive lines of a poem. As mentioned, narrative presents its content in a logical, linear fashion and tells a story from one point to the next, and in this way buttresses the meaning of the story. In poetry, the poet communicates the content in a thematic way that is not necessarily linear. The writers support the themes with two or more poetic lines that parallel one another in a meaningful fashion. For instance, Isaiah 40:31 contains three lines of parallel thought about the renewal of strength that takes place when people trust in the Lord:

> they will soar on wings like eagles;
> they will run and not become weary;
> they will walk and not faint.

The writer uses three images: soaring like eagles, running without becoming tired, and walking without fainting to make a single point—God strengthens those who trust in him.

While parallelism may not be the single most defining characteristic of Hebrew poetry, it is one of the most distinctive. While the success of English poetry depends to large measure on the correspondence of meter and rhyme, Hebrew poetry depends on the relationship of thought from one line to the next.

IMAGERY

Imagery is an important characteristic of Hebrew poetry. It "refers to images produced in the mind by language, whose words and statements may refer either to experiences which could produce physical perceptions were the reader actually to have those experiences, or to the sense-impressions themselves."[4] Hebrew poets used imagery to emphasize the greatness of God. Yahweh is a warrior (Exod. 15:3–4) or has great power (Exod. 15:8: "the waters heaped up at the blast of your nostrils"). While narrative does use imagery, their use in Hebrew poetry produces significant differences in the magnitude and impact. Poetic imagery stimulates the imagination and evokes a strong emotional response.[5]

TERSENESS

Hebrew narrative typically uses clauses composed of sentences that relate events in straightforward, flowing words, and uses paragraphs to add new elements to the story. Hebrew poetry, however, uses short clauses that attempt to pack a great deal of meaning into just a few words in a single line. This tight structure requires a great deal of skill so that the poet can balance the wording and ideas with the poetic line(s) that follow(s) it. This creates one of the difficulties in translating Hebrew poetry, for it is almost always impossible to bring across the ideas in a given Hebrew verse with English words that are equivalent in meaning but retain the terseness of the Hebrew.

LITERARY DEVICES

As is the case with all types of literature, poets often used literary devices to add flavor or emphasis or help the reader identify the main point of a portion of a poem or even the entire poem.[6] Some of these, like word pairs and alliteration, are purely literary; others, such as acrostic poems and chiasms, are more structural in nature. The problem with identifying these is that, unless there is an effort by translators to make them

---

4. Friedman, "Imagery," 363.
5. Longman, "Literary Approaches to Biblical Interpretation," 174.
6. Lists of literary devices can be found in virtually any discussion of Hebrew poetry. Of considerable help is the presentation of VanGemeren, "Psalms," 23–28.

obvious, the interpreters, who are not fluent in Hebrew, are almost completely dependent upon commentaries to identify them.

METER

Meter refers to the rhythm determined by the syllables of the words in a line of poetry. While there is no doubt that Hebrew poetry uses meter, and that meter does have an effect on how it is to be interpreted, there is little agreement about exactly how this is so, and even less agreement as to how to go about relating meter to meaning. When combining this uncertainty with the fact that few English words can match syllable for syllable with Hebrew words in translation, the utility of routinely considering meter is doubtful.

Hebrew poetry generally has very distinct characteristics. This is important because readers cannot interpret every poem as if it is part of the same context. Accurate interpretation requires identifying the type of poetry under investigation. For instance, Song of Songs is an example of love poetry, where the author structures all of its images and parallelisms to emphasize the mystery and significance of love. The book of Lamentations, however, is a long lament, emphasizing the spiritual and physical devastation of Jerusalem at the hands of the Babylonians. While they both use vivid imagery and parallelism, the imagery evokes different emotional responses. Just as it is improper to read poetry with the same mindset with which one would read narrative, it is equally improper to read all poems as if they are the same. What they share in common is that both attempt to evoke a strong emotional response.

There are, in fact, several broad categories of Hebrew poetry. Among the purely poetic works are Song of Songs (a collection of love poems), Lamentations (an extended lament connected to a specific event in Israel's history), and the book of Psalms. The collection of 150 psalms represents poems and songs used in Israel's worship. In these cases, there is little in the way of explicit historical context from which to interpret them. So, as is the case with most type of poetic literature, the primary context for interpretation is within the poem itself. In this sense, a poetic text provides its own interpretative context. Readers should interpret them internally rather than in the context of the poems around them.[7]

---

7. We make this assertion with some degree of hesitation. A growing consensus among

Another category of poetic works includes the Wisdom Literature, of which there are three almost entirely poetic works. The first is Proverbs. Proverbial wisdom in general, and the book of Proverbs in particular, requires a different mindset to reading and interpretation (chap. 7). Proverbs is a collection of wise sayings intended to be passed on to young people to help them learn proper behavior, to learn the art of reason and application of judgment in light of what they know and what they experience, and to help them find success in life. One should read and interpret each proverb or extended discourse as discrete poetic units; it is rare to find any real dependence between proverbs that occur in the same general context.

Another of the wisdom books is Job, which is an extended dialogue whose focus is on the question of God's justice in the light of suffering. It includes all the broader categories of Hebrew poetry discussed above, and it is undoubtedly part of Israel's wisdom tradition. But unlike Proverbs, its structure has a series of interchanges between the characters. Whereas Proverbs covers virtually every possible topic of concern to a student of wisdom, Job does not. Its single focus is theodicy—a study of the relationship of God's goodness and providence in relation to the existence of evil. Also, unlike Proverbs, Job has a narrative framework that provides a setting for the debates that appear within it. Since the author arranged its content around a narrative framework into which the poetic elements have been interwoven, it is important to use the surrounding context when interpreting them.

The third wisdom book is Ecclesiastes. It is largely poetic in nature, and like Job, it is set in a narrative framework that provides a measure of context for understanding it. Further, it contains proverbial poems much like those in the book of Proverbs. However, Ecclesiastes is a monologue, that is, the main voice that speaks in the book belongs to one person.

We may add a third discrete type of poetic literature: the prophetic works of the Old Testament.[8] These works are composed mainly of

---

Psalms scholars exists that indicates that one or more thematic arcs unite the Psalter. Among those who are advocating this approach is Howard, "The Psalms and Current Study," 23–40. See also Snearly, "The Return of the King: An Editorial-Critical Analysis of Psalms 107–50."

8. We are using the term "prophetic" different from we did in chapter 5. Here we are referring to those works that make up the prophetic corpus in the English canon of the Old

poetry of a high rhetorical character. Their main purpose is to exhort the people either to remain faithful to Yahweh or to turn away from their unfaithfulness. They relate to discernible historical and social circumstances that are the main impetus for the prophetic word from God. And, because these prophetic books tend to maintain certain historical or thematic contexts over long stretches of text, it is often best to consider the larger literary context in which one finds the poems.

To summarize, Hebrew poetry occurs in four main contexts: narrative, books of poetry, wisdom books, and prophetic works. Each of these broader literary contexts has its own conceptual framework. The interpreter must therefore have some understanding of these differing contexts.

ANALYZING HEBREW POETRY

After recognizing the broader context in which a poem appears, the next step is to analyze the various ways in which Hebrew poetry communicates. Hebrew poetry uses literary and structural devices in conjunction with each other to produce greater effect.

LITERARY DEVICES

Literary devices are the threads an author uses to weave a story or poem. Among the more effective are imagery and hyperbole.

IMAGERY

Poetic imagery creates a vivid image by evoking the senses. It is figurative language; that is, if taken literally, these images would make little sense. Imagery is pervasive in Old Testament poetry. Exodus 15:3 uses military imagery to magnify God's mighty work of deliverance at the Red Sea: "The LORD is a warrior; the LORD is his name." The image is further developed in the verses that follow by speaking of the destruction of Pharaoh's army (vv. 4–5, 7–9) and describing how Yahweh caused the elements to be the instruments of war by which the enemy was defeated (vv.

Testament. We exclude the books of Joshua–2 Kings from this list. Also, in keeping with the English canon, we will include the book of Daniel, though it is not listed among the Prophets in the Hebrew canon (it is listed among the Writings) and despite the fact that it also is an example of apocalyptic literature.

6 and 8) by using further images: "your right hand shattered the enemy" and "the waters heaped up at the blast of your nostrils." While God does not have human hands or nostrils, the words evoke images in the mind of a mighty warrior wielding a weapon and of an angry bull snorting its rage through flared nostrils.

Obviously, imagery is more than the sum of its words. The interpreter must experience the nature of the image. Many images are perceptual; that is, they set up comparisons understood in the context of the five senses.[9] The writers evoke the reader's memories of sights, smells, sensations, and sounds to provide a vivid picture, as in Ecclesiastes 7:6: "for like the crackling of burning thorns under the pot, / so is the laughter of the fool."

Others focus on items that are part of everyday life, and set up a comparison between the items, as in Isaiah 10:5, where God talks of Assyria as "the rod of my anger." Clearly, the imagery here speaks of a rod as an instrument of discipline. In this case, God is threatening to use Assyria as an instrument to punish the rebellious northern kingdom.[10]

HYPERBOLE AND OTHER DEVICES

Poets use hyperbole and other devices that intensify their poems. Hyperbole intentionally overstates or overemphasizes an act or characteristic in order to make it stand out. If taken literally, such a comparison will seem ridiculous or impossible, so that the interpreter must see behind the emphatic language to its real intention.

Synonymous parallels and word pairs in comparative combinations that bring emphasis to the main point are other examples. In Proverbs 8:10, the writer emphasizes the value of accepting the teachings of a wise master by comparing its value to gold and silver: "Accept my instruction instead of silver, / and knowledge rather than pure gold."

Finally, merism uses items together that separately are opposites. For instance, Psalm 121:2 expresses the totality of God's creation by placing "heavens and earth" together: "My help comes from the LORD, / the maker of heaven and earth."

---

9. Longman, *Literary Approaches*, 175–76.
10. Ibid.

STRUCTURAL DEVICES

Hebrew poets use structural devices to communicate their message. The most important of these are parallelism and chiasm.

PARALLELISM

Along with imagery, parallelism is the most frequently encountered feature of Hebrew poetry. At the most basic level, parallelism refers to the coordination of corresponding ideas or images between poetic lines. Three main types of parallelism are synonymous, antithetical, and synthetic.

Synonymous parallelism involves placing two similar ideas together in such a way that the subsequent lines repeat or reinforce the thought of the first. Psalm 1:1 is a good example:

> How happy is the one who does not
> walk in the advice of the wicked
> or stand in the pathway with sinners
> or sit in the company of mockers!

Notice how the final three lines represent parallel thoughts. Though the wording is different, they communicate similar ideas. It is important to note, however, that in this example, the lines are not exact repetitions of a single thought. Readers must take into account the progression inherent to the parallel lines. It is important to recognize that "synonymous" does not imply an exact correspondence in every case.

In *antithetical parallelism*, the second line reinforces the first by supplying a contrast to it. While it does occur elsewhere, it most frequently occurs in the Wisdom Literature, especially Proverbs. Proverbs 10:1 is a good example:

> A wise son brings joy to his father,
> but a foolish son, heartache to his mother.

The key to identifying antithetical parallelism is the use of "but" in the second line. The conjunction sets up a contrast with the first line. The key to understanding this type of parallelism lies in identifying the nature of the contrast.

In *synthetic parallelism*, subsequent lines in the poem provide additional information to the first, so that there is clear movement or progression of thought from one line to the next. It differs from synonymous parallelism in that it has less to do with similarity of thought and more to do with a progression of thought, as in the case of Ecclesiastes 11:2:

> Give a portion to seven,
> Or even to eight,
> for you do not know what disaster may happen on earth.

In this case, the significance lies in determining the progression the poet is emphasizing. Psalm 29:3–9 is a more extensive example.

CHIASM

Chiasm is a structural device related to parallelism. It has parallel thoughts, but they are not necessarily in consecutive lines. A chiasm will usually look something like the following:

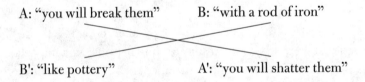

A: "you will break them"   B: "with a rod of iron"

B': "like pottery"   A': "you will shatter them"

Notice how the A and B elements correspond to each other. The line that links the corresponding parts looks like an *X*. This is where the term "chiasm" comes from; it looks like the Greek consonant *chi*, which is similar to the English *X*. Another way to illustrate the relationship among the elements is

A

    B

    B'

A'

While this structure has two central items, there are times when there will be only one central item:

A

    B

       C

    B'

A'

The examples above are a very simple example of chiasm. Chiasms can have complex patterns. However, the central item or items will typically be the central idea of the structure.

Remember, chiasms appear in narrative prose as well as poetic literature with great frequency. In fact, they appear in every kind of literature in every language, and at times are not necessarily intentional structures. Sometimes interpreters succumb to the temptation to force poetic verse or narrative texts into a chiastic structure that they never had. These realities make it important to search for the original intent of the author when interpreting chiastic structures.

INTERPRETING HEBREW POETRY

Understanding the various broader contexts in which Hebrew poetry occurs, and the various modes of expression Hebrew poets used to construct their poems, is not the end of the discussion. It is important to have some kind of broad plan for interpreting Hebrew poetry. These broad guidelines below will have the advantage of providing direction and boundaries for interpretation, without being so constrictive that creativity and exploration are lost.[11]

Identify the literary context in which the poem appears. In all cases, the proper starting point for interpreting a poem is within the poem itself.

---

11. This rather broad list of interpretative steps generally follows those suggested by Osborne, *The Hermeneutical Spiral,* 238–41.

However, this first step is an important one, because it is quite helpful to identify the literary context in which a poem appears before beginning the process of addressing the meaning of the poem itself.

If the writer embedded the poem in a narrative, determine how it fits into the narrative of which it is a part. How does the poem help the narrator tell his story? What point is the narrator trying to communicate, and what does the poem add to this point?

If a poem is part of a prophetic work, determine the historical context in which it occurs and the circumstances or persons it addressed.[12] How does this particular poem relate to those around it? Is it part of a chronological or thematic sequence of oracles united by a central issue? If so, what is different about how this poem addresses the issue within this sequence?

If it appears in the book of Psalms, begin by treating each psalm as an isolated, independent poem. It is also important to remember that the book of Psalms is rather unique in the Bible. In other biblical texts, God is speaking—directly or indirectly—to the reader. The poems in the book of Psalms, however, are people speaking—either directly or indirectly to God.

Note the structural elements of the poem. Identify parallel elements and label them as synonymous, antithetical, or synthetic, and group the parallel elements together so that the parallelisms are obvious. Most modern translations have already done this, so the task then becomes determining how the corresponding ideas relate to each other. Determine what they mean independently, and then what they mean together. What does the poet intend the reader to understand?

If there is a chiastic structure, identify it (commentaries will be of great help for this), and try to find the central elements of the chiasm. The central item in a chiasm will typically perform one of three functions:

1. It will represent the climax of an argument that the poet is trying to make.
2. It will indicate the purpose of the chiastic structure in particular or the poem in general.

---

12. They could speak to the past, the present, or the future, or use various combinations of the three.

3. It will give the principal idea of the chiastic structure or of the poem. The outer items will reinforce the central idea.[13]

Identify and study the imagery. Does the imagery evoke sensory responses, or does it refer to everyday items and create a correspondence between them? What does the poet intend for the reader to understand about the referent (the person, thing, or idea with which the poet is concerned)? Are there broader ancient Near Eastern social or religious matters that lie behind the image? How does the image intend the reader to understand the use of the image; is it a positive image or a negative image?

Identify the historical context of the poem. Does the poem itself provide a historical context? If so, what attitudes does the author express about that particular context? Remember, most psalms do not necessarily have an expressed historical context. That is because they are worship literature, intended for use in any time and any place, and tying them to a particular historical event would tend to limit this timelessness. However, poems will often refer or allude to certain events in Israel's history, and in these cases, it is important to understand how the poet views these events—positively or negatively.

What is the literary form of the poem? This is particularly applicable to the book of Psalms, but all Hebrew poems fit into one or more categories determined by their structure or by the content: war songs, love poetry, hymns, thanksgiving poems, wisdom poems, and imprecatory (cursing) psalms. Each has its own characteristics.

SERMON SAMPLE FROM HEBREW POETRY

Writing sermons based on Hebrew poetry requires experiencing the meaning of the text, not just understanding it. These are slow-cooked sermons—it takes time to achieve the fall-off-the-bone, hickory-smoked flavor of a transformative sermon that touches the head and the heart.

It takes time because you will need to do more than exegete the text; you will also need to spend time meditating on it (Ps. 1:1-2). This is necessary if the meaning and impact of the text is going to flow through you to the audience.

---

13. Deppe, *All Roads Lead to the Text*, 359–60.

In the past when I have preached on Psalm 1, I put primary emphasis on the first verse and created the sermon structure around it. Here is an example from early in my ministry:

Title: How to Live a Happy and Fruitful Life
Text: Psalm 1:1
Thesis: Happiness is a byproduct of living a good life
  I. Be careful how you walk
      a. Walk spiritually by faith (2 Cor. 5:7; Gal. 5:25)
      b. Walk worthy of your calling (Eph. 4:1)
  II. Be careful how you stand
      a. Take a stand for worship (Jude 24)
      b. Take a stand for evangelism (Acts 2:14)
      c. Take a stand for ministry (Ezek. 22:30)
  III. Be careful how you sit
      a. God disapproves of the scoffer (Prov. 3:34)
      b. People disapprove of the scoffer (Prov. 24:9)
      c. Scoffers hurt people (Job 16:20–17:2)
      d. Scoffers should not be allowed to continue their destructive behavior (Prov. 22:10)
      e. God will judge the scoffers (Prov. 19:29)
  IV. You can be happy and fruitful (Ps. 1:2–6)

In this outline, written in my early twenties, I demonstrate a misunderstanding of the function of the synonymous parallelism in verse 1, seeing it as three distinct points instead of a single concept.[14] I used the structure it provided as a skeleton to support a multi-point, topical, self-help sermon, and ignored the power of the imagery in the poem, using it as a conclusion that supported my thesis statement.

Below is a more recent sermon that helps the members of the audience understand the text, experience the full impact of the text, and apply it to their lives.

---

14. VanGemeren, "Psalms," 54: "These three descriptions do not represent three kinds of activities of the wicked or a climactic development from walking to sitting or an intensification in the depraved activities of the wicked. Instead, the parallelism is synonymous and profoundly portrays the totality of evil."

Contrasting Choices

Psalm 1:1–6

How happy is the one who does not
walk in the advice of the wicked
or stand in the pathway with sinners
or sit in the company of mockers!
Instead, his delight is in the LORD's instruction,
and he meditates on it day and night.
He is like a tree planted beside flowing streams
that bears its fruit in its season
and whose leaf does not wither.
Whatever he does prospers.
The wicked are not like this;
instead, they are like chaff that the wind blows away.
Therefore the wicked will not stand up in the judgment,
nor sinners in the assembly of the righteous.
For the LORD watches over the way of the righteous,
but the way of the wicked leads to ruin.

This wisdom psalm occupies the prestigious real estate of the first page of the ancient songbook. It is especially important for that reason, and because it introduces the entire songbook. But its value is greater than that. It provides a stark contrast in lifestyle choices that is helpful for young people considering what kind of person they want to be, middle-age people doing mid-course changes in their lives, and older people reflecting on the choices they have made in the past and evaluating how they want to spend the rest of their lives. In the tradition of other contrasting choices throughout the Bible, the psalmist offers a choice between prospering as a genuinely happy person and perishing as a foolish relic.

An example of contrasting choices in the Pentateuch is Deuteronomy 30:15. As Moses is relaying the terms of God's renewed covenant with the children of Israel in the land of Moab, he says, "See, today I have set before you life and prosperity, death and adversity." Here the choice is between life and death, prosperity and adversity. The choice is obvious, right? Obvious, yet the children of Israel did not always make the right choice.

An instance of contrasting choices in the Former Prophets is in Joshua. As Joshua spoke on the occasion of the covenant at Shechem he said, "But if it doesn't please you to worship the LORD, choose for yourselves today: Which will you worship—the gods your fathers worshiped beyond the Euphrates River or the gods of the Amorites in whose land you are living? As for me and my family, we will worship the LORD" (Josh. 24:15).

Here the choice is between serving the God they knew and serving the unfamiliar, foreign gods. The choice is obvious, right? Obvious, yet the children of Israel did not always make the right choice.

An example of contrasting choices in the Gospels is Jesus' words as he concludes the Sermon on the Mount:

> Therefore, everyone who hears these words of mine and acts on them will be like a wise man who built his house on the rock. The rain fell, the rivers rose, and the winds blew and pounded that house. Yet it didn't collapse, because its foundation was on the rock. But everyone who hears these words of mine and doesn't act on them will be like a foolish man who built his house on the sand. The rain fell, the rivers rose, the winds blew and pounded that house, and it collapsed. It collapsed with a great crash. (Matt. 7:24–27)

In this text, the choice is between building a house on the sand or on a rock. Again, the choice is obvious; everyone knows you build a house on a solid foundation. Obvious, yet the audience did not always make the right choice. We will come back to this issue in a minute, but first, we will explore the choices the psalmist gives.

Because it is poetry, Psalm 1 uses vivid imagery that invites listeners to do more than understand its teachings; it calls them to experience the contrast between genuinely happy people and those with wasted lives, but before it does, it helps them to understand the difference. The genuinely happy people resist the temptation to allow ungodly people to influence them, to negatively influence others, or to stir up strife in the community. Psalm 1:1 says:

How happy is the one who does not
walk in the advice of the wicked
or stand in the pathway with sinners
or sit in the company of mockers!

With this verse, the psalmist is not addressing three separate things (sitting, walking, and standing), but is illustrating the happy person's approach to the totality of life. Evildoers, who take advice from ungodly people, try to lead others astray, and stir up strife, are not genuinely happy—they are miserable, as we shall see in a moment.

Instead of participating in these activities, genuinely happy people soak their souls in God's word. Psalm 1:2b says:

Instead, his delight is in the LORD's *instruction,*
and he meditates on it day and night.

Genuinely happy people do not merely include the Lord's instruction in their lives—it is not an add-on item, or one of the many things they do—it is their delight, their lifestyle, their primary goal. Later, the psalmist would write, "Hallelujah! Happy is the person who fears the LORD, taking great delight in his commands" (Ps. 112:1).

As a result, they are genuinely happy, living stable lives in an ever-changing environment. With verse 3, the psalm shifts from explaining the concept to helping the listener experience it at a visceral level. Look at verse 3:

He is like a tree planted beside flowing streams
that bears its fruit in its season
and whose leaf does not wither.
Whatever he does prospers.

This comparison (simile) should allow you to experience the distinction, not just understand it.

This verse reminds me of the famous exchange Barbara Walters had with Katharine Hepburn in 1981. During the interview, Hepburn described herself as a "strong tree" in her old age. Walters followed up the observation with a question, "What kind of tree are you?" Hepburn said she preferred "to be an oak rather than an elm, in order to avoid Dutch elm disease."[15]

The psalmist did not get as specific as Hepburn did in his poem, just that it was a fruitful tree. However, there is a significant detail found in the original language. The Hebrew word for planted literally means transplanted.[16] It is not that the tree started out next to the ample source of nourishment, the streams of water. Its caretaker transplanted it there.

Genuine happiness is a gift. People cannot find it without God. Left to their own devices, people will not immerse themselves in the Lord's instruction. They will not be firmly planted anywhere, much less by a nourishing stream, and instead, they will be blown about by outside forces. Exactly what the psalmist says in verse 4:

> The wicked are not like this;
> instead, they are like chaff that the wind blows away.

In verse 4, the psalmist describes the evildoers as chaff. They are not fruitful trees, receiving nourishment from an ever-flowing stream. They are chaff, a wasteful, irritating byproduct that the prevailing wind blows until it evaporates in the distance.

Have you ever encountered chaff up close and personal? I have.

One hot, windy West Texas day, my grandfather invited me to ride on his combine with him to harvest wheat. His combine did not have air conditioning, or even a cab, it was just a plain working-man's machine.

He let me play in the grain bin, and even steer the machine—it was great to be with him. But after a few hours, I was ready to go home. The chaff itched. I was miserable.

I begged him to take me home, but he did not.

The itching was unbearable. When we arrived home after sunset, I ran to the bathroom and took a hot bath. I was the first 10-year-old in the history of the world that ever wanted to take a bath. Why? I was covered in chaff.[17] The psalmist could not have used a more powerful

15. http://variety.com/2014/tv/news/barbara-walters-probing-questions-and-a-tall-tale-of-the-tree-1201152684/

16. Carson, *New Bible Commentary*, 489.

17. Wilson, *Fresh Start Devotionals*, 2:12–13.

simile for the futile lives of evil people than chaff. They are a wasteful, irritating byproduct that the prevailing wind blows until it evaporates in the distance. They have no purpose. No direction. No future.

Verse 5 says:

> *Therefore the wicked will not stand up in the judgment,*
> *nor sinners in the assembly of the righteous.*

This is not the outcome for the genuinely happy person. They do not live ruined, meaningless lives. Their caretaker, who transplanted them next to the nourishing stream, does not abandon them to the elements. He watches over them. Look at verse 6:

> *For the LORD watches over the way of the righteous,*
> *but the way of the wicked leads to ruin.*

This is a poem about two choices. The correct choice is obvious. No one wants to be like chaff, a wasted life driven by the wind. Who would want that? The obvious choice is to be a transplanted tree, next to a refreshing stream, bearing fruit. It may be the obvious choice. But not many people make it. Why?

Earlier in the message, I mentioned a choice that Jesus gave his listeners between building their house on the sand or the rock. A few verses before that, he said, "How narrow is the gate and difficult the road that leads to life, and few find it" (Matt. 7:14). The right choice, the obvious choice isn't always the popular choice. Why?

It is far easier for people to build a house on sand, than to build something on rock—not everyone is willing to exert the upfront energy for the long-term payoff; instead, they would rather live for the fleeting moment, but when it is gone, they have nothing left—the remnants of their life is blown away with the wind.

Many people choose to allow evildoers to influence them and join them in their destructive direction. Paul wrote, "Do not be deceived: 'Bad company corrupts good morals'" (1 Cor. 15:33). Going against the grain takes courage. It takes courage to do the right thing. It takes energy, and rarely is it easy.

Today, I want to encourage you to do the right thing, not the easy thing. Immerse yourself in God's instruction, and then live your life according to it.

Just as the caretaker transplants the fruit-bearing tree by the nourishing stream, God makes his instruction available to you. Your response must be to drink deeply. Immerse yourself in his Word—or to use the words of the psalm—meditate on it day and night. Genuinely happy people do not merely include the Lord's instruction in their lives—it is not an add-on item, or one of the many things they do—it is their delight, their lifestyle, their primary goal. If you want to be genuinely happy—commit to doing the right thing: know and live God's instruction.

REFLECTIONS ON THE SERMON

This sermon follows a similar structure that you have encountered in the other sermon examples in the book, but it did not come from narrative plot dynamics. Because the sermon text comes from a psalm, not a narrative passage, the dramatic arc is more subtle. The movements of this sermon are:

> ↓ People do not always make the right choice when presented with contrasting choices.

> > ↑ Genuinely happy people make the right choice to meditate on God's instruction. They are nourished like a tree planted by a stream of water.

> ↓ Ungodly people do not make the right choice. They are like chaff that blows in the wind.

> > ↑ You can make the right choice—God will transplant you by the stream of waters and you can experience the nourishment he provides.

My hope in preaching this psalm was to encourage the audience to experience the truth they are learning, which is the way Psalm 1 unfolds. It is both deductive and inductive in nature. By verse 2, the psalmist reveals the truth he is teaching, which makes it a deductive text. The information is upfront. However, his proof is not a multi-point argument, as most deductive texts contain; instead, the texture of the words is more *pathos* than *logos*, inviting the listener to experience the text, not just understand it.

Aristotle taught that there are three artistic proofs—three tools that speakers use to convince their hearers: ethos, pathos, and logos.[18] Ethos is the overall impression an observer has about another person's honesty and integrity. Though ethos is unquantifiable, it is persuasive. We tend to believe believable people.[19]

The second of Aristotle's trilogy is pathos. It is a gut feeling about the rightness of something and requires the listener to be in a certain frame of mind. It is experiential in nature and is persuasion from within.

Logos is the final word—the truth that convinces beyond any doubt. It is indisputable, logical evidence. These proofs do not work against each other; they combine to form a strong, persuasive cord.

In this sermon, I leaned on the *logos* as in verses 1–2, but approached the teaching of the verses that followed with *pathos*, because that was the approach the psalmist used and I wanted to keep the meaning and the impact of the text intact throughout the hermeneutical and homiletical processes.

In verses 3–4, the psalmist uses a powerful simile as a point of comparison—the stable, fruitful, transplanted tree versus the useless chaff carried away by the wind. One had a caretaker watching over it, the other did not.

My goal was to get the members of the audience to experience what they knew to be true, to evaluate their life trajectory against the teaching, and to commit to align themselves with the Lord's instruction.

---

18. Aristotle, *Rhetoric*, 5: "Of the modes of persuasion furnished by the spoken word there are three kinds. The first kind depends on the personal character of the speaker; the second on putting the audience into a certain frame of mind; the third on the proof, or apparent proof, provided by the words of the speech itself."

19. Ibid., 6: "It is not true, as some writers assume in their treatises on rhetoric, that the personal goodness revealed by the speaker contributes nothing to his power of persuasion; on the contrary, his character may almost be called the most effective means of persuasion he possesses."

For Further Reflection

- What challenges does poetry bring to multi-point or verse-by-verse preachers?
- Remember to identify the main point of the poem/song as you study the passage. How can you build a sermon around that one idea?
- If the poem is in the psalms, you can treat each as an isolated, independent poem, but if it appears in a narrative, pay particular attention to the context. How does the writer use the poem to emphasize the narrative's point?
- If the psalm has a connection to a narrative elsewhere in Scripture, consider how the narrative provides background for better understanding and experiencing the poem.
- Poetry often conveys information that the reader should understand and experience. Consider how to communicate the truth in the poem in such a way that your audience can experience what they learn in the poem.
- Resist the temptation to microwave a sermon based on a poetic text. I do not mean to suggest that preparing a sermon based on a Hebrew poem will require more hours writing it; rather, that you will need to spread out the preparation time. Because you need time to meditate on the text to experience it, you might plan to meditate on the Scripture the week prior to when you will write the sermon.

---[C H A P T E R   7]---

Proverbs

Interpreting the wisdom literature in the Old Testament requires hermeneutical and homiletical muscle memory.[1] It takes time, effort, and patience to develop the skill and knowledge to move comfortably within the world of biblical wisdom literature. The key is to persevere until the intentional process transforms into muscle memory. With practice, and a growing amount of knowledge, understanding, and skill, preachers will become more efficient and accurate.

In order to interpret and preach wisdom literature in general and Proverbs in particular, it is important to have an understanding of two things: the objective of wisdom and the mindset of wisdom thought.

THE DEFINITION AND OBJECTIVE OF WISDOM

Giving a concise, one-sentence definition of wisdom is difficult, as the opening lines from Proverbs illustrate:

The proverbs of Solomon son of David, king of Israel:
For learning wisdom and discipline;
for understanding insightful sayings;
for receiving prudent instruction
in righteousness, justice, and integrity;
for teaching shrewdness to the inexperienced,

---

1. Athletes train their bodies to be fit for the physical demands of their sport, but they also work to build muscle memory so that their actions become second nature. The athlete not only acquires the physical necessities to succeed, but also the experience to know how to act and react in realtime circumstances, even when the circumstances are completely new and unexpected. In short, it takes hard work and patience, but over time skills and aptitudes that were virtually non-existent at the beginning of the training will become second nature after prolonged effort.

knowledge and discretion to a young man—
let a wise person listen and increase learning,
and let a discerning person obtain guidance—
for understanding a proverb or a parable,
the words of the wise, and their riddles.
The fear of the LORD
is the beginning of knowledge;
fools despise wisdom and discipline.

In Proverbs 1:1–7, the repetition of related characteristics associated with wisdom (discipline, understanding, righteousness, justice, integrity, discretion) and the modes of relating wisdom (learning, understanding, receiving, teaching, listening) serve as the basis for embracing proverbial wisdom. Also notice that the use of the word "for" expresses purpose; the clauses that follow spell out the purpose of wisdom, in this case, as communicated through the collection.

Finally, notice that verse 7 is set apart from the rest of the passage. The opening clause literally reads "the fear of Yahweh (is) the beginning of wisdom." "Fear" in this context refers to an intimate, worshipful understanding of God, which has its source ("the beginning") in and with God.[2] The book of Proverbs begins (1:7) and ends (31:30) by mentioning the fear of Yahweh. In the same way, wisdom begins and ends with the fear of Yahweh.

Within the Old Testament context, wisdom is not merely the pursuit of a prescribed list of wise or unwise actions or thoughts. It is a mindset that knowledge, understanding, and experience provide the impetus for correct action or thought in any given circumstance.[3] At the heart of this mindset is a constant awareness of and relationship with the God who is the source of wisdom.

The Role of Wisdom Books in the Old Testament

Preachers cannot interpret Proverbs like they would the laws found in the Pentateuch. The laws of the Old Testament are prescriptive; they lay down in plain terms how God's people are or are not to act. Obedience is

---

2. Van Pelt and Kaiser, "יָרֵא", 2:531.
3. Fee and Stuart, *How to Read the Bible for All Its Worth*, 225.

required of God's people; obedience is a response of love to and for God (Deut. 30:16). Proverbs and other forms of wisdom literature are not prescriptive. Preachers must develop an intuitive sense—muscle memory—of what is right and wrong from them. They deal with the mindset God's people carry with them each day that enables them to act obediently—wisely—in whatever circumstance might be encountered.

This requires a fear of the Lord, which includes more than just terror at the thought of offending God through disobedience. Fear of the Lord is a loving, worshipful understanding of God, resulting in a desire to act wisely. Wisdom literature addresses the attitudes that lead to obedience.

Two Types of Wisdom Literature

There are two different types of wisdom literature in the Old Testament. Each guides the reader in living and thinking in God's world.

The speculative wisdom books, Job and Ecclesiastes, question the way things should work in light of the way they actually work. Whereas the book of Proverbs takes a highly optimistic perspective on life, the books of Job and Ecclesiastes do not. In fact, both books give evidence that while the characters and speakers in the books affirm the optimistic tradition, they seem at a loss to explain the rather negative realities they experienced in their lives.

The book of Proverbs represents the second type of wisdom literature, the proverbial or optimistic wisdom writings. Proverbs are short, highly impactful statements that often use the literary devices of imagery and hyperbole (chap. 6) to make their points. Proverbs do not supply universal prescriptive actions or thoughts. Individual proverbs do not apply to every situation a person might encounter. In fact, if a reader does not consider an individual proverb in light of the greater context of the rest of the book, and the entire Bible, it is highly likely that it will be misinterpreted and misapplied. This raises a special caution to those who select an isolated proverb as the text for an entire sermon.

Take for example Proverbs 26:4: "Don't answer a fool according to his foolishness / or you'll be like him yourself." Taken by itself, the wisdom in this seems self-evident. Answering the foolishness that proceeds from the mouth of a fool is, well, foolish. It would be easy simply to cite this as the primary word from God on how to deal with fools.

However, a quick look at the next verse shows it is not that simple: "Answer a fool according to his foolishness / or he'll become wise in his own eyes." So should the fool be answered or not?

The point is that individual proverbs do not prescribe one action for every situation. Rather, they convey a response to any number of situations. It is up to the individual to decide what response is appropriate in a given circumstance, and the best way to do that is to place the proverb in context with similar proverbs and the whole counsel of Scripture.

Another aspect of proverbial wisdom is that it assumes a principle of retributive justice, which means that God blesses people for wise or righteous choices and he curses them for unwise or unrighteous choices. This type of wisdom expresses a sense of what ought to be or perhaps a better way to say it is the way God intended things to be. Conceptually, then, Proverbs expresses a moral perspective on the world God created and the behavior of humans in that world.[4] The righteous ought to thrive; justice ought to prevail, though in life it does not always seem to be so. Job and Ecclesiastes take up this last observation with a will. Both presuppose that things ought to operate according to the principles God has established, but when they appear not to, how is one to respond? The natural response is to question God's justice.

A final observation about the nature of Proverbs is that wisdom literature is firmly rooted in the undeniable truth that God created the world (Prov. 8:22–31; Job 38–41). In modern terms, this means that not only has God established the workings of the universe in terms of physical laws and principles, but God also established morality within the fabric of the universe he created. What is more, this connection with creation means that people of any race or religious orientation can detect God's truths, whether they recognize them as such or not. Multiple examples of works like Proverbs, Job, and Ecclesiastes exist in the ancient Near East that emphasizes many of the same themes of what ought to be.

In other words, wisdom thought is rooted in general revelation; people everywhere can recognize what is true or right and apply this understanding to life. The intent is to navigate life's challenges and triumphs

---

4. At the risk of oversimplification, morals refer to, as is stated above, "what ought to be." One definition expresses it in this way: "Morals are the principles on which one's judgments of right and wrong are based" (http://grammarist.com/usage/ethics-morals/).

in a successful manner. What distinguishes Old Testament wisdom literature from other wisdom literature is that it is intensely Yahwistic. Proverbs contains limited religious language and limited mention of the major Old Testament themes of covenant and worship. However, there is enough included to support those ideas, which are at the heart of the worldview presented in the biblical wisdom tradition.

INTERPRETING PROVERBS

When interpreting Proverbs, it is important to keep the following five principles in mind. First, proverbs are not intended or designed to represent absolutes. Proverbs are not laws, and therefore preachers should not treat them as if they were. Proverbs are generalized statements of wise action that apply in some situations, but not in every situation. In addition, once preachers identify the principle of a particular proverb, they must compare it with other proverbs that express the same or even an opposite principle in order to narrow down as closely as possible the circumstances under which one should use that principle. In short, always determine the interpretation in relation to the rest of the biblical testimony. The most obvious starting point is Proverbs 1:1–7, the introduction to the entire book of Proverbs.

Second, proverbs express their truths in order to be memorable, not universally applicable.[5] Though it is not easy to discern in English translations, Hebrew proverbs tend to be short, poetically composed lines, usually of four to five words, mainly composesd of one-syllable or two-syllable words. Proverbs are short, pithy, compact, and easy to remember.

Third, not all proverbs are the same. Proverbs contain two broad types of expression: extended discourses (Prov. 1–9, 13; 30–31) and individual proverbs (Prov. 10–29). Also, there are various types of individual proverbs: proverbs, instructions, riddles, sayings, admonitions, and beatitudes. Each has its own characteristics that readers should take into consideration as they interpret them. Most commentaries, dictionary and

---

5. Fee and Stuart, *How to Read the Bible for All Its Worth*, 238. This is a rewording of Fee and Stuart's principle of interpreting Proverbs. They provide general wisdom, and as such, it may not apply to every circumstance.

encyclopedia articles, and books on interpretation and hermeneutics will cover these in detail.[6]

Fourth, Proverbs use poetic devices to communicate their principles. As mentioned in chapter 6, poetry is symbolic or figurative, not literal (like historical narrative or legal texts). Pay attention to the metaphorical, allegorical, or hyperbolic language used in the proverb in order to bring emphasis to the intended point. The book contains every type of parallelism, and each line of a proverb relates to the others.

Finally, proverbs use imagery and vocabulary from the social life of the ancient Near Eastern people in order to communicate their principles. This is a matter of relevance: people have to have an understanding of the language of a proverb to understand and apply its meaning. Therefore, preachers will need to "translate" some proverbs so the modern audiences can understand them.[7] The imagery and the meaning that the original audience likely understood are not always clear to modern audiences. It is important, then, to communicate the argument of the proverb in language that clarifies what is otherwise unclear before proceeding to elucidate the principle.

Sermon Samples from Proverbs

We provide two sermon samples. The first one is from an individual proverb and the second one is from an extended discourse. Our colleague Joe Slunaker wrote the first sermon based upon Proverbs 13:24. As you read, notice how he relates the individual proverb to the overarching theme of discipline in the book of Proverbs, and how he helps define the terminology as other authors use it elsewhere in Scripture.

Do You Love or Do You Hate Your Child?

Proverbs 13:24
The one who will not use the rod hates his son,
but the one who loves him disciplines him diligently.

---

6. See the bibliography for specific references.
7. Fee and Stuart, *How to Read the Bible for All Its Worth*, 239–40.

In 2013, Ethan Couch killed four people and seriously injured two others while driving drunk. In his defense, psychologist Dick Miller testified that Couch was a victim of parents who never set limits for him, and he coined the word "affluenza"[8] to describe what happens to children who grow up without proper parental discipline. Prosecutors asked for twenty years behind bars, but the court sentenced him to ten years of probation.[9]

I am not an attorney and certainly do not understand the nuances of the law, but one thing appears clear to me in this case: the court acknowledged that this young man's privileged upbringing did not prepare him for responsible adulthood. He would have been better off to have parents who would give him fewer things and discipline him more. While his lenient parents gave him plenty of things, they did not give him the most important thing: discipline.

Overall, the book of Proverbs definitely views those who provide financial means for their heirs in a favorable light (13:22), but it also stresses the importance of discipline. It is obvious that the Couches were willing to provide for their son financially and give him anything he wanted. It is also obvious that they did not give him what he really needed: discipline, something a loving parent should always provide.

Our text says, "The one who will not use the rod hates his son, / but the one who loves him disciplines him diligently."

It is striking that the two powerful words, *love* and *hate*, are juxtaposed in this text, based on the action (or non-action) of the parent. The parallelism stands like this:

[A1] The one who will <u>not use the rod</u> [B1] *hates his son;*
but [B2] *the one who loves him* [A2] <u>disciplines him</u> diligently.[10]

---

8. http://www.cnn.com/2013/12/12/justice/texas-teen-dwi-wreck/, (accessed 7/1/16): "I wish I hadn't used that term. Everyone seems to have hooked onto it, we used to call these people spoiled brats."

9. http://www.cnn.com/2016/04/13/us/texas-affluenza-ethan-couch/, (accessed 7/1/16).

10. Developing a way for the audience to visualize the parallelism structure of Hebrew poetry can drive the point home, as the most obvious parallel issues are *love* and *hate*. A breakdown of this verse in Hebrew shows that the *athnak* (a Masoretic accent marker which essentially splits the verse in half) intentionally places these two concepts at the center of the proverb.

The very structure of this verse seems to be asking a question: do you *love* or do you *hate* your child? According to this verse, the answer to that question hangs on whether or not the parent uses "the rod."

Before we go further, I want to remind you of two very special things to keep in mind when studying Proverbs. First, proverbs are not absolutes; and second, proverbs express their truths in order to be memorable, but not to be universally applicable.[11] With those two things in mind, let's explore the text further.

The Hebrew word for "rod" is very flexible in its Old Testament usage. Used 190 times in 178 verses, it has ranges in meaning from rod, staff, club, scepter, to tribe. In the context of discipline, this word most often refers to a thin rod that people used specifically for physical punishment.[12]

This text obviously instructs parents to exercise discipline, but to what end? Remember that not using the rod and exercising discipline are contrasting concepts just as hating and loving children are. In its simplest terms: parental discipline is a necessary component of parental love.

Of course, this is not a green light for child abuse and does not necessarily mandate the use of a literal rod. Proverbs 23:13–14 says:

> Don't withhold discipline from a youth;
> if you punish him with a rod, he will not die.
> Punish him with a rod,
> and you will rescue his life from Sheol.

It reminds us that the point of physical discipline is that the child

---

11. For detailed explanations of these reminders, see "Interpreting Proverbs" above. These two are extremely important to communicate often while preaching Proverbs because of the frequent and misguided tendency of readers to take Proverbs to be absolutes. In the case of our verse in view, the parent who has been diligent in godly discipline could easily question their actions and become discouraged if their child does not follow the Lord.

12. See 2 Samuel 5:14; Isaiah 30:31; Ezekiel 21:15; Micah 4:14; Psalm 89:33; Proverbs 10:13, 22:13–14, 26:3, 29:15. The Hebrew word here is שִׁבְטוֹ (*shiv-toh*). I refrained from pronouncing the word in this sermon, because it is not prudent to force the phoneticization of the ancient language words in an English language sermon because it seldom adds to the actual point when few listeners will know enough Hebrew to know the difference anyway.

"not die," but rather that the *rod* might "save his soul from death." Unlike abuse, which threatens a child's safety, physical discipline done with love, though seemingly harsh, actually contributes to our children's physical safety by warning them away from harm and the deadly consequences of sinful actions.

"Hate" is a very strong word to use of the parents who avoid their responsibility of disciplining their children. Yet Solomon uses it here unambiguously—it is clear, those who do not discipline their children hate them, due in part to the fact that through their apathy, apprehension, ambivalence, or whatever, they are intentionally missing an opportunity to teach their children about God. We will return to this idea in a moment.

Furthermore, parents should discipline *diligently*. What does it mean to discipline diligently? It actually means to *seek* opportunities to do it. As strange as that sounds, look at the way the writers use this word elsewhere in the book of Proverbs:

- Then they will call me, but I won't answer; / they will search for me, but won't find me." (1:28)
- So I came out to meet you, / to search for you, and I've found you. (7:15)
- I love those who love me, / and those who search for me find me. (8:17)
- The one who searches for what is good seeks favor, / but if someone looks for trouble, it will come to him. (11:27)[13]

In each case, there was intentionality to the seeking. Parental discipline should not be an afterthought, but in love, there should be a plan in place to impart wisdom through discipline (29:15).

Proverbs 13:24 is not the only passage in the Proverbs to speak about parental discipline. Proverbs 19:18 describes discipline as a source of hope, that a parent might steer his child away from death;

---

13. Other examples are Isaiah 26:9, 47:11(this usage is strange when brought into English); Hosea 5:15; Psalms 63:2, 78:34; Job 7:21, 8:5, 24:5. I only used the Proverbs examples in the sermon because of time limits. Many of these other examples could serve as cross references to demonstrate what the concept of diligent searching looks like.

22:15 upholds the rod of discipline as able to drive folly from the heart of a child; and 29:17 tells parents that if they discipline their child, he will give them rest and be a delight to their heart.[14]

Perhaps what is most compelling about Proverbs 13:24, along with the rest of the content concerning parental discipline in the Proverbs, is the fact that these prescriptions do not come out of a vacuum, but are actually based on the way God interacts with his people. In the extended discourse of the first part of Proverbs, the author reminds his readers of why God disciplines his children and how to respond appropriately to it. Proverbs 3:11-12 says,

> Do not despise the LORD's instruction, my son,
> and do not loathe his discipline;
> for the LORD disciplines the one he loves,
> just as a father disciplines the son in whom he delights.

With this in mind, the importance of parental discipline becomes clear: parental discipline is a necessary component of parental love because it reflects the way God loves his children.[15] Therefore, if you really want to love your children, you must do more than simply provide for their physical needs, you *must love them enough to discipline them, just as God disciplines you out of his love for you.*

When parents exercise love through corrective discipline they actually teach children about God's character and actions: His character in that just as a father disciplines his sons, he disciplines us; his actions in that, on this side of the cross, he punishes his only son with

---

14. This quick synopsis helps show the frequency and consistency of the texts concerning discipline in the Proverbs.

15. While parental discipline that is a necessary component of parental love is most definitely a part of Proverbs 13:24, the concept of discipline reflecting God's love is not apparent from this verse alone. The inclusion of this phrase comes from the presumption that though the individual Proverbs in chapters 10–29 are discrete units, the book of Proverbs is a literary whole and the beginning chapters set up much of what comes later. In the same way that the concept of "fear of the Lord" frames the book (see first part of this chapter) so does Proverbs 3:11–12 set up all further discussion of discipline in the book. Furthermore, we also presuppose that "at the heart of this mindset [in this case disciplining children] is a constant awareness of and relationship with the God who is the source of wisdom." (See the first part of this chapter.)

a punishment we could not bear in order to save our souls through Jesus' substitution.[16]

Since the fear of the Lord is the beginning of wisdom, it is also a crucial aspect of parental discipline. This is especially significant in light of the first half of Proverbs 29:15: "A rod of correction imparts wisdom." Proverbs 13:24 on its own imparts to the people of God that parental discipline is a necessary component of parental love, but within the whole context of the Proverbs also reminds God's people that this is because it reflects the way God loves his children.

REFLECTIONS ON THE SERMON

This sermon begins with a *Fresh Illustration*[17] to challenge the listeners to consider what parental love is. Parental love is not giving children everything they want; it is giving them what they need: discipline that helps prepare them for adulthood. While lenient, indulgent parents would never say they hate their child, it is clear that they do not love them properly.

The first and second movements of the sermon are the following:

⬇ Indulgent parents do not love their children as they should.

⬆ Loving parents will discipline their children.

Slunaker transitions from the introduction to the text by showing the parallel juxtaposition of love/hate and disciplining/not disciplining. This, along with the introduction, upsets the equilibrium and prepares the people to receive the biblical instruction.

So that the audience does not misunderstand the meaning of the stark love/hate contrast, he reminds the audience of the fundamental nature of proverbs, which is they are not absolutes and not intended to be seen as universally applicable. They speak more of probabilities than they do of absolute cause and effect outcomes.

---

16 One test of a good Old Testament sermon is the way it responsibly deals with the text in context before it points to Christ.

17. http://www.freshsermonillustrations.net.

It is always important to place proverbs in context with the biblical record and other proverbs. Slunaker did this with the biblical record as he discussed the usage of שִׁבְטוֹ (*shiv-toh*) in the Old Testament. This summary helped the reader gain an understanding of the likely meaning of the word in this particular verse.

He paused from his exposition long enough to give some immediate application of the text. He underscores that this verse is not promoting child abuse. This constituted the third movement:

⬇ Abusive behavior is not the same as discipline.

There is a line that parents cannot cross when using corporal punishment with their children.[18] Slunaker made sure his audience knew that he was not encouraging anyone to cross that line. It was important for him to do this in light of some probable reactions. For instance, how would a victim of child abuse be hearing this sermon? Without this pause, they would likely shut down and stop listening. What about abusers? Could they attempt to justify their non-biblical actions with the preacher's words? How about new parents who are deciding how they will discipline their children?

Slunaker returns to the text to explain what discipline is. It is diligent and it is intentional. He places this teaching in the context of how "seeking" is used in other proverbs. To save time, he chooses not to go beyond the scope of Proverbs; however, he does have other citations in a footnote in the sermon. This is a good practice, because someone may ask him to expound the concept further after the service. By including this information in a footnote, he has the information available to share if asked.

Now he expands the scope of the teaching to other proverbs. As previously mentioned, this is sound practice when preaching on a single proverb. It helps provide the proper context to understand and apply the

---

18. https://www.bhwlawfirm.com/spanking-corporal-punishment-texas/: "In Texas, it is a known practice for parents to spank their children and it is perfectly legal to do so, but the main question is when does spanking or other corporal punishment cross the line to child abuse. The Texas Penal Code states that child abuse occurs when the force results in bodily injury. Bodily injury means 'physical pain, illness, or any impairment of physical condition.' Tex. Penal Code §1.07(8)." While laws will vary from state to state, this citation illustrates that there is a line that cannot be crossed.

proverb. By examining a broader context, Slunaker is able to make the statement that "parental discipline is a necessary component of parental love because it reflects the way God loves his children," which leads to the transformative point: *you must love them enough to discipline them, just as God disciplines you out of his love for you.* This ushers in the fourth movement (which is the same as the second movement) of the sermon:

↑ Loving parents will discipline their children.

The proverb is impactful because of its terse, succinct, vivid truth. This sermon keeps the impact intact by contrasting loving discipline with abusive behavior. The third movement helps clarify the biblical teaching. Slunaker provided the third movement in response to possible congregational misunderstanding, and in doing so, carried the impact of the text over into the sermon.

In the sermon below, I examine an extended discourse from Proverbs 31, which contains advice from King Lemuel's mother about how to handle his powerful position. In it, I place the teaching of this proverb in light of other proverbs and the whole counsel of Scripture, especially to interpret the words of King Lemuel's mother about alcohol. Because it is an extended discourse, there is a narrative structure evident in the wisdom passage, which I follow in the sermon.

Powerful Living

Proverbs 31:1–9

The words of King Lemuel,
a pronouncement that his mother taught him:
What should I say, my son?
What, son of my womb?
What, son of my vows?
Don't spend your energy on women
or your efforts on those who destroy kings.
It is not for kings, Lemuel,
it is not for kings to drink wine
or for rulers to desire beer.

Otherwise, he will drink,
forget what is decreed,
and pervert justice for all the oppressed.
Give beer to one who is dying
and wine to one whose life is bitter.
Let him drink so that he can forget his poverty
and remember his trouble no more.
Speak up for those who have no voice,
for the justice of all who are dispossessed.
Speak up, judge righteously,
and defend the cause of the oppressed and needy.

We know Proverbs 31 better for the verses that follow this morning's reading, not our text itself. Pastors often use Proverbs 31:10–31 as a selection for Mother's Day as an example of an ideal mother. If you've been in church for very many years, you are likely to have heard a sermon on that text. The verses that precede it are not as familiar, but are also valuable. They provide a strong example of how people in positions of power should conduct themselves.

With few exceptions, the book of Proverbs contains the wisdom of King Solomon, the wisest man who ever lived. One of those exceptions is Proverbs 31, which contains the wisdom of King Lemuel's mother. While we know nothing about King Lemuel, we do know quite a bit about the influence parents have on their children. Proverbs 22:6 says, "Start a youth out on his way; / even when he grows old he will not depart from it."

We must take care to remember that this verse, and all the verses contained in the book of Proverbs, are just that: proverbs, not promises. Some have mistaken these sayings as ironclad guarantees that bind God to deliver a certain outcome based upon our conduct. For instance, Proverbs 22:6 is listed in the book *God's Promises for Your Every Need* as a promise for your family.[19] This proverb, like all proverbs, speaks of probabilities; it does not make a promise. It underscores the importance of children's early years for their lifelong behavior and indicates that there is connection between what parents teach

---

19. Gill, *God's Promises for Your Every Need*, 290.

their children when they are young and the way the children behave when they are old.

One of my sons recently told me, "I've got you in my head. I hear you speaking to me all the time." I've had the same experience. Words of my parents and grandparents guide me to this day.

Parents' influence does not end when the children leave home. It is not just that they remember our words from when they lived under our roof, but that we continue to speak to them at important times of their lives. That is what is happening in this text. It contains the wisdom that his mother gave to Lemuel when he ascended to a position of power. Specifically, she tells him not to squander his power on instant gratification. She says, "Don't spend your energy on women or your efforts on those who destroy kings. It is not for kings, Lemuel, it is not for kings to drink wine or for rulers to desire beer. Otherwise, he will drink, forget what is decreed, and pervert justice for all the oppressed" (31:3–5).

Lemuel didn't become king so he could live large, chase women, or overindulge with strong drink.

Notice she said women, not a woman; she is discouraging him from being a philanderer. Elsewhere in the book of Proverbs, chasing women is discouraged:

- Drink water from your own cistern,
  water flowing from your own well. (5:15)
- Don't lust in your heart for her beauty
  or let her captivate you with her eyelashes.
  For a prostitute's fee is only a loaf of bread,
  but the wife of another man goes after a precious life.
  Can a man embrace fire
  and his clothes not be burned? (6:25–27)
- My son, give me your heart,
  and let your eyes observe my ways.
  For a prostitute is a deep pit,
  and a wayward woman is a narrow well. (23:26–27)
- A man who loves wisdom brings joy to his father,
  but one who consorts with prostitutes destroys his wealth (29:3)

However, in Proverbs, finding a good wife is encouraged:

- A gracious woman gains honor,
  but violent people gain only riches (11:16)
- A wife of noble character is her husband's crown,
  but a wife who causes shame
  is like rottenness in his bones. (12:4)
- Every wise woman builds her house,
  but a foolish one tears it down with her own hands (14:1)
- A man who finds a wife finds a good thing
  and obtains favor from the Lord. (18:22)

Later in this chapter is her wisdom about a capable wife (31:10–31)—the kind of woman that a mother wants her son to marry. Lemuel's mother is not trying to dissuade him from marriage; she is advising that he not use women as sex objects.

But she doesn't stop with that advice, for in verses 6–7 his mother underscores that he does not need strong drink by saying, "Give beer to one who is dying and wine to one whose life is bitter. Let him drink so that he can forget his poverty and remember his trouble no more."

The first part of verse 6 appears to extol the medicinal qualities of strong drink for those who are dying. Likely most people would want a dying relative to have relief from their pain. However, the second part of the verse, if taken out of context, appears to teach that anyone with a bitter life can justify indulging in intoxicating drinks. If that is the case, it is counter to the attitude of the rest of the book of Proverbs about strong drink. A common theme in the book of Proverbs is that strong drink creates problems; it does not alleviate them. Here is a sample:

- Who has woe? Who has sorrow?
  Who has conflicts? Who has complaints?
  Who has wounds for no reason?
  Who has red eyes?
  Those who linger over wine;
  those who go looking for mixed wine.

Don't gaze at wine because it is red,
because it gleams in the cup
and goes down smoothly.
In the end it bites like a snake
and stings like a viper.
Your eyes will see strange things,
and you will say absurd things.
You'll be like someone sleeping out at sea
or lying down on the top of a ship's mast.
"They struck me, but I feel no pain!
They beat me, but I didn't know it!
When will I wake up?
I'll look for another drink." (23.29–35)

- Wine is a mocker, beer is a brawler;
whoever goes astray because of them is not wise. (20:1)
- Don't associate with those who drink too much wine
or with those who gorge themselves on meat.
For the drunkard and the glutton will become poor,
and grogginess will clothe them in rags. (23:20–21)
- The one who loves pleasure will become poor;
whoever loves wine and oil will not get rich. (21:17)

The purpose of saying strong drink is for the terminally ill or habitually miserable is to draw attention to the fact that Lemuel is neither. Even if people could justify its use for those on the disadvantaged end of the spectrum, Lemuel is not one of them. He is on the advantaged end of the spectrum, and there is no excuse for him to use hard drink to escape from his privileged reality.

While Proverbs 31:1–9 does stress the importance of advantaged people avoiding self-indulgent behavior, it teaches something much more profound than that. In this gem of wisdom, a caring mother tells her powerful son that he has responsibility to use his power and advantage to serve others—to ensure justice. That is part of the reason she encourages him not to self-indulge since she does not want him to be distracted from his main duty—administering justice. Remember that Proverbs 31:5 says: "Otherwise, he will drink, / forget what is decreed, / and pervert justice for all the oppressed."

Like Proverbs 31:5, the wisdom found in the book of Proverbs places a priority on *justice* and sees those who seek after it favorably:

- Justice executed is a joy to the righteous
  but a terror to those who practice iniquity. (21:15)
- The evil do not understand justice,
  but those who seek the LORD understand everything. (28:5)
- The righteous person knows the rights of the poor,
  but the wicked one does not understand these concerns. (29:7)

According to his mother, Lemuel became king so he could serve the people and ensure justice for the oppressed people. His mother encouraged him to give his attention to serving the oppressed,

It is easy for people in a position of power, who can have whatever they want, to abuse that power to satisfy their own desires, while forgetting the real reason they have the position: to serve others. Jesus said, "You know that the rulers of the Gentiles lord it over them, and those in high positions act as tyrants over them. It must not be like that among you. On the contrary, whoever wants to become great among you must be your servant, and whoever wants to be first among you must be your slave" (Matt. 20:25b–27).

Lemuel's mother made it clear that she expected him to use his position for the sake of justice: "Speak up for those who have no voice, / for the justice of all who are dispossessed. / Speak up, judge righteously, /and defend the cause of the oppressed and needy" (Prov. 31:8–9).

While we are not kings, we do have power and influence. *You must use your advantages to serve others and the cause of justice.*

We should not be guilty of self-indulgent behavior, but should devote ourselves to meeting the needs of others, especially the disenfranchised and disadvantaged.

REFLECTIONS ON THE SERMON

In the introduction of the sermon, I provide some background information about the specific proverb we were studying and some information about how to interpret proverbs. Using Proverbs 22:6 as an example served two purposes. First, it showed the value that the wisdom literature placed on parental influence. Second, it allowed me to explain the difference between a proverb and a promise.

I bridge from the introduction to the main body of the sermon with the statement: "However, parents' influence does not end when the children leave home. It is not just that they remember our words from when they lived under our roof, but that we continue to speak to them at important times of their lives. That is what is happening in this text. It contains the wisdom that his mother gave to Lemuel when he ascended to a position of power."

As I work through the text, I place each teaching in light of other proverbs to show three things. First, her instruction is consistent with the principle of not chasing women, but finding a good wife and settling down. Second, I use other proverbs to provide context for Proverbs 31:6–7, which on the surface appears to encourage drinking among the dying and less fortunate. Finally, I show that justice is a major theme in Proverbs.

In light of the mother's wisdom, I make the following statement, "While we are not kings, we do have power and influence in life." This leads to the transformative point: *"You must use your advantages to serve others and the cause of justice."*

Preaching proverbs requires special care. Preachers must interpret them in light of other wisdom literature and the Scripture as a whole, paying special attention not to present them as promises. However, as they develop hermeneutical and homiletical muscle memory, they will gain confidence and skill in promoting a healthy "fear of the Lord" among the people they are blessed to serve.

FOR FURTHER REFLECTION

- How does moving from a thesis statement to a transformative truth/point enhance your preaching from the book of Proverbs and other wisdom literature?
- While the sermons in this book use a one-point sermon structure, there are also times when other structures would work well with proverbs. Read Proverbs and note where the two-point compare/ contrast sermon form would be appropriate for a sermon.
- How could you use modern proverbs or cultural expressions of truth as counter examples of truths expressed in Proverbs?

- How does preaching the morals that emerge from wisdom literature differ from moralistic preaching described in chapter 3?
- What steps can you take to keep from preaching the book of Proverbs like hard and fast rules?
- Make sure to place an individual proverb in context with other proverbs and the Scripture as a whole.

─────────────{ C H A P T E R   8 }─────────────

Narrative Episodes from the Gospels and Acts

The Gospels' writers placed Jesus as the cornerstone of redemptive history. Because of their reports, the church knows the events surrounding Jesus' life, death, and resurrection. Because of the Gospels, we know how God addresses the sin problem, through the life and ministry of Jesus Christ, and how his death, burial, and resurrection make eternal life possible for all who believe.

As a continuation of the Gospel of Luke, The Acts of the Apostles demonstrates God's empowerment of the church to bring the good news to a lost world.[1] In Acts, Luke retold the events, the struggles, and the successes that the gospel encountered as it spread from Jerusalem to the uttermost parts of the earth (see Acts 1:8). Acts inspires and informs the church about its mission.

THE NATURE OF THE GOSPELS

At one time, most New Testament scholars believed that the Gospels followed a literary form unique to the first-century Greco-Roman world. They have abandoned this view in favor of the Gospels reflecting characteristics of several ancient Greco-Roman types of literature, including history, novel, and biography. This shift does not diminish the scholars' view of the truth or accuracy of the Gospels; rather, it is an attempt to understand the literary structures of the Gospels in comparison to similar types of literature, which helps the readers know how to interpret

---

1. Though Acts is not one of the four Gospels, we are addressing it in this section of the book because it is a continuation of Luke's Gospel.

the Gospels.[2] Jonathan Pennington says, "Our canonical Gospels are the theological, historical, and aretological (virtue-forming) biographical narratives that retell the story and proclaim the significance of Jesus Christ, who through the power of the Holy Spirit is the restorer of God's reign."[3]

While the four Gospels share much in common, the synoptic Gospels Matthew, Mark, and Luke have garnered a great deal of discussion among scholars because of their differences.[4] Even where they use the same or similar stories or teaching, they sometimes place them at different places in Jesus' earthly ministry. Each of these Gospels has its own unique focus, and the authors of each have arranged the stories, teachings, and sayings of Jesus accordingly.

The Gospel of John brings the issue of distinctiveness to a new level. Whereas the synoptic Gospels contain stories of exorcisms and parables, the Gospel of John does not. In fact, about 90 percent of John's portrayal of Jesus' ministry is unique.[5]

PRINCIPLES FOR INTERPRETING NEW TESTAMENT NARRATIVES

While interpreting the Gospels and Acts, it is important to allow each book to speak to the in-breaking of God's kingdom with its own voice. Many times interpreters want to use the Gospels to harmonize the accounts of Jesus' ministry. While this is a very important aspect of studying them, it can often obscure the individual emphases the writer was communicating. Remember, allow each Gospel to speak with its own voice.

The same is true of Acts. From a literary perspective, Luke and Acts share more than the same author; they also share the common goal of tracing the spread of the gospel.

---

2. For discussions on the genre of the Gospels, see especially Pennington, *Reading the Gospels Wisely*, 3–35. Also valuable are Hurtado, "Gospel (Genre)," 276–82; and Vorster, "Gospel Genre," 2:1077–79.

3. Pennington, *Reading the Gospels Wisely*, 35. Pennington speaks of his dependence on Strauss, *Four Portraits, One Jesus*, 27–29.

4. Known as the synoptic Gospels because of the large amount of material they share in common. For discussions of the Synoptic Problem, see Tuckett, "Synoptic Problem," 6:263–70; Carson and Moo, *An Introduction to the New Testament*, 77–112.

5. Strauss, *Four Portraits, One Jesus*, 288–89.

The distinctive emphases among the Gospels are important keys to accurately interpret and preach from them. Each episode, parable, teaching, or saying connects to the unique purpose of the Gospel writer that uses them.

Of the four Gospels, the Gospel of John is the most unique. While all Gospel writers share the firm conviction that Jesus is the Son of God, the Messiah for the Jews and the world, none emphasizes that truth more clearly than John does. His Gospel combines an emphasis on the eternal deity of Christ and his position as the "Lamb of God, who takes away the sin of the world" (1:29 ESV), with the singular idea that Jesus Christ is God himself incarnate in the world. Love is the central concept that binds all these together.

Matthew emphasizes the rule of Jesus the Messiah (1:1–16), the son of David and the Son of God. Matthew also shows concern for Gentiles by including four women who were not Israelites in Jesus' genealogy: Tamar, Rahab, Ruth, and Bathsheba (1:1–7), the confession of faith by the Roman officer (8:10–12), and the Great Commission (28:18–20).[6]

Mark shows Jesus as the Suffering Servant of Isaiah, and he makes the effort to relate Jesus' to Israel's mission. Mark ties these themes together in a way that redefines and sharpens what messianic rule in God's kingdom is.

Luke's Gospel is unique among the four Gospels because it has a sequel in the book of Acts. Readers must consider one when they interpret the other. In Luke and Acts, Luke recounts the story of Jesus from his birth (complete with a genealogy) to his ministry, death, and resurrection, and then his legacy into the first years of the church and beyond, describing the spread of the gospel from Jerusalem, to Judea, Samaria, and to the uttermost parts of the world. Central to this theme is his assertion that God's deliverance of Israel continues, bringing attention to the inclusion of the Gentiles and socially marginalized people into his kingdom. The Holy Spirit plays an elevated role in both the Gospel (Luke 1–4) and in the book of Acts (Acts 2; 10:38).

As previously mentioned, the book of Acts is the second part of Luke's account of the spread and proclamation of the gospel from its beginning in Jerusalem to the last notice about Paul's ministry in Rome. The

---

6. Turner, *Matthew*, 46; Fee and Stuart, *How to Read the Bible Book by Book*, 269–72.

Gospel of Luke left off outside Jerusalem in Bethany with Jesus giving final instructions that emphasized his identity as Messiah and promising empowerment to the witnesses of his Messiahship as he was carried up into heaven (24:36–53).

Acts picks up the story by mentioning Jesus' appearances to his apostles over a forty-day period (1:1–3). It was during this time that the risen Jesus gave the promise of the Holy Spirit and asked them to wait in Jerusalem until he imparted that matchless power to them. He ends his words to them in Acts 1.8: "But you will receive power when the Holy Spirit has come upon you, and you will be my witnesses in Jerusalem in all Judea and Samaria and to the ends of the earth" (ESV). Note the joining of the power of the Holy Spirit with the mission to carry the gospel to the ends of the earth. This is the key theme in the book of Acts: the spread of the gospel through the Spirit-empowered proclamation of Jesus Christ as the risen Lord. It is important to recognize that the phrase "to the ends of the earth" is intended to show that it was Jesus' intent to include the Gentiles in the growth and expansion of God's kingdom and that the Holy Spirit would empower them as members of that kingdom.

Acts 1:8 provides the thematic arc that binds Luke's account of the movement of the gospel into the world.[7] While the locations indicated in the verse do provide a good outline of the gospel's expansion, the narrative has six distinct stages.[8] Each stage ends with a summary statement that emphasizes the success of the gospel and shows an increasing opposition to the gospel's proclamation:

1. *Acts 1:1–6:7.* This section recounts how the church fared during its early days in Jerusalem. It concludes with a comment: "And the word of God continued to increase, and the number of the disciples multiplied greatly in Jerusalem, and a great many of the priests became obedient to the faith" (ESV).

2. *Acts 6:8–9:31.* This section begins with the preaching of Stephen. After a lengthy sermon, it recounts his martyrdom, an

---

7. Jerusalem, Judea and Samaria, the uttermost parts of the world.

8. I (Watson) developed this division of Acts based upon the work of Fee and Stuart, *How to Read the Bible for All Its Worth*, 111–12. Though Fee and Stuart present it as only a suggested outline, it is a dependable place to begin a study on how Luke depicts the Spirit-empowered movement of the gospel from Jerusalem to the rest of the world.

outcome that Saul applauded. It is on the heels of this notice that Luke mentions the spread of the gospel outside of Jerusalem to Samaria, and the first mention of Gentile conversions. Paul's conversion as he was traveling to Damascus is a real coup for the early church, for it is through God's most committed opponent that Jesus would greatly increase the conversion of the Gentiles to the faith. This section ends in 9:31 with another summary: "So the church throughout all Judea and Galilee and Samaria had peace and was being built up. And walking in the fear of the Lord and in the comfort of the Holy Spirit, it multiplied" (ESV).

3. *Acts 9:32–12:24.* It is at this point that Luke begins to focus on the ministry of the apostle Peter. God's revelation to Peter in 10:9–16 marks a turning point for both Peter and the spread of the gospel: not even food regulations were to be a hindrance to the evangelization of the Gentiles. Despite the cultural and ethnic difficulties that attended this unfettered inclusion of Gentiles, Acts 12:24 once again summarizes the result: "But the word of God increased and multiplied" (ESV).

4. *Acts 12:25–16:5.* Section 4 recounts the resolution of the matter of table fellowship with Gentiles (15:1–35). It also recounts the initial missionary efforts of Paul and the spread of the gospel into Western Europe. The section ends with the following summary in Acts 16:5: "So the churches were strengthened in the faith and increased in numbers daily" (ESV).

5. *Acts 16:6–19:20.* This section presents the second missionary journey to Europe led by Paul. As he moves farther into Western Europe, the nature and scope of resistance grows more threatening. Yet, as the summary in Acts 19:20 reports, "So the word of the Lord continued to increase and prevail mightily" (ESV).

6. *Acts 19:21–28:30.* As Paul and the gospel travel farther west toward Rome, two seemingly opposite things happened. Paul faced growing local and official opposition, giving him the opportunity to preach and share the gospel with more people, both Jew and Gentile. Even as opposition and persecution increased, so did the numbers that God added to the church. Despite the conflict the gospel encountered as it spread, Acts 28:30–31 says, "Paul stayed two whole years in his own rented house. And he welcomed all

who visited him, proclaiming the kingdom of God and teaching about the Lord Jesus Christ with all boldness and without hindrance" (ESV).

Preaching Gospel Narratives

Gospel narratives are well suited for the one-point expository sermon. While the stories can have secondary points, typically, the biblical author included the story in his Gospel to drive home a main point.[9] However, the narratives do more than make a point for readers to understand; they include information that moves their hearts also. Because of this, preachers should not strip-mine the story reducing it to a proposition; instead, they should preach it in a holistic way.[10] If preachers work hard at keeping the meaning and impact of the text intact through the hermeneutical and homiletical processes, their sermons from New Testament narratives will speak to the heads and hearts of their listeners.

Preaching New Testament narratives has much in common with preaching other biblical narratives. For instance, preaching them well requires the preacher to do the following four tasks:

- Take care in keeping a narrative episode whole and not separating it from its larger purpose or context;[11]
- Focus on the theocentric nature and purpose of the story and not

---

9. The four Gospels and Acts use different genres to add depth and color to their narratives. In the Gospels, miracle stories, sermonic materials, parables (covered in chap. 9), and several other narrative forms are incorporated in the overall narrative. When the Gospels share a story or any of the other smaller literary forms in common, be careful not to transfer the meaning from one to the other.

10. Sweet, McLaren, and Haselmayer, *A is for Abductive*, 294: "For modern Bible readers, the Scriptures became like a mountain from which we strip-mine for its modern treasure—abstract propositions or principles. The native stories, poetry, genres, and language were surface distractions—like flowers, trees, elk and butterflies—that kept us from our real interest that lay beneath all that superficiality." Long, *Preaching and the Literary Forms of the Bible*, 69–70: "In the Bible, narrative is not a device; it is an expression of the way things are. . . . The first order work of the biblical writers was to 'reveal the enactment of God's purposes in history.'" Wiarda, *Interpreting Gospel Narratives*, 48–49: "Gospel stories communicate definable theological truths in a way that impacts the whole person."

11. Greidanus, *Modern Preacher and the Ancient Text*, 221: "Narratives are particularly susceptible to the abuse of isolating a detail which appears to fit a particular preaching occasion."

look for moral virtues in the characters;[12]

- Discover the main point by following the plot movements to the end of the story (see chap. 2);
- Be careful not to confuse movements with points (see chap. 2).

However, preaching New Testament narratives offers unique challenges because many of the stories about Jesus appear in more than one New Testament Gospel, and when they do, the authors do not arrange them in the same chronological order or provide the same details. One way to approach preaching the New Testament narratives is to blend the details from different Gospel accounts together. However, this approach works against understanding authorial intent.

The following principles of interpretation should be helpful in discerning how to develop sermons on the New Testament narratives:

1. *Always be aware of the overall perspective of each individual book.* Keep in mind that each Gospel writer views the story of Jesus from a different perspective. The same is true of Acts. The overall purpose of the author should guide any interpretative decision you make about a particular passage. The brief summaries above are good starting points for this exercise. When you study the accounts from other Gospel writers, do so primarily to inform your understanding of the authorial intent of your text, not to provide additional details to the story.

2. *Pay attention to the major transition points in each narrative.* For instance, there are several such transition points in the book of Acts. One is the geographical pattern established in Acts 1:8, but there are others. The activities of Peter in chapters 1–12 are the book's focus, but except for a brief appearance in chapter 15, the focus shifts from Peter to Paul as the central character throughout the rest of the book. Such transitions are signposts for the expansion of the gospel into the greater world.

3. *Understand individual episodes in the light of their immediate*

---

12. Fee and Stuart, *How to Read the Bible for all Its Worth,* 74: "[The narratives'] purpose is to show God at work in his creation and among his people. The narratives' glorify him, help us to understand and appreciate him, and give us a picture of his providence and protection."

contexts. For instance, within the six geographical segments of Luke's narrative there are many individual stories and summary statements. Interpreters should consider these individual portions of text in light of their immediate literary context.

SERMON SAMPLES FROM GOSPEL NARRATIVES

The following sermon uses a weaver structure (chap. 2), where I parallel each movement from the text with a personal story. The listeners will provide their own third strand as they listen.

In His Time

Luke 1:13 (NASB)

But the angel said to him, "Do not be afraid, Zacharias, for your petition has been heard, and your wife Elizabeth will bear you
a son,
and you will give him the name John."

Elizabeth had long since resigned herself to the fact that she would never hear the patter of little feet in the home where she and her husband, Zechariah, lived. Elizabeth was barren. "Barren"—the very word elicits thoughts of sand blowing across a desert wasteland.

Zechariah was in the sanctuary carrying out his priestly duties when God interrupted him. Gabriel, the angel that stands in the very presence of God, left his coveted place to stand in the presence of God's priest. Shocked by the angelic sight, Zechariah became frightened. Zechariah wasn't expecting to hear a word from the Lord while he was doing his religious duty.

Gabriel had some good news: "But the angel said to him, 'Do not be afraid, Zacharias, for your petition has been heard, and your wife Elizabeth will bear you a son, and you will give him the name John'" (Luke 1:13 NASB).

"Your prayer has been heard"—what prayer? Likely, Zechariah hadn't done any praying for a child in years. He'd forgotten about the prayer, but God hadn't. In his perfect timing, God answered a young man's prayer when he was too old to remember it and gave his wife a son, when she was too old to conceive on her own.

How could a religious man be surprised to find a word from God in the sanctuary? Why would a priest doubt that God could answer his stale prayer?

Even spiritual men have moments when their faith flickers. Let me explain what I mean.

When the angel of the Lord told him he would have a son, Zechariah doubted the prophecy. *It is impossible*, Zechariah thought, *for an old man and a barren woman to have a son.* After fifty-plus years of disappointment, perhaps I'd doubt too. How about you?

After he expressed his doubt, Zechariah was speechless.

Literally, Zechariah was speechless. "And now, since you didn't believe what I said, you won't be able to speak until the child is born. For my words will certainly come true at the proper time" (Luke 1:20 NLT).

I don't know what constitutes the greater miracle—an elderly woman having a baby or a preacher being quiet for nine months. Though I have no experience having a baby, I did have a time in my life when I couldn't speak. It was a humbling experience.

During a surgery to remove a cancerous thyroid, the doctor tapped on my recurrent laryngeal nerve, thinking it was fatty tissue. The assistant surgeon assured the doctor it was not the nerve and advised that he cut it. Twice he asked for an instrument to sever the structure, but when he tried, his hand froze. "Because I tapped on the nerve," the doctor explained to me, "it no longer transmits the signal from the brain to the vocal cord," The result was a paralyzed vocal cord.

"But doctor," I whispered, "I'm a preacher, what do I do without a voice?"

I stared into my doctor's eyes. "Will my voice come back?" He blinked and looked away. "I don't know, maybe, since I didn't cut the nerve. Normal function could return in a few months, or it could be permanent."

In that moment faced with an impossible situation, my theology and this unfortunate reality rammed together, full force in a head-on collision. In that moment, I had more questions than answers. *Will I ever preach again? How will I earn a living? What about my family? WHERE ARE YOU, GOD?*

Like Zechariah, I doubted.

That night I lay in bed as a thick silence surrounded me. "God, I'm over here," I prayed. "Are you watching? Why are you doing this to me? Why don't you heal me?"

God's people were good to me. The church supported me, and preachers from our state convention office in Albuquerque filled my pulpit as I waited for my healing.

My wife and my mother were my greatest encouragers throughout the ordeal; they pumped me with hope and calmed me when I had soul seizures. I worried about paying the bills, the welfare of the church, and our future. Susan never worried. "Everything is going to be fine," Susan would say. "God will take care of us." Her strength buttressed my crumbling faith. "God will heal you," my mother said, "He wouldn't call you to preach without supplying you a voice." These words were my lifeline. I held to them like a drowning man.

Clearly God's hand kept the surgeon from cutting the nerve, and I fully expected to get my voice back. Every morning when I awoke, I said, "I love you, Susan." When the words came out in a whisper instead of a normal voice, I swallowed and thought, *tomorrow—tomorrow will be the day. My miracle will come.*

Tomorrow never came. I was confused the day I checked into the hospital for additional surgery to correct the problem. *God, where are you, and why didn't you heal me?*

Immediately after the surgery, my voice was strong, but after the swelling went down, I had a coarse, breathy voice that projected slightly above a whisper. With every tick of the clock, it got weaker, and I grew more confused. Though the congregation encouraged me, I knew I was no longer a good preacher. My voice was too weak.

The disability had its accompanying trials. Drive-through windows were the absolute worst. On one occasion, the operator mocked my breathy whisper when he took my order. His immaturity brought out my own; I wanted to squash him like a bug.

The only time I cried through the ordeal happened about a month after I lost my voice. I stood next to the guest preacher as we began to sing: "I love you Lord, and I lift my voice. . ." Of course, I didn't try to sing—it hurt too badly to force the wind. I just mouthed the words. But when I got to the word "voice," I began to cry. "What good am I to you, Lord," I prayed. "I can't even worship with your people."

Occasionally, I got a chuckle out of my disability. I wrote the name of a person I wanted to visit on my notepad and showed it to a hospital volunteer to get a room number. The kind woman slanted her head and asked, "Can you hear me?" Of course, I could hear, but I couldn't speak to tell her, I had to write yes on the pad.

Notice that Zechariah's friends did the same thing when Elizabeth followed the angel's instructions to name her baby "John."

"'What?' they exclaimed. 'There is no one in all your family by that name.' So they asked the baby's father, communicating to him by making gestures. He motioned for a writing tablet, and to everyone's surprise he wrote, 'His name is John!' Instantly Zechariah could speak again, and he began praising God" (Luke 1:61 64 NLT).

Did he praise God because he could speak, or did he speak because he could praise God? This isn't a chicken-or-egg type of question. Think about it. A man communicating with a pencil and tablet doesn't even try to speak. His praise erupted. Praise burst through his sealed lips and flowed to the glory of God.

Like Zechariah, my voice is back. After a third surgery, I have a near-normal voice. Though I thanked God for giving Dr. Netterville the skill to heal me, I still wondered why God didn't intervene. That is, until a comment the doctor made during a follow up visit. "Your nerve is transmitting enough signal that the vocal cord is staying healthy—not enough that it can ever move again, but enough to give a rich sound when supported by the silicone implant."

"Dr. Netterville," I asked, "what would my voice have been like if the surgeon had cut the nerve instead of tapping it?" I heard his voice and God's at the same time. He said, "Your voice would have always sounded hoarse." God said, "See, you got your miracle after all."

Because he is faithful, you can trust in God, even while you wait on his response to your need.

This side of my miracle, I view life a little differently. I praise God that though my faith may flicker from time to time, it never fails! Zechariah probably had the same thought when he bounced his newborn baby prophet on his knee.

REFLECTIONS ON THE SERMON

Writing a weaver sermon requires writing the biblical story first. (There will not be time for multiple second and third movements; it will need to be a simple, four-movement sermon.) Next, write the personal story that corresponds to the movements of the text. (Typically, I caution against using too many personal illustrations in sermons because it can create a split-focus, but with the weaver sermon, it is an essential element.)[13] After you have written both, you can cut and paste the stories together, adding the transition sentences and the transformative point. This sermon had the following movements:

↓ Zechariah and Elizabeth were unable to have children.

↑ The Lord's angel appeared to announce they would have a child.

↓ Zechariah doubted and lost his voice/I lost my voice to cancer.

↑ God was faithful—he gave them a child and Zechariah's voice returned/God was faithful to me, restoring my voice and strengthening my faith.

Notice that the third and fourth movements included my personal story woven into the structure of the sermon.

---

13. Before deciding to use a personal story in a sermon, it is wise to ask the following questions:
   1. Is there a compelling reason to interject myself into the story?
   2. Would using this story glorify me or God?
   3. Will telling this violate a trust?
   4. Will this story diminish or enhance the message?
   5. Would it diminish the office of pastor for me to tell this story?
   6. Could this story create a stumbling block to others?
   7. Can I obtain the same result without making it personal?
   8. Have I talked about myself too much lately?
   9. Will this illustration assist in my goal of spiritual transformation?
   10. Does this have the potential to hurt someone or keep them from hearing my message?
   11. Will the audience be able to relate to this story?
   For a discussion on "split-focus," see Buttrick, *Homiletic*, 94.

In the following sermon, I show several places in the narrative where Pilate should have decided not to order Jesus' crucifixion. It is a straightforward retelling of the biblical narrative with a surprise ending.

Why Did He Do It?

Matthew 27:11–26 (NASB)

Now Jesus stood before the governor, and the governor questioned Him, saying, "Are You the King of the Jews?" And Jesus said to him, "It is as you say." And while He was being accused by the chief priests and elders, He made no answer. Then Pilate said to Him, "Do You not hear how many things they testify against You?" And He did not answer him with regard to even a single charge, so that the governor was quite amazed.

Now at the feast the governor was accustomed to release for the multitude any one prisoner whom they wanted. And they were holding at that time a notorious prisoner, called Barabbas. When therefore they were gathered together, Pilate said to them, "Whom do you want me to release for you? Barabbas, or Jesus who is called Christ?" For he knew that because of envy they had delivered Him up.

While he was sitting on the judgment seat, his wife sent to him, saying, "Have nothing to do with that righteous Man; for last night I suffered greatly in a dream because of Him." But the chief priests and the elders persuaded the multitudes to ask for Barabbas, and to put Jesus to death. But the governor answered and said to them, "Which of the two do you want me to release for you?" And they said, "Barabbas." Pilate said to them, "Then what shall I do with Jesus who is called Christ?" They all said, "Let Him be crucified." And he said, "Why, what evil has He done?" But they kept shouting all the more, saying, "Let Him be crucified!"

When Pilate saw that he was accomplishing nothing, but rather that a riot was starting, he took water and washed his hands in front of the multitude, saying, "I am innocent of this

Man's blood; see to that yourselves." And all the people an-
swered and said, "His blood be on us and on our children!"
Then he released Barabbas for them; but after having Jesus
scourged, he delivered Him to be crucified.

When the Roman soldiers drove the spikes through the hands of Jesus, they were driving our sins to the cross. Think for a moment about that day. They moved him from one clandestine courtroom to another to achieve their goal: crucifixion. Finally, Pilate sealed his fate when he took the bowl of water and declared, "I wash my hands of the blood of this man," and he turned Jesus over to the angry mob.

They beat him with a cat-o'-nine-tails; 39 strokes some say, following Jewish law. The truth is, we don't know how many lashes he took. The whip was not in the hands of a Jew; it was a Roman who beat him.

"Hail, King of the Jews," they cried, as they put a crown made of thorns on his head. They spat in his face, they pulled his beard, and they mocked his holy name.

They put a cross on his back, and in his weakened state, he stumbled beneath the load. Simon of Cyrene carried the cross for him as Jesus walked up the hill to his destiny.

The soldiers ripped his robe from him, reopened his wounds, and forced him on the rough-hewn cross. Though it was customary to use ropes to tie a criminal to the cross, the soldiers used 14-inch spikes to nail him and our sins to the cross. First one spike and then another through the quivering flesh of his hands.

Then just as they had raised the serpent in the wilderness, they raised him from the ground and dropped the cross into its resting place.

He stayed on the cross for six hours before the ridiculing, mocking crowd, and then he became sin for us. Paul wrote, "He made Him who knew no sin to be sin on our behalf that we might become the righteousness of God in Him" (2 Cor. 5:21 NASB).

There he forgave our trespasses, and there he nailed our sin to the cross. And the Father turned his back on his Son refusing to look at the sin he'd become.

The earth trembled, the skies blackened, and the veil in the temple split, and Jesus exclaimed, "It is finished."

Why did he do it? Why did Pilate acquit Barabbas and crucify Jesus?

He did so, even though he knew Jesus was the King of the Jews (Matt. 27:11) and Barabbas was a notorious criminal (Matt. 27:16). Pilate even knew that the accusations against Jesus came from envious people (Matt. 27:18) and had no grounding in fact. Pilate's wife begged him to release Jesus, but he did not listen to her (Matt. 27:19). This was an innocent man (Matt. 27:23), yet Pilate chose to set the guilty man free and kill the innocent man. Why?

I'm sure that part of the reason was to avoid an uprising among the people that could eventually cost him his job, but, in the final analysis, he did it because he was too weak to do the right thing. Notice the mistakes that Pilate made.

He tried to take the easy way out and force the people to make the decision for him by offering to release someone they would never want back in their community. Matthew 27:16–17 says: "And they were holding at that time a notorious prisoner, called Barabbas. When therefore they were gathered together, Pilate said to them, 'Whom do you want me to release for you? Barabbas, or Jesus who is called Christ'?" (NASB). I'm sure Pilate thought he was being clever and had discovered a way that he could avoid making a decision, but he was wrong. He was wrong because he underestimated the extent of the religious leaders' hatred for Jesus.

Pilate failed to act on sound advice from his wife who urged him to be a man and do the right thing. Matthew 27:19 says: "And while he was sitting on the judgment seat, his wife sent to him, saying, 'Have nothing to do with that righteous Man; for last night I suffered greatly in a dream because of Him'" (NASB). Again, Pilate suffered from indecision, refusing to follow the advice his wife gave him. He was paralyzed by his own inability to make a decision.

Pilate asked others to make a decision that only he could make. In Matthew 27:22–23 we read that "Pilate said to them, 'Then what shall I do with Jesus who is called Christ?' They all said, 'Let Him be crucified!' And he said, 'Why, what evil has He done?' But they kept shouting all the more, saying, 'Let Him be crucified!'" (NASB)

When all this failed, he acted, but he chose to take the path of least resistance and do what the people wanted. Look at Matthew 27:24: "And when Pilate saw that he was accomplishing nothing, but rather that a riot was starting, he took water and washed his hands in front of the multitude, saying, 'I am innocent of this Man's blood; see to that yourselves'" (NASB).

Pilate deluded himself into thinking that he wasn't responsible, but he was. His indecision led him to endorse the decision of others, making him culpable for their actions and his inactions. He wasn't successful in avoiding the decision when he tried to pass the buck off to the Jews in the beginning, or when he tried to make the people "an offer they couldn't refuse" by releasing Jesus, not Barabbas. He failed to listen to his wife's encouragement to do the right thing, but chose to listen to the ranting of an angry mob instead. In the end, he tried to say that his indecision didn't have consequences, but it did. No matter how many times he washed his hands, he would be responsible.

Why did he do it? Bottom line, he did it because he was a sinner. Just like you and me. He did it because he ignored the consequences of his decision, thinking that God would somehow make an exception for his sin. Did he really think he could wash away his guilt with a basin of water?

Why did he do it? He did it because he loves us. No, I'm not talking about Pilate now, I'm talking about Jesus Christ, who loves us so much that he bore our sins on the cross and made a way possible for our guilt to be removed. Not with a basin of water, but with his own blood.

Love made salvation possible. Believe in Jesus today and make salvation personal.

Has there ever been a time in your life when you've accepted Jesus as your Savior and surrendered your life to him as your Lord? Won't you pray with me now? With a simple prayer, tell him that you've sinned and that you're sorry for your sins. Ask him to forgive you of your sins and to take them away from you. Tell him you'll live the rest of your life for him and that you'll serve him until your dying day. Tell him that you are willing to exchange your life for his death. Ask him to save you.

REFLECTIONS ON THE SERMON

The sermon has a twist—a surprise answer to the question, Why did he do it? I shifted from Pilate's point of view to Jesus' point of view because

I wanted to underscore that Pilate did not drive the crucifixion; it was all a part of God's redemptive plan. Other than that, it is a straightforward retelling of a Gospel narrative.[14]

    ↓ The Romans crucified Jesus.

        ↑ Pilate could have stopped the crucifixion.

    ↓ Pilate allowed the crucifixion. He did it because he was a weak sinner.

        ↑ Pilate did not have the final say—Jesus laid down his life willingly. He did it because he loves us.

As I look back on forty years of preaching, I regret that I did not preach the gospel message more often. Hearing the gospel is transformative for believers and for nonbelievers. As I said, this is not a sophisticated sermon; it is a straightforward retelling of a part of the Passion Week, which ends with a clear call for people to believe the gospel message. This is the reason I am including it as an example. Preaching Gospel narratives does not require a deep understanding of sermonic structure. Just tell the story. The story is powerful. God will use it to transform lives.

For Further Reflection

When writing a sermon from a Gospel narrative, it is helpful to ask yourself the following questions:

- Does my sermon fit within the purpose of the Gospel writer for this passage?
- Does my sermon focus on what God is doing, or who he is?
- Does the transformative point flow out of the main point of the narrative?

---

14. Normally it is not wise to shift points of view in a sermon, because it usually works against clear communication. In this case, I intentionally broke the rule of thumb to produce a surprise ending.

- Do the movements of the sermon correspond to the movements in the narrative?
- Where is the gospel in this sermon? Does the sermon communicate the gospel effectively?

Parables

Scholars do not agree on the number of points parables have. While Stein and other contemporary scholars would say, "a single point," that view does not enjoy universal acceptance and would have little to no support prior to the late nineteenth century.[1] This discussion is vital for expository preachers who want their sermon structures to emerge from the text.

APPROACHES TO PARABLES

ENDLESS NUMBER OF POINTS APPROACH

Prior to 1899 preachers reinterpreted and spiritualized each element in a parable to describe Christian truths. A popular example of the allegorical approach is the parable of the Good Samaritan:[2]

TABLE 3: GOOD SAMARITAN ALLEGORICAL APPROACH

Scripture	Allegorical Interpretation
A certain man went down from Jerusalem to Jericho	Adam
Jerusalem	the heavenly city from which Adam fell

---

1. Stein, *Basic Guide to Interpreting the Bible*, 141. For examples of those who disagree with the one point per parable postion, see Buttrick, *Speaking Parables*, 18–19; Hultgren, *The Parables of Jesus*, 12–14; Köstenberger and Patterson, *For the Love of God's Word*, 224–25; McCartney and Clayton, *Let the Reader Understand*, 221–24. For in depth treatments on how parables have been interpreted through history, see Wright, *Jesus the Storyteller*, 9–42; Snodgrass, "From Allegorizing to Allegorizing," 3–29; Stein, *Introduction to the Parables*, 42–71; Osborne, *Hermeneutical Spiral*, 308–11; and Köstenberger and Patterson, *Invitation to Biblical Interpretation*, 43–35. Finally, a full treatment is available in Gowler, *The Parables after Jesus*.

2. Adapted from Fee and Stuart, *How to Read the Bible for All Its Worth*, 155.

Jericho	the moon, and thereby signifies Adam's mortality
robbers	the devil and his angels
stripped him	taking away his immortality
beat him	by persuading him to sin
left him half-dead	as a man he lives, but he died spiritually, therefore he is half-dead
the priest and Levite	priesthood and ministry of the Old Testament
the Samaritan	means guardian, thus Christ himself
bandaged his wounds	binding the restraint of sin
oil	comfort of good hope
wine	exhortation to work with a fervent spirit
beast	the flesh of Christ's incarnation
inn	the church
the next day	after the resurrection
innkeeper	apostle Paul

Opposition to the excesses of this approach came from Tertullian, Chrysostom, Augustine, and later Aquinas. Yet these church fathers themselves perpetuated allegorical teaching. For example, the Good Samaritan interpretation above comes from Augustine. The allegorical approach resulted in a wide and wild variety of interpretations. Worse, it had nothing to do with Jesus' original intention for his listeners or the Gospel writers' intent for their readers.

Reformers joined in the opposition. They reintroduced a literal hermeneutic, which considered the historical setting and grammatical structure of parables. Nevertheless, Martin Luther, John Calvin, and especially their successors permitted allegorical exegesis to creep into their own interpretations. This practice continued into the nineteenth century.[3]

---

3. Stein, *Method and Message of Jesus' Teachings*, 45–49. For an example of the continued practice, Trench's popular *Notes on the Parables of Our Lord*, first published in 1841, followed the allegorical approach.

ONLY ONE-POINT APPROACH

In response to the practice of allegorical interpretation of parables, Adolf Jülicher published *Die Gleichnisreden Jesu* (*The Parable Discourses of Jesus*), which broke the grip of allegorical interpretation for parables for most interpreters.[4] Jülicher said that every parable had only one point and that all other details are incidental storytelling.

C. H. Dodd, Joachim Jeremias, and others built upon Jülicher's foundational work to promote the one-point, no allegory approach. Dodd argued that since parables are metaphors, interpreters should find the one point of comparison, and defended Jülicher's anti-allegorical approach as well as a three-pronged classification of parables.[5] Following Dodd, Jeremias called for interpreters to hear the parable as Jesus' original audience heard it. For Jeremias, this meant the in-breaking of the kingdom of God in Jesus' ministry. Jeremias foreshadowed later redaction critics who recognized that the parables reflected the needs of the early church.[6]

Redaction critics developed Jeremias' emphasis further, stressing the theological editorial contributions of the Gospel writers. In other words, the context of the parable gives readers editorial clues for the proper interpretation of parables. For instance, the Prodigal Son (Luke 15:11–32) must be understood in light of what Luke states in 15:1–2.

Robert Stein, a leading contemporary redaction critic, who champions the one-point, no allegory approach to parables, stresses four stages of interpretation:

1. Interpreters must discover the one main point of the parable.
2. Interpreters must "seek to understand the *Sitz im Leben* [situation in life] in which the parable was uttered." This point stresses what the parable meant to the original audience.
3. Readers must seek to understand how the Gospel writer

---

4. Long, *Witness of Preaching*, 95. Stein, *Method and Message of Jesus' Teachings*, 50: "Jülicher's main contribution to the investigation of the parables was that he pointed out the difference between parables and allegories. In so doing, he laid to rest the allegorical method of interpreting the parables that had plagued the church for centuries."

5. C. H. Dodd, *Parables of the Kingdom*, 2–3, 12 (figurative sayings, similitudes, and parables proper).

6. Jeremias, *The Parables of Jesus*, rev. ed. The book was originally published in 1947 and revised in 1963.

interpreted the parable. This brings in the fruit of redaction criticism and the editorial influence of the writers.

4. Finally, readers must seek to find out what God is saying to them
today. Personal application, therefore, must be a part of contemporary interpretation.[7]

Jülicher, Dodd, Jeremias, and Stein all attempted to divorce allegory
from parables and stress one basic point per parable. Jülicher's reaction
against extreme allegorizing pushed the pendulum toward the other extreme—no allegory and one point only. Jülicher's approach, in an attempt
to save the parables from wanton allegorizing, ended up obscuring important allegorical features.[8] Today, some scholars are pushing against
the rigidity of the one-point interpretation that refuses to see any allegorical features.

Multi-Point Approach

Among evangelicals, a major voice for the multi-point approach is Craig
Blomberg, who says the interpreter should look for one point per main
character, not one point per parable and allow those points to shape
the sermon.[9] A turning point for Blomberg was Jesus' own words. The
only interpretations of parables supplied by Jesus had allegorical elements (Matt. 13:1–23; Mark 4:1–12; Luke 8:4–10). Moreover, several parables reveal obvious allegorical features, including the Wicked
Tenants (Mark 12:1–12), the Wedding Feast (Matt. 22:1–14), and the
Great Banquet (Luke 14:16–24). Therefore, Blomberg claimed that
parables are much more allegorical than the one-point only approach
allows. If Blomberg is correct, then many parables have more than one
main point.[10] Blomberg does not argue for making every detail of a
parable allegorical. Instead, interpreters must limit allegorical features
to characters, actions, or symbols that correspond to the rest of the
parable.[11]

---

7. Stein, *Introduction to Parables*, 56–81.
8. Wright, *Jesus the Storyteller*, 18.
9. Blomberg, *Preaching the Parables*, 15.
10. Blomberg, *Interpreting the Parables*, 24–25.
11. Ibid., 64–65.

While Blomberg's contribution is significant, his response against the one-point per parable formula resulted in him creating a new formula: one-point per character. His arguments have not persuaded all modern interpreters, who continue to follow the one-point principle for parables.[12] Perhaps a measured, non-formulaic approach is preferred.

No One-Size-Fits-All Approach

Klyne Snodgrass writes, "In short, some parables make one point, and some make several points. A formulaic approach to parable interpretation does not work. One must discern from context the intent of the analogy."[13] While it is true that not all parables have only one-point, it is also true that many do. This makes it very important for pastors to pay attention to the text when choosing the sermon form.[14]

Our recommended approach is a measured one, avoiding the extremes (allegory, one-point only, one-point per character). With some careful exegetical work, preachers can discover which parables are right for the one-point expository preaching approach. This begins with an understanding of what parables are.

---

12. Stein maintains his approach most recently in *A Basic Guide to Interpreting the Bible*, 140–50. The title of Fee and Stuart's chapter on parables in their 2014 edition of *How to Read the Bible for All Its Worth* is "What's the Point?" 154–67. Robertson McQuilkin's recent revision of *Understanding and Applying the Bible*, 209–22, follows suit.

13. Snodgrass, *Stories with Intent*, 29.

14. Blomberg, *Interpreting the Parables*, 197–407. Blomberg lists several three-point parables. Some are easy to figure out, with his one point per character rule, such as the Prodigal Son (Luke 15:11–32: father, prodigal son, and older son). Others are not as apparent until Blomberg discloses them. Examples here include the Two Sons (Matt. 21:28–32: father, son who refused but went, and son who promised to go but did not); the Ten Virgins (Matt. 25:1–13: bridegroom, foolish virgins, and wise virgins); the Rich Man and Lazarus (Luke 16:19–31: rich man, Abraham, and Lazarus); the Laborers in the Vineyard (Matt. 20:1–16: master, eleventh-hour laborers, and rest of laborers); and the Sower (Mark 4:3–9, 13–20: sower, fruitful seed, and three unfruitful seed). Examples of two-point parables from Blomberg include the Rich Fool (Luke 12:16–21: God and the rich man); the Barren Fig Tree (Luke 13:6–9: master and fig tree/vinedresser); and the Unjust Judge (Luke 18:1–8: judge and widow). Even Blomberg allows for some one-point parables. They include the Hidden Treasure and the Pearl of Great Price (Matt. 13:44–46); the Tower Builder and the Warring King (Luke 14:28–33); and the Mustard Seed and the Leaven (Luke 13:18–21). All six are simple comparisons on what the kingdom of God is like.

WHAT ARE PARABLES?

While Jesus taught in other ways, his primary teaching method was with parables.[15] Parables may have common characteristics, but it is difficult to have a single definition that applies in all instances. Snodgrass says, "In fact, possibly no definition of parables will do, for any definition that is broad enough to cover all the forms is so imprecise that it is almost useless."[16] Nevertheless, Snodgrass produces a helpful definition: "In most cases then *a parable is an expanded analogy used to convince and persuade.*"[17] This definition takes into account that the Hebrew word *mâshâl* and the Greek word *parabolē* offer a wide range of meanings: proverb, satire, riddle, aphorism, dialogue, discourse, legal axiom, figurative saying, extended simile, full-fledged story, and allegory.[18] Scriptural parables include all of these variations. Scholars often mention three kinds of parables: similitude ("the kingdom of God is like…"), metaphor ("You are the salt of the earth"), and story parable (Good Samaritan, Prodigal Son, etc.). But this explanation misses other potential categories. Snodgrass classifies parables into these six categories:[19]

Similitudes. The parable of the Leaven is an example. "The kingdom of heaven is like leaven that a woman took and hid in three measures of flour, till it was all leavened" (Matt. 13:33). Similitudes are simple, straightforward comparisons. They have action but no plot.

Interrogative parables. Like similitudes, these parables present no plot development. Questions are the key element. "Who from you. . ." (*tis ex hymōn*) is the key phrase signaling this category. These parables set up a hypothetical situation that forces hearers to answer a question.

---

15. Teaching techniques include overstatement (Matt. 5:29–30), hyperbole (Mark 10:24–25), puns (Matt. 16:18), similes (Luke 13:34), metaphors (Matt. 9:37–38), proverbs (Luke 9:62), *a fortiori* (lesser to greater) statements (Matt. 6:28–30), irony (Matt. 16:2–3), questions (Mark 8:27–30), parabolic actions (John 13:1–17), and poetry (Luke 6:27–28). Many of these are embedded within parables. For details, see Stein, *The Method and Message of Jesus' Teachings*, 7–32; Köstenberger and Patterson, *For the Love of God's Word*, 216–22; and Duvall and Hays, *Grasping God's Word*, 282–86. One-third of his teaching was delivered in parabolic form in the synoptic Gospels.

16. Snodgrass, *Stories with Intent*, 7.

17. Ibid., 9; Köstenberger and Patterson, *For the Love of God's Word*, 222, agree: "A parable is a short narrative that demands a response from the hearer."

18. Stein, *An Introduction to the Parables of Jesus*, 16–21.

19. Snodgrass, *Stories with Intent*, 9–15.

Examples include the Friend at Midnight (Luke 11:5–13) and the Lost Sheep (Luke 15:1–7).[20]

Juridical parables. Because they hide their referent, these parables produce self-condemnation from the hearer through the aid of an image. The parable forces the hearers to judge the situation, but later realize that they are the ones who are the offending party. Nathan's indictment of David with "You are the man!" (2 Sam. 12:1–14) serves as an Old Testament example. In the Gospels, the Two Sons (Matt. 21:28–32), the Wicked Tenants (Matt. 21:33–45), and the Two Debtors (Luke 7:40–47) qualify as examples of juridical parables.

Single indirect parables (also known as example stories). These parables show plot development. Snodgrass limits this category to only five parables, all found in Luke's Gospel: the Good Samaritan, the Rich Fool, the Unjust Steward, the Rich Man and Lazarus, and the Pharisee and the Tax Collector. They are indirect since they speak of another person, but are direct concerning the subject at hand. Thus, the Rich Fool addresses the hearer indirectly through the rich man, but the story treats the hearer directly on the subject of wealth.

Double indirect narrative parables. These parables reveal the deepest plot development. Something happens in the parable that creates a problem or possibility. Then other actions happen that bring resolution or potential resolution to the problem. The parable of the Banquet (Luke 14:15–24) serves as an example. Dialogue between characters often signals the start of resolution. Other times the conclusion is open-ended, forcing hearers to ponder what should happen next, such as in the parable of the Fig Tree (Luke 13:6–9).

"How much more" parables. This grouping includes some interrogative parables with no plot development and some narrative parables with plot development. These parables contrast human action with God's actions. For instance, "If you then, who are evil, know how to give good gifts to your children, how much more will your Father who is in heaven give good things to those who ask him!" (Matt. 7:11 ESV). God's actions, therefore, far exceed the actions of the person in the parable.

---

20. Ibid., 12. Snodgrass mentions that modern English translations mask this category by exchanging the question with "Suppose one of you." Among modern versions, only the ESV retains "Which of you."

Parables with plot development (*single indirect* parables, *double indirect narrative* parables, *"how much more" narrative* parables) are a good place to start when looking to preach one-point expository sermons. A close look at which of the parable characteristics they have will help with making the decision whether or not to use a one-point structure.

CHARACTERISTICS OF PARABLES

Not all parables share the same characteristics. While scholars are prone to make long lists with exacting details,[21] some general characteristics are self-evident, including:

- Concise, simple, and engaging
- Focused on people
- Fictional descriptions that emphasize everyday life
- Repetition of key points
- Gracious God demanding a decision
- Kingdom-centered ethics required
- Parables appear in collections
- Parables often include Old Testament allusions
- Gospel writers stress their own characteristics (e.g., Luke and money)

Some characteristics, however, demand more description; they are described in the following sections.

MAJOR AND MINOR POINTS

This characteristic reveals the debate on whether there is one-point to a parable (e.g., Stein) or multi-points (e.g., Blomberg). Yet even those who choose one-point still recognize secondary points and are open to finding minor points. This also means the possibility of finding allegorical features.[22] While it is appropriate to limit the one-point sermon structure to the major point, the other points could occupy a brief aside in the sermon.

---

21. Snodgrass, *Stories with Intent*, 17–22, lists eleven characteristics. Osborne, *Hermeneutical Spiral*, 296–302, lists ten. Osborne's list is repeated but summarized differently by Köstenberger and Patterson, *For the Love of God's Word*, 227–33.

22. Osborne, *Hermeneutical Spiral*, 297; Snodgrass, *Stories with Intent*, 28.

CONCLUSION AND CLIMAX

Jesus often pronounces a terse dictum at the end of the parable. This is the "rule of end stress." It is much like the punch line of a joke. The Rich Fool concludes with, "So is the one who lays up treasure for himself and is not rich toward God" (Luke 12:21 ESV). Or Jesus may use an open-ended question that forces the hearers to respond. The Two Debtors concludes with, "Now which of them will love him more?" (Luke 7:42 ESV). The conclusion therefore often provides the main point of the parable, or applies its teaching to a broader situation. Parables with this characteristic are good candidates for one-point expository sermon structures.

LISTENER RELATEDNESS

This characteristic underscores the definition and purpose of parables. Jesus intended to elicit a response from his hearers. Parables provide an encounter mechanism and function differently depending on the audience. Hearers respond either positively or negatively. Unbelievers rejected the truths, whereas believers responded to the truths. Parables with this characteristic make good two-point expository sermon texts.

REVERSAL OF EXPECTATION

Parables often produce unexpected turns of events that startle hearers and force them to consider the deeper implications of the parable. The Good Samaritan story was shocking because there was no such thing as a *good* Samaritan in first-century Palestine. Likewise, for the tax collector to be the good person at the expense of the Pharisee was an outrageous thought. Reversal of expectations is a type of parable that delivers a point with power.[23] Parables with this characteristic have potential as a one-point expository sermon.

KINGDOM-CENTERED ESCHATOLOGY

The theme that runs throughout the parables is the kingdom of God. Parables reflect the already-not yet aspect of the kingdom. The kingdom is present but also future. Growth parables (the Mustard Seed, the

---

23. Snodgrass, *Stories with Intent*, 19: "Not all parables implement reversal, but when they do, they are among the most powerful instruments for change that Jesus used." See also Osborne, *Hermeneutical Spiral*, 299.

Leaven) reflect its present-ness and the cost of discipleship (Rich Man and Lazarus). Parables with an urgency of decision (the Talents, the Ten Virgins) reflect its future-ness.[24] When parables have two levels of meaning, the preacher's goal is to bridge those levels and find the main point(s) of the parable. Remember, just because there is likely a double application for parables with this characteristic, there could still be opportunity to preach a sermon with a one-point structure.

Interpreting Parables

Preaching the meaning of the parable implies precision in interpreting the parable. While there are numerous and varying guidelines on interpreting the parables,[25] the following steps, while not exhaustive, are helpful:

Determine the Structure of the Parable

Köstenberger and Patterson say, "Make note of plot development, literary style, and narrative flow. Ensure that you correctly identify transitional phrases, literary inclusions, and other textual markers."[26] Work toward establishing the points of reference in the parable. Discover the climax of the story, its turning points, and the key dialogues. Pay particular attention to the end of the parable.

Determine the Historical Context of the Parable

This principle stresses the task to discover the original audience and the original intent of the parable. Snodgrass claims, "Any interpretation that does not breathe the air of the first century cannot be correct."[27] Biblical culture, historical context, and ancient religious life must be uncovered.

Determine the Literary Context of the Parable

Here the interpreter must take note of how each writer used the parable. Remember that the parables are twice-used stories—once by Jesus and

---

24. Osborne, *Hermeneutical Spiral*, 300–301; Fee and Stuart, *How to Read the Bible for All Its Worth*, 167.

25. Snodgrass, *Stories with Intent*, 24–31, delivers eleven guidelines. Köstenberger and Patterson, *For the Love of God's Word*, 234–35, offer nine steps. Osborne, *Hermeneutical Spiral*, 302–308, produces eight guidelines.

26. Köstenberger and Patterson, *For the Love of God's Word*, 234.

27. Snodgrass, *Stories with Intent*, 25.

once by the Gospel writer. They are stories within larger stories woven into the full Gospel itself.[28]

DETERMINE THE MAIN POINT OF THE PARABLE

Osborne reminds us that the point of a parable may come at the introduction (Luke 18:9; 19:11) or the conclusion (Matt. 15:13; Luke 16:9). Or it may come as a question introducing the parable or its application afterward (Matt. 18:21–35; 20:1–15; Luke 12:16–20).[29] The main point uncovered must be one that Jesus' original audience understood and that the Gospel writer intended.

Stein provides several questions interpreters can ask to isolate the main point, including:

- What terms are repeated in the parable? Which are not?
- Upon what does the parable dwell, that is, to what or to whom does the parable devote the most space?
- What is the main contrast in the parable?
- What comes at the end of the parable (end stress)?
- What is spoken in direct discourse in the parable? (Frequently what is most important in the parable appears in direct discourse.)
- What characters appear in the parable? Which are the least important? Which are the two most important characters? (Usually a parable zeroes in on two characters to establish its main point.)[30]

APPLY THE CENTRAL TRUTH(S) OF THE PARABLE

How do the parable's truths apply to my life? My current situation? How should its message change my behavior? For example, knowing that the Good Samaritan story is about loving my (unlovable) neighbor, what concrete actions will flow out of this truth's significance in my life today?

SERMON SAMPLES FROM PARABLES

I have likely heard more sermons on the parable of the Prodigal Son than any other passage of Scripture. My father, who was my pastor when I

---

28. Ibid., 26.
29. Osborne, *Hermeneutical Spiral*, 305.
30. Stein, *Introduction to the Parables*, 56.

was a child and teenager, loved this parable and preached from it often, sometimes more than once a year. Through the years, I have preached it a fair number of times, usually in a three-point sermon, divided by the three main characters in the story. However, in the sermon that follows, I chose a larger literary unit, which changed the shape of the sermon I preached. Because the parable cluster was a direct response to the Pharisee's comment in Luke 15:2, I shaped the sermon as an expository one-point sermon.[31]

I developed a one-point sermon that places the parable of the Prodigal Son in context with the other parables in Luke 15.

Celebrate!

Luke 15:4–32

"What man among you, who has a hundred sheep and loses one of them, does not leave the ninety-nine in the open field and go after the lost one until he finds it? When he has found it, he joyfully puts it on his shoulders, and coming home, he calls his friends and neighbors together, saying to them, 'Rejoice with me, because I have found my lost sheep!' I tell you, in the same way, there will be more joy in heaven over one sinner who repents than over ninety-nine righteous people who don't need repentance.

"Or what woman who has ten silver coins, if she loses one coin, does not light a lamp, sweep the house, and search carefully until she finds it? When she finds it, she calls her friends and neighbors together, saying, 'Rejoice with me, because I have found the silver coin I lost!' I tell you, in the same way, there is joy in the presence of God's angels over one sinner who repents.

"He also said: A man had two sons. The younger of them

---

31. See earlier section "Only One-Point Approach" in this chapter: "Redaction critics developed Jeremias' emphasis further, stressing the theological editorial contributions of the Gospel writers. In other words, the context of the parable gives readers editorial clues for the proper interpretation of parables. For instance, the Prodigal Son (Luke 15:11–32) must be understood in light of what Luke states in 15:1–2."

said to his father, 'Father, give me the share of the estate I have coming to me.' So he distributed the assets to them. Not many days later, the younger son gathered together all he had and traveled to a distant country, where he squandered his estate in foolish living. After he had spent everything, a severe famine struck that country, and he had nothing. Then he went to work for one of the citizens of that country, who sent him into his fields to feed pigs. He longed to eat his fill from the pods that the pigs were eating, but no one would give him anything. When he came to his senses, he said, 'How many of my father's hired workers have more than enough food, and here I am dying of hunger! I'll get up, go to my father, and say to him, Father, I have sinned against heaven and in your sight. I'm no longer worthy to be called your son. Make me like one of your hired workers.' So he got up and went to his father. But while the son was still a long way off, his father saw him and was filled with compassion. He ran, threw his arms around his neck, and kissed him. The son said to him, 'Father, I have sinned against heaven and in your sight. I'm no longer worthy to be called your son.'

"But the father told his servants, 'Quick! Bring out the best robe and put it on him; put a ring on his finger and sandals on his feet. Then bring the fattened calf and slaughter it, and let's celebrate with a feast, because this son of mine was dead and is alive again; he was lost and is found!' So they began to celebrate."

When was the last time something really good happened to you? What did you do to celebrate it?

In our text today, we see several people who had something very good happen to them. I want you to notice what they did to celebrate.

There was a shepherd who had a hundred sheep but lost one of them. He cared so much for the lost sheep that he left the other ninety-nine behind to go find the lost sheep. When he found it, he called his friends and neighbors together to celebrate his good fortune. I want you to notice the pattern in the story: lost, found, celebrate. The sheep was lost, and then it was found, which was reason to celebrate.

There was a woman with ten coins who lost one of them. She searched her house until she found the lost coin and when she found it, she called her friends and neighbors together to celebrate her good fortune. I want you to notice the pattern in the story: lost, found, celebrate. The coin was lost, and then it was found, which was reason to celebrate.

Then Jesus raised the stakes. It wasn't an animal or a coin that was lost this time; it was a son. The father lost one of his sons, who asked for his inheritance early, left home, and squandered it in a foreign land. This father didn't leave his older son at home to search for the prodigal, he just waited and hoped that his son would return. When he returned, the father was ready to celebrate. Notice the pattern in the story: lost, found, celebrate. The son was lost, and then he was found, which was reason to celebrate.

Is the message of these parables that we are to celebrate when something good happens to us? I don't think so, mainly because we don't need guidance to do that. It is what comes natural.

Let's dig a little deeper to see if we can discover the meaning. A parable is a story that Jesus "throws alongside" (literal meaning of the word "parable") of a truth to help define it. It provides a contextual "aha" moment for the listener. Jesus uses common, earthy things to illustrate the truths he taught.

Prior to the twentieth century, interpreters viewed the parables allegorically, assigning a meaning to every element of the story and drawing conclusions. Sometimes this process yielded wild conclusions based upon the most inconsequential detail.

Near the end of the nineteenth century, Adolf Jülicher pointed out the inconsistency of the allegorical interpretations and argued that instead of assigning an allegorical meaning to every detail, Bible students should look for one main point per parable. Recently Craig Blomberg has argued that there is one main point per character in the parable. Klyne Snodgrass gives a helpful perspective when he writes, "In short, some parables make one point, and some make several points. A formulaic approach to parable interpretation, as for all biblical studies, just does not work. One must discern from context the intent of the analogy."[32]

---

32. Snodgrass, *Stories with Intent*, 29.

To find the heart of this parable cluster, you have to look at two things. First, you look at the patterns in the text, and then you look at the situational context of the parable. Following Snodgrass's advice, I believe there is one point in the parable cluster, not a different point in each parable.

Thus far, we've looked at two parables and a part of the third: the parable of the lost sheep, the lost coin, and the lost son. In each instance, we've seen the unmistakable pattern of lost, found, celebrate; and it would be easy to draw the conclusion from Jesus' teaching that we should celebrate when good things happen to us. However, we've failed to look at the end of this parable cluster—the portion of the third parable that speaks of the older brother.

Robert Stein adds to our understanding of interpreting parables with his "end stress." He points out that in most stories the climax comes at the end, so if you want to really know the point of the parable look at the concluding words. So let's look at the end of the parable cluster Luke 15:25–32:

> "Now his older son was in the field; as he came near the house, he heard music and dancing. So he summoned one of the servants, questioning what these things meant. 'Your brother is here,' he told him, 'and your father has slaughtered the fattened calf because he has him back safe and sound.'
>
> "Then he became angry and didn't want to go in. So his father came out and pleaded with him. But he replied to his father, 'Look, I have been slaving many years for you, and I have never disobeyed your orders, yet you never gave me a goat so that I could celebrate with my friends. But when this son of yours came, who has devoured your assets with prostitutes, you slaughtered the fattened calf for him.'
>
> "'Son,' he said to him, 'you are always with me, and everything I have is yours. But we had to celebrate and rejoice, because this brother of yours was dead and is alive again; he was lost and is found.'"

With this final parable, the older son breaks the patterned response. When the shepherd found his lost sheep, he called his friends and neighbors together and they celebrated. When the woman found her lost coin, she brought her friends and neighbors together and they celebrated. When the father found his lost son, he killed the fatted calf and wanted to celebrate. But when the brother found his lost little brother, he didn't celebrate—he became angry. Parable 1: lost, found, celebrate. Parable 2: lost, found, celebrate. First half of parable 3: lost, found, celebrate; second half of parable 3: lost, found, *anger*.

There is one more place where the pattern breaks down. In the case of the lost sheep, the shepherd left the ninety-nine to seek for it. In the case of the lost coin, the woman of the house set aside all other duties to focus on finding the coin. But when the prodigal was lost, the father did not leave his older son to search for the prodigal. He stayed home.

However, when the older brother did not come to the celebration, the father left the party to find the older brother. This leads me to believe that the main point in this parable cluster does not have to do with the younger son, but the older one. The shepherd searched for the sheep, the woman of the house searched for the coin, and the father searched for the older brother.

We've explored the patterns, now let's look at the context. Luke writes in 15:1–3, "All the tax collectors and sinners were approaching to listen to him. And the Pharisees and scribes were complaining, 'This man welcomes sinners and eats with them.' So he told them this parable."

The Pharisees were grieved because Jesus was being gracious to sinners, just as the older brother was grieved because the father was being gracious to the prodigal.

This parable cluster isn't about celebrating when something good happens to you. Rather, it is celebrating God's grace when something good happens to someone else—even your rival brother that doesn't deserve grace.

I've spent the first half of my ministry preaching against Pharisees. Now I've come to understand I am one. I am the older brother who dutifully does the right thing and takes notice of others who do the wrong thing. Having come face to face with the teachings of Jesus in these parables, I know I need God's grace in my life as desperately as the prodigal son did. I'm learning the issue isn't who is better, but that we're brothers. And brothers celebrate when something good happens in the other's life—especially when it isn't deserved.

Because God is gracious, extend God's grace to others, and celebrate it in your own life, and theirs.

Do you love God's grace? The real test of how much you love the grace of God isn't how you respond to it when you receive it, but whether you can celebrate when someone who doesn't deserve it receives it. And whether you can acknowledge that you don't deserve it when you get it either.

REFLECTIONS ON THE SERMON

In this sermon I used the *who done it* structure (see chap. 2) to guide the congregation through interpretative choices to discover the point of the parable cluster.

> ↓ Do these parables teach us to celebrate when something good happens to us? Isn't that something that comes natural?

>> ↑ Yes, but there is an unmistakable pattern of celebration with the shepherd who found the sheep, the woman who found the coin, and the father that found the son.

> ↓ That's true, but it didn't happen with everyone. The older brother who found his younger brother did not celebrate, he got angry.

>> ↑ Exactly. That is why the father left his youngest son's party to minister to the older brother. We are to celebrate God's grace when others experience it just as we do when we experience it.

Preachers teach hermeneutics every time they preach. Usually it is more subtle than it was in this sermon, but nonetheless we model how to interpret Scripture in the way we handle it in our sermons. In this sermon, some of the conclusions Mike Kuykendall and I presented in the previous part of this chapter made their way into the sermon to help the congregation understand the interpretative choices I was making in the sermon. Both the immediate context of the parables and the "end stress" of the parable cluster were important elements that shaped the sermon as a one-point sermon with the transformative point's emphasis on extending grace to the undeserving.

* * *

In the Luke 15 sermon, I preached a one-point sermon based on a parable cluster. In the following sermon, I preach a one-point sermon based on a single parable, which is a more typical approach.

The Reward for Faithfulness

Matthew 25:14–30

"For [the kingdom of heaven] is just like a man about to go on a journey, who called his own slaves, and entrusted his possessions to them. And to one he gave five talents, to another, two, and to another, one, each according to his own ability; and he went on his journey. Immediately the one who had received the five talents went and traded with them, and gained five more talents. In the same manner the one who had received the two talents gained two more. But he who received the one talent went away and dug in the ground, and hid his master's money.

"Now after a long time the master of those slaves came and settled accounts with them. And the one who had received the five talents came up and brought five more talents, saying, 'Master, you entrusted five talents to me; see, I have gained five more talents.' His master said to him, 'Well done, good and faithful slave; you were faithful with a few things, I will put you in charge of many things, enter into the joy of your master.'

"Also the one also who had received the two talents came up and said, 'Master, you entrusted to me two talents; see, I have gained two more talents.' His master said to him, 'Well

done, good and faithful slave; you were faithful with a few things, I will put you in charge of many things; enter into the joy of your master.'

"And the one also who had received the one talent came up and said, 'Master, I knew you to be a hard man, reaping where you did not sow, and gathering where you scattered no seed. And I was afraid, and went away and hid your talent in the ground; see, you have what is yours.'

"But his master answered and said to him, 'You wicked, lazy slave, you knew that I reap where I did not sow, and gather where I scattered no seed. Then you ought to have put my money in the bank, and on my arrival I would have received my money back with interest. Therefore take away the talent from him, and give it to the one who has the ten talents.' For to everyone who has shall more be given, and he shall have an abundance; but from the one who does not have, even what he does have shall be taken away. And throw out the worthless slave into the outer darkness; in that place there shall be weeping and gnashing of teeth." (NASB)

In this parable, Jesus gives three people differing numbers of talents. What is a talent? In the church, we often make a distinction between a talent and a spiritual gift. We usually define a talent as something we come by naturally, something we were born with. A spiritual gift, however, is something mystically given to us by God when he saves us. In other words, it is something we were *born again* with.

Certainly, there needs to be a distinction between talents and spiritual gifts, but part of that distinction does not need to be the source of the ability. Whether we were born with it, or God mystically bestows us with it after our conversion, the source is the same: God. James 1:17 says, "Every good gift and every perfect gift is from above, and cometh down from the Father of lights, with whom is no variableness, neither shadow of turning" (KJV). So whatever the talent is that the master gives his servants, we must note that the source of the gift is the master; the servants would not have it without his act of giving.

As I've said, when we use the word "talent," we immediately think of it as a special ability that someone has; therefore, we interpret this parable in that light. We condense the teaching by saying that if God gives you a talent—meaning a special ability—you'd better develop it or he will take it away. This sounds good on the surface, except the word "talent" in this usage does not mean a special ability.

In Palestine, a talent was a weight of money. The master in this parable isn't giving special abilities to his servants (something a man couldn't do anyway). He was giving money. How much? Likely it was worth around sixty days' wages of a worker. With a minimum wage at $10.50 an hour, it would be worth just over $5,000 in our current context. Regardless of the details, it was enough money that the master cared what they did with it.

Beyond the linguistics involved, there is another issue that we have to deal with in this text: the master didn't distribute the talents fairly. To one he gave five, to another he gave two, and the other he gave only one. In a day where it doesn't matter whether you win or lose, it just matters if everybody gets to play and has a good time, this seems inequitable. Is it fair for the master to give more to one and less to another? Doesn't that give one an unfair advantage?

Okay, let's stop here for a moment; let's leave the parable to talk about how popular culture tends to view God. In a cartoon strip of Calvin and Hobbes, the mischievous imp Calvin is climbing on a rock when he says: "This whole Santa Claus thing just doesn't make sense." In the next frame, he continues, "Why all the secrecy? Why all the mystery? If the guy exists, why doesn't he ever show himself and prove it?" Then, jumping off the rock, he says, "And if he doesn't exist, what's the meaning of all this?" Hobbs responds, "I dunno—isn't this a religious holiday?" Calvin quips, "Yeah, but actually, I've got the same questions about God."[33]

Like cartoon characters, people often try to fit God in their mold and get him to show and explain himself. They don't just want him to be just; they want him to be fair.

God is just. He judges each man based on the opportunities and responsibilities he's given him. But he isn't fair. He doesn't give every man the same opportunities and responsibilities. I like the attitude of Captain David Fortune of the Monterey Police Department. Captain Fortune has had three different types of cancer. His first round was

---

33. http://www.goodreads.com/quotes/tag/christmas.

with cancer of the larynx in 1979. That cancer led to surgery, radiation, and an artificial voice box. Later, in 1988, he got cancer again but in his left kidney, and then skin cancer in 1993. The odds of getting two types of cancer are great, but the odds of getting three types are astronomical. What was his response? "I don't feel picked on. I don't feel I'm a marked man," he said. "I feel blessed to be able to handle the challenges and keep going."[34] Instead of complaining about the hardships we face in life, perhaps we need to develop an attitude of gratitude, like Captain Fortune has.

Why would the master distribute the talents unfairly? He gave them to the people according to their ability. Wouldn't you do the same? Aren't you doing the same? Those of you who are in the age group investing for your retirement, think about how you are allocating your resources. Do you put the same amount of money in every stock so you can be fair? Or do you put the greater amount of money in funds that you believe will perform well and lesser amounts in funds that you are uncertain about? That's exactly what the master did. He placed the greater amount of his wealth in the person he believed would give him the greatest return on his investment.

When he returned, he found what he'd expected. The one he gave five talents to and the one he gave two talents doubled his money, but the one he gave only one talent did not earn a return at all. As it turns out, he took the money and buried it in the ground so it would be safe. His concern was with keeping things the way they were instead of achieving his potential. The master was livid with him and called him lazy. Okay, no argument here. Obviously, the man was lazy—he didn't do anything except bury the money and dig it back up. The other two were wheeling and dealing—working hard to make a profit, but not this one. He was lazy. But the master called him more than lazy, he called him wicked. Wait a minute, that's a strong word: *wicked.* The punishment was as startling; the useless servant was cast into darkness where there is weeping and gnashing of teeth.

The rewards to the faithful are just as surprising. I'd expect him to give them a cut of the profit and send them away on vacation; instead, he gives them more responsibility.

---

34. *Monterey County Herald,* June 19, 2002.

God does not exist to make your life easier. You exist to serve and worship him and the greatest reward you can ever receive is to have the honor of having more responsibility, and the greatest thing you can ever do in life, is to fulfill the potential that God has given you.

The rewards and punishments seem strange to us because we usually view the world through the eyes of the leading man or woman and think of God as playing a supporting role. He isn't! Life isn't about us; it is about God!

REFLECTIONS ON THE SERMON

The parable of the talents has some abrupt twists and turns and a surprise ending. For one, calling the man who buried the talents wicked along with lazy is startling. That the master took from the one who had little and gave to the one with the most is another; it upsets the Western concept of fairness. Then rewarding the faithful person with more responsibility, not time off, would not be anticipated by most people listening to the story. The abruptness helps build the tension and keep the audience's attention.

This is a parable with a narrative plot that I followed closely.

↓ God does not operate by our sense of fairness.

↑ God does give each person opportunities (according to their abilities).

↓ God punishes those who do not fulfill their potential.

↑ God does reward the faithful, but he does so by giving them more responsibilities.

While there was enough tension supplied by the text itself, I chose to use a Fresh Illustration[35] about Police Captain David Fortune, who exemplified a positive response to life's inequities. While the illustration likely would work in any setting, the story was familiar to the congregation who

35. http://www.freshsermonillustrations.net.

heard the sermon for the first time, which was located on the Monterey Peninsula, near where Captain Fortune served.

FOR FURTHER REFLECTION

When preaching on parables, it is helpful to ask yourself these questions:

- Have I been faithful to the original intention of the Gospel writer in this parable?
- Have I captured the moment when the true meaning of the parable came through for Jesus' hearers?
- Does the sermon communicate what the Gospel writer wanted to say to the readers in his own day?
- Does the transformational point of the sermon relate back to the parable and into the lives of my hearers?
- Is the transformational point a preferred response to the transformational truth from the text?

Epistles

Epistles are the dominant literary form in the New Testament, representing twenty-one of the twenty-seven books. They are popular for study, devotional reading, and as texts for expositional sermons. Taken together, Epistles create a picture of life in the early church, give instruction for Christian behavior in a largely pagan culture, and define orthodox Christian teaching and theology. For these reasons and more, we preach them.

In its most basic form, an epistle is a letter. However, the modern reader is not the original recipient; we are reading someone else's mail, and we are only getting one side of the communication.[1] This observation is critical when it comes to understanding what the writer is saying to the original recipient(s) and applying its significance to the modern hearer. Details like the name of a writer, recipient, and date are useful for cataloging an old letter as a historical artifact, but understanding the message requires more information. To preach the text faithfully, we must have the rest of the story.

THE REST OF THE STORY

The rest of the story—authorship, culture, and context—provides needed information to understand the meaning. This is true of any letter. Modern readers can only understand the meaning of Dietrich Bonhoeffer's *Letters and Papers from Prison*, C. S. Lewis's *Letters to Malcolm: Chiefly on Prayer*, or even Martin Luther King Jr's *Letter from a Birmingham Jail* after taking into account the person, the current culture, and the imminent context of the circumstances that prompted the writings. The same is true with the letters of the New Testament. It is impossible to ignore

---

1. Arthurs, *Preaching with Variety*, 151.

authorship, culture, and context if readers want to gain any significant understanding of the meaning as defined by authorial intent.

The Epistles are not all the same. Different writers, recipients, and circumstances produce a variety of correspondence from highly personal to much more philosophical.[2] Sometimes the circumstances are clear. Sometimes they are not.[3]

Most Epistles identify the author in the letter, and scholars provide additional information in their exegetical commentaries about cultural issues. But the best way for preachers to understand context is to spend a substantial amount of time reading it. This gives them a feel for the tone and flow of the passage. To see how the text functions within the chapter and the letter itself they should read it aloud, multiple times, in a variety of translations, with different inflections and emphases. This helps preachers get a flavor of how the original audience would have heard the epistle. Remember, the Epistles were oral communication —the writers wrote them so the recipients could read them aloud during a church gathering.[4] It makes sense, then, that one of the best ways to connect with the context is through reading and speaking them.

Another way to connect with the context is to ask questions of the text. Why is this being said at this point in the letter? What is the writer trying to communicate? How does the writer want the reader(s) to respond?

These questions help us think about the text in a fresh way. Sometimes familiarity with the text is the enemy of good exegesis and effective preaching. As with other genres in the Bible, it is wise to go to the text first and then go looking for the answers to the questions raised in the text in commentaries.

Preaching the Epistles

Preachers can preach Epistles with passion and impact. Most would agree that preaching should not be dramatic to manipulate an audience

---

2. Greidanus, *Modern Preacher*, 313: "Letters written for specific occasions, to respond to specific concerns."

3. Fee and Stuart, *How to Read the Bible for All Its Worth*, 58: "We have the answers, but we do not always know what the questions or problems were—or even if there was a problem."

4 Arthurs, *Preaching with Variety*, 163: "Not only were the epistles received aurally, they were also composed through speech."

or to draw attention to the preacher's oratory skills. However, few would defend boring preaching. The challenge for the preacher is to be faithful to the text and interesting to the audience.

William Willimon says, "What ought to cause me to lie awake at night is not that somebody said he found me boring, but whether I've been faithful to my appointed calling to preach the word."[5] My question is, is it possible to be a faithful preacher and be boring? Preachers have a responsibility to be faithful to the text and to communicate it well.[6] Faithful preachers preach the message of the text, but they also keep the impact of the text intact. If they do not, they hinder the message. Haddon Robinson says, "Boredom is not just poor communication, it is a destroyer of hope."[7]

It is hard to imagine the apostle Paul writing his letters dispassionately. Think of the white-hot polemic of the Galatian letter against the legalism of the Judaizers. It leaves no option than to stand fast in the liberty of Christ and not return in the yoke of slavery (5:1). Even the more measured argumentation of the book of Romans contains impassioned points of reference to its readers. Sermons on these profound texts should not be void of the emotional impact of the text, and the best way to do that is to gain cues from the text itself.

MULTIPLE POINTS PREACHING APPROACH

There are many times that a text from the Epistles has multiple points that work well with the common three-point sermon structure. One example is Ephesians 2:1–10, which divides naturally into thirds. However, it is important to allow the impact of the text to remain intact while preaching the text at all times, even when preaching a multi-point sermon. Often pastors feel free to rearrange the text to suit their purposes, emphasizing something that the author did not intend. One way to arrange Ephesians 2 is to reorder it by time: past, present, future as illustrated by this outline:

---

5. Willimon, "Pumping Truth," 137.

6. Chartier, *Preaching as Communication*, 61: "Preachers must communicate clearly if the power of the gospel is to be comprehended and felt in the lives of the people."

7. Robinson, April 27, 2012. Preaching into the Wind National Ministry Conference, Talbot School of Theology, Biola University, La Mirada, CA.

> Title: Salvation for All Times
> Text: Ephesians 2:1–10
> Thesis: Salvation is for now and in eternity
> Outline:
>   1. What you were: *spiritually dead* (2:5)
>   2. What you are: *God's masterpiece* (2:10)
>   3. What you will be: *resident of heaven* (2:6)

However, by changing the order, the preacher inadvertently alters the impact of the message. The thrust of this text is to encourage people to walk in God's good works that he prepared for them. The reordering changed the thrust from earth to heaven, and made this great passage something to understand, not something to live. A better approach would be to trust Paul's intent and leave the impact of the text intact. Here is an alternative outline:

> Title: God's Purpose in Salvation
> Text: Ephesians 2:1–10
> Outline:
>   1. Be alive *in* Christ (2:5)
>   2. Be alive *with* Christ now and in eternity (2:6)
>   3. Be alive *for* Christ in this life (2:10)
> Transformative point: *Find and follow God's design for your life.*

Because this multi-point text has incremental steps (chap. 2), where one point leads to another, it is important to keep the emphasis where Paul had it—in the here and now. God did not make us for heaven; he made heaven for us. We are God's masterpiece, created to bring him glory, honor, and praise. One day we will do that in heaven, but Paul's emphasis in this text was on living out God's grace and call upon our lives on earth.

While preaching for information is necessary, preaching for transformation (chap. 3) is preferred. Preaching for transformation requires paying attention to the intent of the author and not altering the meaning or impact of the text to fit the need of the moment.

EXPOSITIONAL PREACHING APPROACH

No literary form in the New Testament is as well suited for expositional preaching as the Epistles. As mentioned in chapter 1, the approach of read, explain, illustrate, and apply works well with the Epistles, which are mostly direct, didactic, and doctrinal. That is the general rule; however, it is important to notice the exceptions.

Some of the Epistles have a compelling background story. For instance, the letter to Philemon has such a strong story behind it that preachers could preach a one-point expository sermon by following its plot.

While the Epistles are letters, they also contain other literary forms, such as hymns, sayings, illustrations, analogies, and quotations; and the writers use a variety of expressions to communicate their point(s).[8] Greidanus identifies eight different rhetorical structures within the Epistles, including repetition (Eph. 4:4–6, "one"), inclusion: opening and closing (1 Cor. 13), chiasm (1 Cor. 12–14), climax (Eph. 4:4–6, "one God and Father"), dialogue (1 Cor. 15:35–36; Rom. 6–7), parallelism (1 Cor. 15:55), antithesis (2 Cor. 4:16–18), and metaphor (1 Cor. 9:24).[9] Some of these elements represent opportunities for one-point expository sermons by using them as a homiletical unit, but there are other opportunities also.

ONE-POINT SERMON OPPORTUNITIES

The Epistles contain "task theology."[10] Hearers of the Word are to do more than listen to it, they are to live it (James 1:22). The sermon text should be a literary unit, which is more than just a verse or part of a verse to prove a predetermined point.[11] The passage should be a complete thought or expression, so that the main idea or theme is apparent from the context. One contextual boundary marker that indicates the presence of a one-point homiletical unit is a shift from the indicative to the imperative mood.

A SHIFT FROM INDICATIVE TO IMPERATIVE

The focal point is to determine the purpose of the passage for the original readers, which preachers will determine by ascertaining the background for and the occasion of the letter, along with the situation of the

---

8. Arthurs, *Preaching with Variety*, 152.

9. Greidanus, *Modern Preacher*, 319–23.

10. Fee and Stuart, *How to Read the Bible for All Its Worth*, 58: "Theology being written for or brought to bear on the task at hand."

11. Greidanus, *The Modern Preacher and the Ancient Text*, 323.

recipients. The message of the text is not always exclusive to the issue at hand. Rather, it can be a deeper, timeless truth. For example, Paul argues for the unity of the church based on the body of Christ (1 Cor. 12). Peter admonishes us to persevere in persecution because of the sufferings of Christ (1 Peter 2). Arthurs refers to this principle of "transcendence" as a "type of argument based on first principles and core values rather than pragmatism."[12] Finding the underlying principle is often the key to communicating the main idea of the text. When we find that truth, we can proclaim it with confidence and accuracy.[13]

A shift from indicative to imperative is a contextual boundary marker that often defines a single point. The movement from doctrinal content to application indicates a thought package that takes the hearer from thought to a transformative action. The indicative mood is truth stated; the imperative mood is truth applied. Because God loves us (indicative), we should love each other (imperative) (1 John). Because Jesus will come again (indicative), we should not grieve like those who have no hope (imperative) (1 Thess. 4).[14] This type of marker will not only help determine the boundaries of the passage under consideration, it will shape the sermon. The key is to find the imperative interruption in the indicative flow of the passage.

For example, the book of 1 Corinthians has around one hundred verbs in the imperative mood. Paul clusters some of them together after shifting from the indicative. They are multiple commands based upon the information provided. For instance, in 1 Corinthians 11:28–34, Paul provides five commands related to the Lord's Supper controversy:

1. All should examine themselves (v. 28);
2. Then eat the bread (v. 28);
3. Then drink of the cup (v. 28);

---

12. Arthurs, *Preaching with Variety*, 157.

13. Greidanus, *Modern Preacher*, 339: "Whenever the passage is so culturally specific that it yields no analogies with the contemporary situation, one can seek to redefine the specific issue or try to discover the principle entailed in the recommended practice. Once one has discovered this principle, one can apply it to the present historical-cultural setting in an analogous way."

14. Arthurs, *Preaching with Variety*, 157: "In the Epistles, action is motivated by the facts of theology."

4. Wait for one another (v. 33);

5. Eat at home if you are hungry (v. 34).

In this case, he shifts from the indicative mood (1 Cor. 11:17–27) to five verbs in the imperative mood (1 Cor. 11:28–34) indicating the need for a multiple-point sermon. [15]

However, there are other times that Paul sprinkles a lone imperative verb (or parallel verbs as in 5:7a, 5:13b, and 15:33b–34 —see table below) in a sea of indicatives, causing an imperative interruption in the flow of indicative information. (One way to spot this pattern is to create a visual filter using Bible Software programs.) These pericopes lend themselves to a one-point expository sermon because they provide a corresponding action to sound doctrine.

TABLE 4: SELECT IMPERATIVE INTERRUPTIONS IN 1 CORINTHIANS

1 Corinthians Passage	Verses Using Indicative Mood	Imperative Interruptions (ESV)
1:4–31	1:4–30	1:31: "so that, as it is written, 'Let the one who boasts, boast in the Lord.'"
3:1–15	3:1–10a, 11–15	3:10b: "Let each one take care how he builds upon it."
4:6–21	4:6–16, 17–19	4:16: "I urge you, then, be imitators of me."
5:1–13	5:1–6; 7b–13a	5:7a: "Cleanse out the old leaven that you may be a new lump."
		5:13b: "Purge the evil person from among you."
8:1–13	8:1–8, 10–13	8:9: "But take care that this right of yours does not somehow become a stumbling block to the weak."

---

15. There are also two imperative verbs in the passage that quotes the words of Jesus in 1 Corinthians 11:24–25.

9:1–27	9:1–23, 24–27	9:24: "Do you not know that in a race all the runners run, but only one receives the prize? So run that you may obtain it."
12:1–31	12:1–30	12:31: "But earnestly desire the higher gifts. And I will show you a still more excellent way."
15:1–34	15:1–33a	15:33b–34: "Do not be deceived: 'Bad company ruins good morals.' Wake up from your drunken stupor, as is right, and do not go on sinning. For some have no knowledge of God. I say this to your shame."
15:35–58	15:35–57	15:58: "Therefore, my beloved brothers, be steadfast, immovable, always abounding in the work of the Lord, knowing that in the Lord your labor is not in vain."

SERMON SAMPLE FROM THE EPISTLES

Our colleague J. T. Reed developed the following one-point expository sermon based on 1 Corinthians 15:1–34. In the past, he had always approached the text using multi-point sermons; here is one of the outlines he used previously:

Title: Resurrection: The Heart of the Gospel

Text: 1 Corinthians 15:1–34

Thesis: Belief in the resurrection is non-negotiable for Christians

Introduction: For Christians the resurrection is not just part of our faith, it is at the very center of our faith. There can be no flexibility about this.

1. Without the resurrection, we have nothing to *stand* on.
   a. If there is no resurrection, the apostles were liars.
   b. If there is no resurrection, we have an empty confession of faith.
2. Without the resurrection, we have no *Savior* to believe in.
   a. The teachings of Jesus depend on the resurrection; he claimed he would rise from the dead.
   b. The deity of Jesus rests on the resurrection
3. Without the resurrection, we have no *salvation* to hope for.

    a. Victory over sin depends on the resurrection

    b. Victory over death depends on the resurrection

Conclusion: The empty tomb declares we have a firm foundation to stand on, we have a living Savior to serve, and we have real salvation that gives freedom from sin.

This outline provides a good structure to teach information about the resurrection. However, in the sermon below, Reed kept the meaning and the impact of the text intact by preaching a one-point sermon from a homiletical unit that makes a single point (as defined by Paul's shift from the indicative to the imperative mood).

Living the Resurrection

1 Corinthians 15:1–34

Now I want to make clear for you, brothers and sisters, the gospel I preached to you, which you received, on which you have taken your stand and by which you are being saved, if you hold to the message I preached to you—unless you believed in vain. For I passed on to you as most important what I also received: that Christ died for our sins according to the Scriptures, that he was buried, that he was raised on the third day according to the Scriptures, and that he appeared to Cephas, then to the Twelve. Then he appeared to over five hundred brothers and sisters at one time; most of them are still alive, but some have fallen asleep. Then he appeared to James, then to all the apostles. Last of all, as to one born at the wrong time, he also appeared to me.

For I am the least of the apostles, not worthy to be called an apostle, because I persecuted the church of God. But by the grace of God I am what I am, and his grace toward me was not in vain. On the contrary, I worked harder than any of them, yet not I, but the grace of God that was with me. Whether, then, it is I or they, so we proclaim and so you have believed.

Now if Christ is proclaimed as raised from the dead, how can some of you say, "There is no resurrection of the dead"? If there is no resurrection of the dead, then not even Christ has been raised; and if Christ has not been raised, then our proclamation is in vain, and so is your faith. Moreover, we are found to be false witnesses about God, because we have testified wrongly about God that he raised up Christ—whom he did not raise up, if in fact the dead are not raised. For if the dead are not raised, not even Christ has been raised. And if Christ has not been raised, your faith is worthless; you are still in your sins. Those, then, who have fallen asleep in Christ have also perished. If we have put our hope in Christ for this life only, we should be pitied more than anyone.

But as it is, Christ has been raised from the dead, the firstfruits of those who have fallen asleep. For since death came through a man, the resurrection of the dead also comes through a man. For just as in Adam all die, so also in Christ all will be made alive.

But each in his own order: Christ, the firstfruits; afterward, at his coming, those who belong to Christ. Then comes the end, when he hands over the kingdom to God the Father, when he abolishes all rule and all authority and power. For he must reign until he puts all his enemies under his feet. The last enemy to be abolished is death. For God has put everything under his feet. Now when it says "everything" is put under him, it is obvious that he who puts everything under him is the exception. When everything is subject to Christ, then the Son himself will also be subject to the one who subjected everything to him, so that God may be all in all.

Otherwise what will they do who are being baptized for the dead? If the dead are not raised at all, then why are people baptized for them? Why are we in danger every hour? I face death every day, as surely as I may boast about you, brothers and sisters, in Christ Jesus our Lord. If I fought wild beasts in Ephesus as a mere man, what good did that do me? If the dead are not raised, Let us eat and drink, for tomorrow we die. Do not be deceived: "Bad company corrupts good morals." Come to your senses and stop sinning; for some people are ignorant about God. I say this to your shame.

"Christi," a non-Christian girl, was dating one of our church member's kids. After attending a few worship services, she dropped by my office to ask me a question, "What is it you believe?"

I asked her if she minded my showing her from the Bible what we believed. She agreed. I began sharing with her a simple gospel presentation.

As I shared the gospel I was mentally preparing myself for her objections, which I anticipated would come in some form of either "I'm not a bad sinner," or "Oh, I've always believed so I'm okay."

I read the final Scripture, "That if thou shalt confess with thy mouth the Lord Jesus, and shalt believe in thine heart that God hath raised him from the dead, thou shalt be saved" (Rom. 10:9 KJV). She interrupted me with a shocked look.

"Is that what you believe?" she asked, "Really—you believe that a dead man came back to life?"

"Yes," I responded, "that is why we celebrate Easter. Jesus died for our sins on the cross, was buried, and three days later came out of the grave alive and appeared to the apostles. This is the heart of the Christian message (1 Cor. 15:3–5)."

This was the first time I ever saw someone wrestle with the idea that Jesus rose from the dead. Most often people had just skipped right over that little detail without blinking an eye. I knew something special was happening.

"I don't know if I could believe that." She said, "If it really is true that changes everything I have ever thought about. I have to really give that some thought."

This really is the center of it all.

After prayer, she left to ponder and struggle with this issue that, in her words, "changes everything."

Today as I reflect on that conversation, I think about the lifeless response of so many believers who have neither passion nor reaction when thinking about the bodily resurrection of Jesus. I suspect that they simply translated those words to mean a belief in some kind of existence beyond death, not realizing that most religions believe in some type of soul existence after the grave.

Maybe that describes you.

What evidence is there for life after death? Is there solid evidence for a happy hunting ground, or any other concept of afterlife? Is there hard evidence of reincarnation, or even becoming one with the universe after death? These are all speculations based on legends and hopeful flights of imagination, but bodily resurrection says somebody went into death's lair and returned, and in doing so, proved that there is life beyond death. The bodily resurrection of Jesus moves this issue from the realm of speculation to historically based evidence. This is a game changer.

After a clear, concise reminder of the gospel of the resurrection, which Paul preached, he asks a pointed question: "If it is preached that Christ has been raised from the dead, how can some of you say that there is no resurrection of the dead?" (NIV).

We do not know the exact nature of what "some" in his congregation were saying, but there are a number of viable suggestions. Perhaps from the influence of Greek philosophy that denigrated the human body as a prison, and viewed salvation as a release of the human spirit from its prison, "some" saw no value in the resurrection of the body. They were in essence substituting the doctrine of immortality of the soul for resurrection of the body, as many people do today as they talk about an afterlife. Paul wanted to nip this weakening of the Christian belief in the resurrection of the body in the bud. He wanted to bury it, if you will.

In a series of "if/then" clauses Paul builds a case for the importance of the resurrection, presenting little vignettes of "if there is no resurrection, then this is the implication." In rapid manner Paul said, "Have you considered this? Have you considered this?" He wanted them to stop and think through what they were saying.

Let's spend some time working through what Paul wrote.

"If there is no resurrection of the dead, then not even Christ has been raised" (1 Cor. 15:13). If it is impossible for a dead person to come back to life, then Jesus did not come back to life. And if Jesus didn't come back to life, then what are we doing here meeting like this on a Sunday? Sunday is a resurrection celebration. Without the resurrection, there is nothing to celebrate folks. Let's go home.

He continues: "And if Christ has not been raised, then our proclamation is in vain, and so is your faith. Moreover, we are found to be false witnesses about God, because we have testified wrongly about God that he raised up Christ—whom he did not raise up, if in fact the dead are not raised" (1 Cor. 15:14–15).

The very core of our preaching is the death, burial, and resurrection of Jesus Christ. If there is no bodily resurrection, then we are preaching a powerless, senseless message; and what you are claiming as faith is of no use, it is trusting in a lie. There is no power here. In fact, we have told an untruth about God. We have been saying God raised Jesus from the dead, but if there is no resurrection, every preacher is a liar, guilty of blasphemy!

He says it again: "For if the dead are not raised, not even Christ has been raised. And if Christ has not been raised, your faith is worthless; you are still in your sins" (1 Cor. 15:16–17).

The gospel teaches the forgiveness of sins—the release of our guilt before God for all our wrong doings. The resurrection of Jesus verifies that he dealt with our transgressions on the cross because sin is what holds people in death. Jesus defeated death and forgiveness of sins is real—but only if the resurrection is real.

One more thing: "Those, then, who have fallen asleep in Christ have also perished" (1 Cor. 15:18).

Without the resurrection, there can never be hope at a funeral. Our Christian loved ones are dead and we will never see them again. No more talk about "I'll see them in heaven." And let's throw out all those songs we sing about gathering on the other side in glory. Lost, lost, lost—all is lost if there is no resurrection.

Paul summarizes: "If we have put our hope in Christ for this life only, we should be pitied more than anyone" (1 Cor. 15:19).

What a pitiful lot of people we are. We have staked our claim for eternal life and forgiveness, for the meaning of life itself, on Christ. But if there is no resurrection there is nothing beyond, and all the things we have given up in this world to follow Christ for are just things we have missed out on. We have wasted our years. Oh, what a hollow empty life we have chosen if there is no resurrection.

No hope.

No faith.

No forgiveness.

No future.

No reuniting with loved ones.

But (and here comes the good news): "But as it is, Christ has been raised from the dead, the firstfruits of those who have fallen asleep" (1 Cor. 15:20).

Listen again, as if for the first time, to the exciting news about the resurrection:

> There is a nice symmetry in this: Death initially came by a man,
> and resurrection from death came by a man. Everybody dies
>   in Adam;
> everybody comes alive in Christ. But we have to wait our turn:
>   Christ is
> first, then those with him at his Coming, the grand consumma-
>   tion when,
> after crushing the opposition, he hands over his kingdom to
>   God the Father.
> He won't let up until the last enemy is down—and the very last
>   enemy is
> death! (1 Cor. 15:21–26 The Message)

As Paul rejoices in the Christian message it is as if he remembers a few other "if/then" statements that he wants to press his point on.

> Otherwise what will they do who are being baptized for the
> dead? If the dead are not raised at all, then why are people
> baptized for them? (1 Cor. 15:29).

This would be a very good place to chase a few theological rabbits. What is this baptism for the dead? There are many speculations and theories about it. Two things we can definitely say. First, Paul and the first readers of this letter knew exactly what he was referring to, even if we don't. Second, theologically and biblically there is no support for building a doctrine of proxy baptism on this passage. Although we do not know what Paul is referring to, the point of his illustration is clear if we don't get sidetracked.

"Baptized in reference to the dead" is another way to translate the phrase "baptized for the dead."[16] Baptism is about death, burial, and resurrection. It is an illustration of the heart of the gospel, the death, burial, and resurrection of Jesus Christ. It is a testimony of what has happened to the believer in uniting with Christ. They have died to an old life and they have been born again to a new, resurrected life in Christ. Baptism is a proclamation of the believer's future hope—to be buried and resurrected to spend all eternity with Jesus Christ.

Paul's point is simple. If there is no resurrection of the dead, why practice baptism? If there is no resurrection, baptism is a silly thing to do.

Paul uses a personal case in point as he rushes to his conclusion: "Why are we in danger every hour? I face death every day, as surely as I may boast about you, brothers and sisters, in Christ Jesus our Lord. If I fought wild beasts in Ephesus as a mere man, what good did that do me? If the dead are not raised, Let us eat and drink, for tomorrow we die" (1 Cor. 15:30–32).

From the near riot, that Paul caused in Jerusalem between the Pharisees and the Sadducees (Acts 23:6), to all the hardships he endured listed in 2 Corinthians 11, he placed himself in daily danger to preach the message of the resurrected Jesus. Why would a person put up with all that if there is no resurrection? The best thing to think would be, *Forget this, I quit. Life is too short for this.*

He then makes his summary statement: "If I fought wild animals in Ephesus with only human hope, what good did that do me?" He continues, "If I fought wild beasts in Ephesus as a mere man, what good did that do me? If the dead are not raised, Let us eat and drink, for tomorrow we die" (1 Cor. 15:32).

If there is no life beyond this life, then there really is no accountability for life. There is no greater purpose. "Let us eat and drink, for tomorrow we die." All the consumerism messages of the world are true. "It doesn't get any better than this." "You only go around once so grab all the gusto you can." "Go ahead, you are worth it." "You deserve this." "Party like there is no tomorrow." "He who dies with the most toys wins." "YOLO, you only live once."

---

16. Fisher, *Commentary on 1 and 2 Corinthians*, 247–48: "Paul meant that Christians were being baptized with a view to the resurrection of the dead."

You would expect Paul to say something at this point in his argument such as he has already said, "But Christ has indeed been raised from the dead." Or perhaps, "So you see how foolish it is for someone who claims to be a believer in Christ to say there is no resurrection." We would think a logical, rational conclusion is in order to such a clear presentation as to why the bodily resurrection is so important.

But that is not what happens.

In an impassioned voice, Paul fires off the point he expects his readers to live. He is not writing this text to convince them to believe that the resurrection occurred. The very tone of his argument is that he thinks they already believe that Jesus rose from the dead (remember, most of the original listeners to this text likely knew someone who had seen the risen Lord). He was not trying to get them to agree that the resurrection happened; he was writing to get them to live out the implications of the resurrection. In the same way that a drill sergeant would bark orders at a new recruit, Paul said, "Do not be deceived: 'Bad company corrupts good morals.' Come to your senses and stop sinning; for some people are ignorant about God. I say this to your shame" (1 Cor. 15:33–34).

Stop being misled. Hanging around those who say you only go around once in life are corrupting your lifestyle. Wake up. Sober up. You are asleep at the wheel. You are out of your mind if you claim to be a Christian and live a life unaffected by the resurrection. You should be ashamed of how you are allowing nonbelievers to shape your lifestyle. *Because Christ rose from the dead, you should influence others with the gospel; don't allow them to influence you.*

Guilt, shame, confrontation—all those things that modern congregations don't want from their preachers are found in this single verse, which begs the point, if the resurrection is not affecting your lifestyle, do you really believe? What you believe is what you apply to your life; the rest is just talk.

Paul was emphatic: "'Bad company corrupts good morals.' . . . Stop sinning" (1 Cor. 15:33). We do not know the specifics of what Paul was referring to when he said "stop sinning," but we have some good clues in "let us eat and drink, for tomorrow we die." While there is a use of this phrase in the book of Isaiah, it can also reflect an Epicurean catchphrase or any other worldview that focuses only on this life. From both epistles to the Corinthians, we see the libertine lifestyle reflected in the life of this church. Paul pointedly said this is a reflection of some not really knowing God. "Let us eat and drink, for tomorrow we die" works for people who believe they only live once, but it does not work for those who believe in the resurrection, who know you can live again in eternity.

The phrase "I say this to your shame" is interesting. He directed his impassioned commands past their minds to penetrate their hearts. Shameful! Paul says shame on you for living like you only live once. Remember, because of the resurrection, there is more to come. This is good news that excites those who live it.

I was on an airline trip when a rough looking, big man dressed as if he had just come off a construction site sat next to me. He noticed that I was reading a book with a Christian title and asked, "You a Christian?" "Yes I am." I said. Without further question, he began telling me his story.

He had been down on his luck, jobless and homeless when his girl-friend's mother said he could sleep on the living room couch for a few weeks, but only if he would agree to go to church with her on Sunday. He had never been to church but he figured that was a small price to pay for a place to stay. He put it off for a couple of weeks but on Easter Sunday, he gave in. He said it was a packed house and a crowded church that day. (I think any place he sat would have been crowded, he was a big guy.) That day, as he sat toward the back of the church, the preacher presented the message of Jesus and the resurrection plainly and clearly. At the end of his message he said, "I want you to get up from where you are sitting and come down here and accept Jesus as Lord." As they stood to their feet, under great conviction of the Spirit, the big man quickly squeezed past everyone in the row and started down the aisle, assuming everyone else would be doing the same thing. When he noticed he was the only one making his way toward the front he looked back at all the stoic faces. He said to me, "I wanted to shout at them, didn't you hear the message? This is the best thing ever, why aren't you coming down here?" He then looked at me and said, "That day changed my life forever, but I still don't understand how all those people could hear such wonderful news and not be excited." He then asked me a pointed question, "Are you excited about Jesus?"

Grasping the resurrection changed his life. He expected it to change all believers' lives. So did Paul. God changed Christi's life too, I had the privilege of baptizing her after she embraced the gospel of Jesus Christ and experienced life transformation. That's the nature of the gospel of the resurrection. If you truly believe, it changes everything.

Don't allow those who have nothing to live for influence how you live. Live like you will live eternally, not like you will only live once.

REFLECTIONS ON THE SERMON

In the introduction of this sermon, Reed upsets the equilibrium by telling the story of a young woman who did not believe in the resurrection. (He later brings resolution to that story and demonstrates the significance of the text in his conclusion.)

In the body of his sermon, he uses a modified expositional approach. He did not read, explain, illustrate, and apply. Instead, he saved the application and the illustration for the final movement of the sermon. The exposition produced a zig zag \/\/\/\/\/ as he explained Paul's instruction and the unstated objections of his readers.[17]

The sermon reached a climax with the transformative point: *Influence others with the gospel; don't allow them to influence you.*

In the final movement of the sermon, he explained the transformative point, and then illustrated how that truth changed the lives of a man he met on an airplane and Christi, the young girl from the sermon introduction. He showed how believing in the resurrection makes a difference in people's lives today.

By resisting the temptation to apply and illustrate in the body of the sermon, he delivered the transformative point with power, and in doing so, he kept Paul's intent and the impact of his writing intact.

ARGUMENTS THAT FOLLOW A PLOT STRUCTURE

There are times in the Epistles where the arguments the author makes follow the plot structure of a narrative (chap. 2). James 5:13–20 does that. One way to preach this passage is with a three-point outline like this one:

---

17. We have to surmise their objections, since by its nature an epistle is only one side of a dialogue.

    I. Reasons to Pray (5:13–16)
       a. Suffering
       b. Cheerful
       c. Ill
    II. Results of Prayer (5:13–20)
       a. Restored health
       b. Forgiveness of sins
    III. Requirements of Answered Prayer (5:16)
       a. Confession
       b. Righteous living

Another way would be to follow the plot dynamics in the text and present it as a one-point expository sermon.

    ↓ Prayers of lament are appropriate when suffering (5:13).

        ↑ Prayer brings hope to the suffering (5:14–15).

    ↓ God does not answer yes to all prayers (implied by the conditional nature of 5:16).

        ↑ God answers yes to the prayers of righteous people (5:16–19) (also 4:3).

Most of the time, the Epistles lend themselves to a multi-point sermon, or an expositional pattern of read, explain, illustrate, and apply. That is the general rule. However, preachers who allow the structure of the text to influence the shape of their sermon will find opportunities to preach a one-point, expository sermon, and in doing so, will keep the meaning and the impact of the text intact through the hermeneutical and homiletical processes.

For Further Reflection

Questions to ask yourself when you prepare a sermon on an epistle:

- Does this sermon reflect the original intent and message of this letter in its original context?

- Does the transformational truth (whether in a one-point sermon or more) of the sermon match the main point of the passage?
- Have you selected a large enough homiletical unit for the sermon? Is it adequate to communicate the intended truth of the passage or is it a few verses without a full context?
- Is this passage in an "indicative" or "imperative" section, or both? Does the sermon relate in a consistent manner to the intent of the writer as indicated by the mood?
- Is the structure of the sermon appropriate to the content and form of the passage? Is something being communicated in the form that is left out of the sermon?

─────────────[C H A P T E R   1 1]─────────────

Revelation

When I (Wilson) was a student/pastor, I took an upper-level elective on the book of Revelation and decided to teach through the book during our church's mid-week service. All went swimmingly until I passed the seven churches and found myself drowning in the apocalyptic portion of the book. It was not that I didn't know what I believed. I knew. In fact, I was surer of my stance then than I am now. What I lacked in intellectual maturity, I made up in confidence. It was not a good experience for me—or for them. This initial teaching experience has made it tempting to avoid Revelation in my preaching ministry.

Revelation can be easy to ignore, or worse yet, misuse from the pulpit. On the surface, it is a controversial book. Some have used Revelation to erect theological fences between their fellow believers, even making a particular interpretation a test of fellowship. It is doubtful that we could settle these longstanding disputes in this chapter, but we would like to see if there is some common ground for people on all sides of the interpretive fences.[1] It is not that we think we can tear down the fences. We just want

---

1. See the discussion by Beale, *Revelation*, 44–49; Osborne, *Revelation*, 18–22; and Köstenberger and Patterson, *For the Love of God's Word*, 274–77. The authors provide five options available for understanding Revelation. First, the *preterist* approach stresses the historical context of John's original audience. Its emphasis rests in the first century. All or almost all of its prophecies have already occurred. Thus, the symbols refer to people and events of John's immediate audience and situation. Second, the *historicist* approach attempts to trace history from John's original audience to the second coming. Revelation serves as a chronological roadmap. Its symbols predict major events and persons who span church history from the first century to the end of time. Third, the *futurist* approach understands the majority of Revelation as events that will transpire in the immediate future. Revelation, therefore, mainly deals with prophecies yet to be fulfilled. The symbols refer to people and events at the very end of earth's history. Fourth, the *idealist* approach emphasizes the symbols of Revelation over any specific references to time or events. The symbols picture eternal and timeless truths, such as the struggle between good and evil that

to build a neighbor gate in them for all people from all viewpoints and approaches.[2] Our goal is to encourage preaching apocalyptic literature "in context that allows us to understand and live out its main message."[3]

BLESSINGS

"Blessed is the one who reads aloud the words of this prophecy, and blessed are those who hear, and who keep what is written in it, for the time is near" (1:3 ESV). While every person of every generation can draw insight from this book, there were some original recipients. Specifically, John wrote to seven churches in Asia Minor (1:4, 11). Each church experienced oppression in various ways. The oppression, persecution, or at least pressure came from three sources: Rome, the Jewish people, and heretics.

ROME

The Roman persecution challenged believers to stand firm in the midst of emperor worship and accommodation to a pagan culture.[4] While official persecution was likely not occurring,[5] there was a pressure to conform, especially in Asia Minor. John himself was in exile (1:9), and Antipas was already dead (2:13).

---

exists in each generation. Finally, the *eclectic* approach attempts to combine the strengths and limit the weaknesses of the aforementioned approaches. Few if any eclectics follow the historicist model, but most attempt to interact with the other approaches. Thus, like every other New Testament book, Revelation's original audience must be heard first (preterist). Revelation's symbolic world presents timeless truths which every generation is challenged to follow (idealist). Ultimately, we must also recognize that future events such as the second coming and great white throne judgment await fulfillment (futurist).

2. This chapter will narrow its focus to preaching from the book of Revelation. Half of Daniel, as well as parts of other Old Testament prophets and the New Testament Gospels, contain apocalyptic elements and language. Revelation, however, comprises the most, and will serve as our guide. It is a great work of theology; it is crucial for preachers to preach from it; it is critical for hearers to live out its main message.

3. Duvall, *The Heart of Revelation*, 2. Duvall speaks specifically of Revelation but the point is true for all apocalyptic literature.

4. Most commentators accept a later date for the composition of Revelation. This means that Domitian (AD 81–96) was the emperor who pressured Christians to conform. Some scholars, however, opt for an earlier date for Revelation. If so, then Nero (AD 54–68) is the emperor in question. An example of an early dater is Gentry, *Before Jerusalem Fell*.

5. Beale, *Revelation*, 12–16; and Osborne, *Revelation*, 7–12.

JEWS

"Judaism was respected within the Roman Empire as an ancient mono-
theistic religion, and Jews were exempted from worshiping Roman gods
and participating in the imperial cult. Some Jews were hostile toward
the church and brought charges against Christians before the Roman au-
thorities, accusing them of being anti-Roman troublemakers."[6] Smyrna
(2:9) and Philadelphia (3:9) clearly reflect this oppression.

HERETICS

John challenged believers to combat false teachers and their enticements
to compromise the faith. Heresy was observable in John's symbols of
Balaam (2:14), the Nicolaitans (2:6,15), and Jezebel and her disciples
(2:20–24).

Therefore, the primary purpose of Revelation was to encourage
Christians who faced pressure and persecution from the outside and/or
faced heresy and accommodation from the inside. Revelation challenges
readers to remain faithful, even if it means martyrdom. This purpose applies to readers of every generation—not just the first or the last.

LITERARY FORMS IN REVELATION

Revelation reflects a mixed genre. John intertwines three distinct literary
types in the book. Many have called Revelation "prophetic-apocalyptic."[7]
Perhaps a better designation is to call it an epistolary-prophetic-apoca-
lypse. Such a label reveals the literary mixture as well as what appears to
be the weightiest of the three genres: apocalypse.

EPISTLE

Revelation begins as a typical epistle written to seven churches in the
province of Asia Minor (1:4). Each church receives its own message from
the glorified Christ (2:1–3:22). The book concludes with an epistolary
postscript (22:21). The implication is that the book of Revelation is one

---

6. Duvall, *Heart of Revelation*, 5: "This Jewish pressure would have tempted some
Christians to maintain a quieter attitude about their faith so that they would not attract too
much attention to themselves before either Jews or Romans." Also see Beale, *Revelation*, 31.

7. For example, see Beale, *Revelation*, 37; and Osborne, *The Hermeneutical Spiral*,
276.

letter intended for all seven churches.[8] Interpreters of epistles must try to reconstruct as accurately as possible the original historical circumstances, remembering that they are occasional in nature, intended for a specific occasion occurring between the original author and audience. Preachers must begin here for proper understanding (see chap. 10).

PROPHECY

Prophecy is the second genre of Revelation (1:3). At times, Old Testament prophecy was predictive, but it mainly concerned itself with calling the prophet's own generation to repentance and obedience. Remember that less than 2 percent of Old Testament prophecy is messianic, less than 5 percent specifically describes the new covenant, and less than 1 percent concerns "end-time" events.[9] As a whole, prophecy concerns itself more with Jesus' first coming and less with Jesus' second coming (the ultimate, eschatological end).

Another way of saying this is that preachers must keep a near view-far view approach in mind. The prophet prophesied what would happen soon if repentance were missing. He was specific in the predictions of the near future. Yet he also prophesied more generally about a day when a Messiah would come, only with less specificity (after all, the Pharisees— the very people looking for the Messiah—rejected Jesus because he did not come in the way they expected). Likewise, when the prophet envisioned even farther into the future to the last days, his words were even more unspecific. Therefore, we must also read the New Testament prophet, John, with broad strokes when he speaks of the end of days, or else risk falling into the same problem the Pharisees did—expecting the coming of the Messiah in a certain, specific, detailed way. Keep this near view-far view in focus when preaching from Revelation.[10]

APOCALYPSE

The third genre of Revelation is apocalypse. The very first word of the book is *apocalypsis*, "revelation" (1:1). Apocalyptic literature was popular

---

8. Bauckham, *The Theology of the Book of Revelation*, 12–17.

9. Fee and Stuart, *How to Read the Bible for All Its Worth*, 188.

10. Duvall and Hays, *Grasping God's Word*, 411–15. For an excellent discussion on the subgenres in prophecy, see Köstenberger and Patterson, *For the Love of God's Word*, 164–81.

in John's day. Modern readers must follow its rules and guidelines for interpretation. Apocalyptic literature such as Revelation is similar to parables, in that the details are often simply a part of the overall scenery (see chap. 9). We must not expect every brushstroke on the painting to carry meaning and demand exegesis. The big picture is the best picture. Notice the following traits in apocalyptic literature.

VISIONS

Apocalypses display a structure that revolves around multiple visions, for instance, 4 Ezra and 2 Baruch both follow seven visions. Revelation has multiple visions.

POETRY

Like prophecy, apocalyptic literature is highly poetic. John's apocalypse includes numerous examples of parallelism and chiasm structures. John uses at least five kinds of poetic elements.[11] Hymns in the worship scenes summarize John's theology.[12]

RECAPITULATION

Apocalyptic literature often recycles or recaps its visions. When a new vision begins, the seer temporally goes back in time and marches forward toward the end again. The book may have numerous *endings*. This literary technique is in Isaiah, Ezekiel, Zechariah, and especially Daniel. Chapters 2, 7, 8, 9, 10–12 of Daniel offer five parallel visions on the same general period of the future. This recapping occurs in Revelation as well. The seals, trumpets, and bowls, for example, are not three separate plagues. They offer an intensifying repetition.[13]

OTHERWORLDLY MEDIATORS

Often a heavenly being interprets the visions, most often angels. Sometimes a great figure from the past (such as Abraham, Moses, or

---

11. Wilder and Easley, *Faithful to the End*, 277–80. Easley lists hymns (17), prophecy (7), lament (4), and portrayal (3) for a total of 31 poetic units.

12. Horn, *Author's Use of Hymns*, 75–109.

13. Recapitulation can be traced as far back as Victorinus, who produced the first commentary on Revelation around AD 304. See the extended discussion by Beale, *Revelation*, 121–51.

Ezra) helps. The apostle John includes numerous angels but no great fig-
ures from the past.

TIME AND SPACE DIMENSIONS

The spatial aspect deals with the supernatural world and discloses the
activities of supernatural beings such as angels and demons. The tem-
poral aspect involves eschatological judgment. This judgment often involves cosmic catastrophe and the public judgment of all humanity.

DETERMINISM AND GOD'S JUSTICE

For the apocalypticist, the course of history is predetermined. It is going
to happen soon. Earth and humanity have run their course. The end of
the age will be in the writer's own lifetime or soon afterward. This de-
terminism led to ethical passivity. Apocalyptic literature also revealed a
deep concern for the justice of God. How can God allow such suffering
and pain to occur upon the righteous by the hands of the unrighteous?
When will God avenge his own? Apocalypses, therefore, attempted to
defend the justice of God.

DUALISM

Two types of dualism are evident in apocalyptic literature. The first is
cosmic dualism. Two worlds are emphasized: heaven and earth; God
versus Satan, present suffering versus future salvation, and present age
versus the age to come. Second, there is social dualism. Apocalypticists
divide humanity into two groups: good and evil, the elect and the rest,
the saved and the perishing. The final struggle between good and evil
involves supernatural powers, but humanity will also participate in the
struggle. In Revelation, Christians will participate in the battle against
Satan only through their witness to Christ and refusal to accommodate
themselves to the evil culture of the beast and great prostitute.

TRIBULATION

A consistent theme found in apocalypses is the intense period of suffering that immediately precedes the end of time and/or advent of a new
era. For some apocalypses, the tribulation was already in the past. For
others, it was present. For still others, it was in the near future. The function of the tribulation also varied. Tribulation for believers was a test

to produce watchfulness and steadfastness. For unbelievers, however, tribulation was judgment and a final opportunity to repent. The book of Revelation correlates closely. The tribulation is in the imminent future (2:10; 3:10); it is before the second coming (e.g., 6:1–8 leads to 6:12–17). It will come upon God's people (6:9–11; 7:1–8) and upon unbelievers (chaps. 14–16). It functions for Christians as a test and motivation to faithfulness (3:10, 19). For unbelievers, it is an opportunity to repent (9:20–21; 16:21).

SYMBOLISM

In order to express the inexpressible scenes revealed to John, he abandoned common narrative and opted for apocalyptic imagery instead. Such language contains fantastic, bizarre symbolism and often includes grotesque creatures, earthquakes, and supernatural catastrophes. But the symbolism also extends to numbers, colors, places, and institutions as well.

DIFFERENCES IN REVELATION

Although Revelation exhibits most of the characteristics listed above, there are numerous differences between other apocalyptic literature and John's apocalypse. For example, John does not use pseudonymity. Moreover, John's symbolism is rooted in Christianity. Unlike other apocalypses, John drew from five primary sources: his own experience (1:9–10), the Old Testament (perhaps as many as five hundred plus allusions), Jewish pseudepigrapha, the New Testament, and ancient mythology (the contemporary combat myth found in Rev. 12). This serves to remind us that Revelation is unique within its own genre.

INTERPRETING REVELATION

MAKING SENSE OF SYMBOLISM

The meaning of a symbol is sometimes clear. Jesus is the lion, the lamb, the male child, the bridegroom. The bride is the church. John interprets some symbols himself (1:20; 4:5; 5:6; 12:9; 17:9–15). Interpreters, however, need more help with the rest of the symbols—over three hundred in all. Readers must come to the text with symbolic readiness. A beast is not a beast; a sickle is not a sickle; a star is not a star; and a mountain is not a mountain.[14]

It is a much better approach to assume symbolic meaning.[15] As you read the book of Revelation, it is helpful to ask what the apparent meaning associated with this image is. In particular, pay close attention to when a symbol reappears in different places. For example, the number seven is an important symbol for perfection, fullness, and completion. But it is also found implicitly in sevenfold patterns. Another example is the lampstands. Their symbolism is defined in chapter 1. Thus, when John mentions lampstands again in chapter 11, readers must keep the previous definition in mind. Nonetheless, you must also remember that not every single image found in Revelation has analogical or symbolic

---

14. Yet many Bible students continue to follow a literal approach toward Revelation, resorting to symbolism only when it is impossible to sustain literalism. Such an approach is inconsistent. For example, in chapter 12 the pregnant woman, clothed with the sun with the moon at her feet, grows eagle's wings. The dragon has seven heads and ten horns. These are obvious symbols. Why, then, would an interpreter suddenly resort to literalizing 1,260 days? Why is the flood of water in an actual desert, which attempts to drown the woman, somehow a literal event? For consistency, shouldn't the water come gushing out of a huge dragon's mouth, attempting to drown a genuine, weird-looking woman? Or what about the second beast of Revelation 13:11–18? It is not a real beast. Some believe it symbolizes a false prophet or false religion. So why is the image he makes suddenly literal? Why is the mark on the right hand or the forehead literal? This picking and choosing is inconsistent.

15. Bandy, "The Hermeneutics of Symbolism," 46–58. See also Bandy's contributions found in Köstenberger and Patterson, *For the Love of God's Word*, 293–97. We must interpret the symbols according to John's intent. In both of these resources, Bandy lists seven helpful steps in interpreting the symbols of Revelation:

- Recognize the symbolic imagery associated with the description of names, people, beings, clothing, colors, numbers, heavenly bodies, nature, animals, places, institutions, and events.
- Look for interpretations of those symbols within the vision.
- Determine if the symbol stems from an allusion to the Old Testament. Scholars disagree on the definition of an allusion (echo, allusion, or near quote) and on their number (250–500 allusions). The most helpful Old Testament books include Isaiah 24–27, Ezekiel 38–48, Zechariah 1–6, and Daniel 7–12.
- Compare it with other apocalyptic writings to see if it is a common symbol with a relatively standard meaning. The most helpful non-biblical works include 1 Enoch, 4 Ezra, 2 Baruch, and the Apocalypse of Abraham.
- Look for any possible connections between the symbol and the cultural-historical context.
- Consult scholarly treatments of the symbol in commentaries and other works.
- Remain humble in your conclusions.

significance. Readers must not separate a symbol from its context. Often, the image simply forms part of the intentional heightening of the picture, much like parables in the Gospels (see chap. 9).

Preachers must keep the original audience in mind when interpreting Revelation, but they must preach it to twenty-first-century hearers. How should God's people live today? This does not mean grabbing the newspaper and attempting to match what America's president has to say about the European Union. Rather, it is applying the themes and truths of Revelation to the battles and fears of everyday living. This book reveals—never conceals—what the current generation of believers should be doing. Every believer should be on mission. Disciples, even in the midst of persecution, must know that they are secure in the eternal protection of God.

LOOKING FOR BOUNDARY MARKERS

There are two basic approaches to Revelation's overall structure. The first is to follow a chronological progression to the end. The second one argues for repetition of its visions. Thus, "the end" occurs several times. Both approaches, however, recognize the same unified message and follow similar paths on delineating John's structure.

The boundary markers that John uses include the demarcation of individual visions, the repetition of key phrases, and the use of numbers, primarily the number seven. Scholars debate the exact number of visions—some find four, based on the key phrase "in the Spirit," and build their entire outline of Revelation around these four references.[16] Others see six, seven, or eight distinct visions.[17]

Obvious boundary markers include a prologue (1:1–8) and epilogue (22:6–21). Additional boundaries are the seven letters (2:1–3:22), seven seals (6:1–8:5), seven trumpets (8:6–11:19), and seven bowls (15:5–16:21).

---

16. For example, Michaels, *Revelation*, 26–32; and Thomas and Macchia, *Revelation*, 2–5. The four references are located at the commencement of significant sections: the seven letters (1:10); the throne room vision (which many extend to the seals, trumpets, and bowls; 4:2); the fall of Babylon (17:3); and the new heaven and new earth (21:10).

17. For example, six visions is followed by Koester, *Revelation*, 112; seven visions is followed by Hendriksen, *More Than Conquerors*, 28; and Beale, *Revelation*, 114, is inclined toward eight visions.

Some minor boundary markers include John's use of key phrases of "hearing" and "seeing" which often signal the beginning of a new vision or subsections within a vision. The two phrases "and I saw/heard" and "after this/these things, I saw/heard" often signify a break.

Preachers should search the markers, which separate individual visions as well as the sections within those visions. These markers help to decide what passages become candidates for sermons.

PREACHING REVELATION

As you preach from the book of Revelation, remember that it reveals the eschatological triumph of Christ. This gives comfort to believers who face persecution and heresy, while also challenging them to remain faithful to the end. The following sections show how to divide Revelation with a view to defining homiletical units.

INAUGURAL VISION (1:9–20)

This vision relates to the seven letters to the seven churches (2:1–3:22). The overriding theme is Christ among and over his church. John's numerous allusions to the Old Testament prepare preachers for the remainder of his visions. Preachers can preach eight multi-point sermons from this section: one sermon for the introductory vision and one sermon for each of the seven churches. Because most of the letters contain commendation, criticism, and instruction, it is best to keep the structure intact and create multi-point sermons (see chap. 2).

THRONE ROOM VISION (4:1–5:14)

This vision can be preached as a three-point sermon emphasizing that the Lord is worthy to receive glory and honor (4:1–11), the Lord is worthy to break the seals (5:1–7), and the Lord is worthy because he redeemed us (5:8–14). Or a portion could be treated as a one-point sermon, as our colleague, Steve Long does in the sermon later in this chapter.

THE SERIES OF PLAGUES (6:1–16:21)

The series of seven seals, trumpets, and bowls take up significant space in Revelation (chaps. 6–16).[18] Their theme, however, is the same: righteous

---

18. Scripture span includes interludes mentioned below.

judgment on unrepentant humanity. The first four of each set of plagues are short; the final three have more detail. Each series of plagues builds, repeats, and intensifies the previous series.

This section, sans the interludes, provides two opportunities for one-point sermons.

The seven seals (6:1–8:5) is a homiletical unit with a plot that lends itself to one-point sermon by following its dramatic arc.

↓   Four horsemen of the apocalypse ride and bring war, famine, and death (6:1–8).

↑ Martyrs cry out to God, "How long . . .?" (6:9–11).

↓ Everyone, rich and poor, powerful and vulnerable, declare they cannot survive the wrath of God (6:12–17).

↑ God will intervene (7:1–8:5).
- He promises to rescue his people (7:1–8).
- God's people and the angels break out in worship (7:9–14).
- The suffering of the tribulation is for a purpose (7:15–17).
- The people's prayers are in God's presence (8:1–5).[19]

The seven trumpets (8:6–11:19) has a similar plot line and makes the same point: God will get the last word!

↓ First six trumpets bring pestilence that intensifies with each blow of the horn, moving from bad to worse (8:6–9:21).

↑ Angel appears in power, bringing anticipation that God is going to rescue the people (10:1–3).

19. Many Bible students understand the conclusion of the seals to be at 8:1. Others, however, recognize that John is using an interlocking technique that introduces the trumpets (8:2) before concluding the seventh seal (8:3–5). The same technique is observable at 15:1. John introduces the bowls but completes the interlude (15:2–4) before launching into the bowls (15:5–16:21). For example, see Beale, *Revelation*, 460–64, 617–22; and Bauckham, *Climax of Prophecy*, 17–18.

⬇ A voice instructs John to seal up what he hears and not reveal it (10:4–11).[20]

⬆ Two witnesses appear who will bring a testimony (11:1–6).

⬇ The beast martyrs the witnesses (11:7–10).

⬆ God raises the witnesses and the seventh trumpet sounds, announcing that God is on his throne! (11:11–19).

INTERLUDES (7:1–17; 10:1–11:14; 12:1–15:4)

Attached to each of the three series of seals, trumpets, and bowls are interludes. The first and second interludes are between the sixth and seventh seals (7:1–17) and sixth and seventh trumpets (10:1–11:14). The third interlude introduces the bowls (12:1–15:4). Whereas the object for the three series of seven plagues is unrepentant humanity, the audience for the interludes is believers. The book promises believers eternal protection, yet charges them with being Christ's witnesses even unto death. They must remain faithful and endure opposition to the end. Like the plagues, each interlude builds, repeats, and intensifies the previous one.

The third interlude contains an opportunity for a one-point sermon. The woman, child, dragon, and beasts (12:1–15:4) and the introduction to the bowls (15:5–8) is a homiletical unit that demonstrates that perseverance while suffering brings glory to God:

⬇ Dragon revolts in heaven (12:1–6).

⬆ Dragon ejected from heaven (12:7–12).

⬇ Dragon persecutes the woman (12:13–15).

---

20. The voice instructs John to seal and not reveal, but is referring only to the seven thunders. A few verses later John is instructed to reveal and be God's witness. Yet this call to witness does lead to the bitterness of persecution.

↑ Earth assists the woman (12:16–18).

↓ Beast emerges from the sea, blasphemes God, and attacks the saints (13:1–10a).

↑ Saints must persevere (13:10b).

↓ Beast from the earth deceives the people (13:11–18).

↑ 144,000 are not deceived and follow the Lamb. Universal praise erupts around God's eternal throne (14:1–15:4).

The fall of Babylon begins a series of upward movements that comprise an extended crescendo declaring the destruction of evil forces and extends to the end of the book declaring the ultimate victory. They are best handled with multi-point sermons.

FALL OF BABYLON VISION (17:1–19:10)

Chapters 17–22 are perhaps the most difficult chapters to outline. Beale lists no less than nine proposals.[21] Nevertheless, all agree that the major theme of chapters 17–18 describes the ultimate fall of Babylon at the end of history.

SECOND COMING VISION (19:11–21)

This vision is the most obvious reference to the second coming. The rider's description and actions are detailed (19:11–16), followed by Armageddon and judgment (19:17–21).

MILLENNIAL REIGN VISION (20:1–15)

This vision is easily divided into the binding of Satan (20:1–3), the thousand years (20:4–6), Satan's release and end-time battle (20:7–10), and the great white throne judgment (20:11–15).

---

21. Beale, *Revelation*, 109.

NEW HEAVEN AND NEW EARTH VISION (21:1–22:5)

The new heaven and new earth arrives (21:1–8); the new Jerusalem is described (21:9–21); and worship in the new Jerusalem (21:22–27) is as it was in the garden of Eden (22:1–5).

OTHER POSSIBILITIES

The subgenre of poetry offers other one-point sermon possibilities. Specifically, the heavenly worship scenes in 7:12–17, 11:16–18, and 15:3–4, and the poems spoken by the loud voice in 12:10–12 and 21:3–4 could all become one-point sermons. Sermons on these texts can help listeners understand what worship was like in the first century, not just what it is like in heaven.[22]

SERMON SAMPLE FROM REVELATION

Our colleague Steve Long examines one portion of the Throne Room Vision (4:1–5:14) in his sermon "Hope in Uncertain Times."

Hope in Uncertain Times

Revelation 5:8–14

When he took the scroll, the four living creatures and the twenty-four elders fell down before the Lamb. Each one had a harp and golden bowls filled with incense, which are the prayers of the saints. And they sang a new song:

> *You are worthy to take the scroll*
> *and to open its seals,*
> *because you were slaughtered,*
> *and you purchased people*
> *for God by your blood*
> *from every tribe and language*
> *and people and nation.*

---

22. Hurtado, *Origins of Christian Worship*, 87–90. Hurtado mentions other passages of Scripture that reflect New Testament era songs in Philippians 2:6–11, Colossians 1:15–20, John 1:1–18, Ephesians 5:14, and 1 Timothy 3:16.

> *You made them a kingdom*
> *and priests to our God,*
> *and they will reign on the earth.*
>
> *Then I looked and heard the voice of many angels around the throne, and also of the living creatures and of the elders. Their number was countless thousands, plus thousands of thousands. They said with a loud voice,*
>
> > *Worthy is the Lamb who was slaughtered*
> > *to receive power and riches*
> > *and wisdom and strength*
> > *and honor and glory and blessing!*
> > *I heard every creature in heaven, on earth, under the earth, on the sea, and everything in them say,*
> > *Blessing and honor and glory and power*
> > *be to the one seated on the throne,*
> > *and to the Lamb, forever and ever!*
>
> *The four living creatures said, "Amen," and the elders fell down and worshiped.*

The apostle John ministered to seven churches in Asia Minor during difficult times. It was under the reign of the Roman emperor Domitian that John was exiled to the island of Patmos, about 37 miles off the coast. While in exile, he wrote these churches a word of encouragement—a word we need today.

Modern day believers have more in common with those who were the original recipients of the book of Revelation than we did when I was a child. For instance, today obedience to the government is valued higher than personal conscience, which closely resembles what was happening in the New Testament era with the imperial cult emperor worship. Some Christians experience persecution for their beliefs today, as they did then. Sexual temptation was rampant in their culture and is rampant in ours. Many people treated abortions as a convenience, not a moral lapse, in their time just as it is in our time.

As they did in the first century, we need a word of hope.

John's message is not John's message, it is Jesus' message—the book of Revelation is a book with Jesus as the source and the subject of the revelation, that is, the revelation is about Jesus. Some people think the book of Revelation is a book with hidden meanings, but that could not be further from the truth. John's purpose is to reveal truth, not hide it. John writes about his visions in Revelation to reveal meaning, not conceal it. Ultimately, it reveals Jesus Christ.

The heart of the message is in chapter 5 in a vision of the throne room of God. While seated on the throne, God is holding a scroll in his right hand. This scroll has writing on both the inside and the outside and has seven seals. There has been speculation about what this scroll contains, but the image would be plain to John's congregations in Asia Minor. Likely, it was a will.[23] After writing the will, the testator rolled up the scroll and seven witnesses would seal the document, with each witness impressing their wax seal with their signet ring.[24] The contents of the will were inside; the identification of the will was on the outside.

Even though God had created a perfect world for his people, that was not the first-century world, nor is it ours, because of sin and rebellion against God. God's purpose is to restore the people to that perfect world. But how will he do it? Inside the sealed document is the answer—it contains God's will—but there is a problem: no one is worthy to open it and reveal it.

John looks to see who will open the scroll and break its seals, but they can find no one who is worthy to break the seals.[25]

John weeps.

Then one of the elders tells John (5:5) that he should stop crying. Because there is one who is worthy—the Lion from the tribe of Judah. He has been victorious and can break the seals and open the book. So John looks, but to his amazement, there is no lion standing there—only a slaughtered lamb. He sees a living, slaughtered lamb. The slaughtered lamb takes the scroll out of the hand of the One seated on the throne and the heavenly host, together with the assembled elders,

---

23. Nowak, *Wills in the Roman Empire*, 54–58; Beale, *Revelation*, 340–42.

24. Maine, *Ancient Law*, 185–87; Osborne, *Revelation*, 249.

25. *Oute blepein auto*, translated by the KJV as "neither to look thereon." Osborne, *Revelation*, 251–52, confirms that it refers to examining the contents, and not just "looking at it."

falls before the Lamb in worship.[26]

What just happened? Why does the imagery change from the powerful to the vulnerable—from the mighty to the weak, from the conqueror to the conquered? Why is a living, slaughtered lamb the one that is worthy to break the seals and reveal God's will?

The testimony of Scripture is that even against great odds, there is hope. Christians can overcome.

If the government demands that you forfeit your Christian conscience as a token of citizenship, you know that the day will come when, at the name of Jesus every knee will bow and confess to the glory of God that Jesus Christ is Lord (Phil. 2:10).

When sexual temptation tries to entrap you, you know that God says he is faithful and with the temptation will provide a way of escape (1 Cor. 10.13).

Even if the majority believes that life is cheap and kill babies for convenience, you know that Jesus values children and calls all the little children—even inconvenient babies, powerless, unborn babies—to come to him because the kingdom of God belongs to such as these (Luke 18:16).

Even if outright persecution breaks out and believers are tortured and murdered, believers take comfort in Jesus' words, "I am the resurrection and the life. The one who believes in me, even if he dies, will live" (John 11:25). We may live in a world where evil thrives and the righteous suffer, but we know there is power in the resurrection (Phil. 3:10).

But back to our question, why a slaughtered lamb? Why does the elder allude to the Lion from the tribe of Judah—the powerful, the mighty conquering lion, but when John looks up he sees the vulnerable, weak, conquered lamb?

During difficult days, whether they are days of uncertainty or suffering, it is important to know why the lion walks off stage when the slaughtered lamb appears. Throughout the Old Testament, prophets

---

26. The good news, the gospel, is that Jesus Christ did not regard equality with God as something to be grasped, but emptied himself and took on the form of a slave, being made in the likeness of all men, and humbled himself by becoming obedient to the point of death, even death on a cross (Phil. 2:6–8).

and poets ask, "How can God allow this suffering?" You never see that question anywhere in the New Testament. Why?

When the slaughtered lamb appears, so does hope. It does not matter how hopeless the situation looked for John's congregations—or for us. From the world's perspective, we may be weak and powerless, but we will overcome just as the Lamb of God did. "God's weakness is stronger than human strength" (1 Cor. 1:25b).

Jesus was born in the likeness of weak, human flesh. He felt pain, both physical and emotional. He experienced times of uncertainty where he chose not to know everything he had a right, as God, to know. He is able to sympathize with our weakness because he was tested in every way just as we are but without sin (Heb. 4.15).

He has been thirsty, hungry, dirty, and exhausted. One of His friends betrayed him. His three closest friends could not stay awake to comfort him in his suffering. He was convicted in an unfair trial because his accusers threatened the judge (John 19:12). And he died by one of the cruelest tortures.

I once heard Henry Blackaby say, "You always have to look at your suffering in the shadow of the cross." When we place our suffering in the shadow of the cross, we find hope.

But the story doesn't end on the cross. On the third day, Jesus rose from the grave and defeated sin, death, and the grave. You will encounter suffering in this world, but you can be courageous. "I have conquered the world," Jesus tells us (John 16:33).

It is not that the slaughtered lamb is worthy—it is that the lamb that lives, even after it was slaughtered, is worthy. The Lamb who is worthy to break open the seals gives hope to those in the first century and to us.

And in the midst of all of our pain, all of our suffering, all of our disappointment, we offer praise to the Lamb of God. Yes, Lord Jesus, you are worthy to receive power, riches, wisdom, strength, honor, glory, and blessing.

Because the living, slaughtered Lamb is worthy to break the seals and reveal God's will, the prayers of the saints enter the throne room (Rev. 5:8) and a new song breaks out in heaven:

> *You are worthy to take the scroll*
> *and to open its seals,*

because you were slaughtered,
and you purchased people
for God by your blood
from every tribe and language
and people and nation.
You made them a kingdom
and priests to our God,
and they will reign on the earth. (5:9b–10)

God created people to be a kingdom and priests and to reign on the earth—and the Lamb makes it happen! This begins a chain reaction of praise. In verse 12, we see that all heaven breaks forth with loud praise when the Lamb takes the scroll: "Worthy is the Lamb who was slaughtered to receive power and riches and wisdom and strength and honor and glory and blessing!" (5:12b).

The reaction spills over to the earth, the sea, and under the earth: "Blessing and honor and glory and power be to the one seated on the throne, and to the Lamb, forever and ever!" (5:13b).

Suffering? Tough times? Cultural decay? Yes, I get it. They are all around us. But don't despair. You may be down, but you are not out. *You can place your trust in the Lion from the tribe of Judah, who is the slaughtered Lamb that lives*—he will never leave you or forsake you (Matt. 28:20), and is returning for you (John 14:3).

REFLECTIONS ON THE SERMON

Preaching a sermon from Revelation, which is not in a series of sermons, creates a unique challenge. Before preachers can explain and apply the text, they must first orient the listeners to the hermeneutical landscape of apocalyptic literature, which is something that Long does well with the introduction to the sermon. He helps the listener get a sense of the setting and gets right to the heart of the message.

The movement of the sermon follows the plot of the text:

⬇ No one is worthy to open the scroll with the seven seals (5:1–4).

↑ One of the elders proclaims that the conquering lion from the tribe of Judah is worthy (5:5).

↓ The conquering lion does not appear; instead, a conquered lamb shows up (5:6).

↑ The slaughtered lamb lives; he is not conquered; he has conquered death and is worthy. This begins a chain reaction of worship (5:7–14).

Long avoids the temptation of time stamping the events of the text and provides a timeless application. Jesus is worthy of worship and we can place our trust in him.

For Further Reflection

Questions to ask when you prepare a sermon on an apocalyptic text:

- Is the sermon reflective of the particular genre of the book and passage?
- Is the transformative point consistent with the original intended meaning of the passage?
- Has a preconceived interpretive slant influenced your approach to the passage?
- Does the transformative truth of the passage come through in the sermon?
- Does the sermon speak faithfully to the original context of the passage as well as the modern reader/hearer?
- How can you preach the truth of the text without time stamping it?
- How does the sermon communicate the ultimate victory of the kingdom of God?

Bibliography

Akin, Daniel L. "The Work of Exposition: Structuring the Message." In *Engaging Exposition*, edited by Daniel L. Akin, Bill Curtis, and Stephen N. Rummage, 138–47. Nashville: B&H, 2011.

Allen, O. Wesley, Jr. *Determining the Form: Structures for Preaching*. Minneapolis: Fortress Press, 2008.

Amit, Yairah, and David R. Bauer. "Narrative Literature." In *The New Interpreter's Dictionary of the Bible*, edited by Katherine Sakenfeld, 4:223–25. Nashville: Abingdon, 2006–2009.

Aristotle. *Rhetoric*. Translated by W. R. Roberts. Stilwell, KS: Digireads, 2005.

Arnold, Bill T., and Bryan E. Beyer. *Encountering the Old Testament: A Christian Survey*. Grand Rapids: Baker, 1999.

Arthurs, Jeffrey D. "Preaching the Old Testament Narratives." In *Preaching the Old Testament*, edited by Scott M. Gibson, 73–86. Grand Rapids: Baker, 2006.

————. *Preaching with Variety*. Grand Rapids: Kregel, 2007.

Bandy, Alan. "The Hermeneutics of Symbolism: How to Interpret the Symbols of John's Apocalypse." *The Southern Baptist Journal of Theology* 14:1 (2009): 46–58.

Bartlett, David L. *The Shape of Scriptural Authority*. Philadelphia: Fortress Press, 1983.

Barth, Karl. *Church Dogmatics*. Vol. 1, part 1. Translated by T. F. Torrance and G. W. Bromiley. New York: T&T Clark International, 1957.

————. *Homiletics*. Louisville: Westminster John Knox, 1991.

Barrett, C. K. *The First Epistle to the Corinthians*. Black's New Testament Commentary. London: Continuum, 1968.

Bauckham, Richard. *The Theology of the Book of Revelation*. Cambridge: Cambridge University Press, 1993.

_____. *The Climax of Prophecy: Studies on the Book of Revelation*. London: T & T Clark, 1993.

Bayley, Peter. *French Pulpit Oratory, 1598–1650: A Study in Themes and Styles, with a Descriptive Catalogue of Printed Texts*. Cambridge: Cambridge University Press, 1980.

Beale, Gregory K. *The Book of Revelation*. New International Greek Testament Commentary. Grand Rapids: Eerdmans, 1999.

Behm, J. "Μορφοω." In *Theological Dictionary of the New Testament*. Edited by Gerhard Kittel, Geoffrey W. Bromiley, and Gerhard Friedrich. Grand Rapids: Eerdmans, 1964.

Blackwood, Andrew W. *Preaching from the Bible*. Grand Rapids: Baker, 1974.

Block, Daniel Isaac. *Judges, Ruth.* The New American Commentary. Nashville: Broadman & Holman, 1999.

Blomberg, Craig L. *Interpreting the Parables*. 2nd ed. Downers Grove: InterVarsity Press, 2012.

_____. *Matthew*. New American Commentary. Nashville: B&H, 1992.

_____. *Preaching the Parables: From Responsible Interpretation to Powerful Proclamation*. Grand Rapids: Baker, 2004.

Briscoe, Stuart. "Filling the Sermon with Interest." In *Mastering Contemporary Preaching*, edited by Bill Hybels, Stuart Briscoe, and Haddon Robinson, 67–75. Portland: Multnomah, 1989.

Bruce, F. F. *Romans: An Introduction and Commentary*. Vol. 6, Tyndale New Testament Commentaries. Downers Grove, IL: InterVarsity Press, 1985.

Bugg, Charles B. *Preaching from the Inside Out*. Nashville: Broadman Press, 1992.

Bullinger, E. W. *How to Enjoy the Bible*. New York: Cosimo, 2008.

Burk, Denny. "The Death of a Mentor, Howard Hendricks (1924–2013)." http://www.dennyburk.com/the-death-of-a-mentor-howard-hendricks-1924-2013/.

Buttrick, David G. *Homiletic: Moves and Structures*. Philadelphia: Fortress Press, 2008.

_____. *Speaking Parables: A Homiletic Guide*. Louisville: Westminster John Knox, 2000.

Carey, Greg. *Ultimate Things: An Introduction to Jewish and Christian Apocalyptic Literature*. St. Louis: Chalice, 2005.

Carpenter, Eugene. "Songs of Praise for Deliverance at the Sea (15:1–21)." In *Exodus*, Evangelical Exegetical Commentary. Bellingham, WA: Lexham Press, 2012.

Carr, David M. *An Introduction to the Old Testament: Sacred Texts and Imperial Contexts of the Hebrew Bible*. Chichester, West Sussex, UK: Wiley-Blackwell, 2010.

Carson, D. A. *Exegetical Fallacies*. Grand Rapids: Baker, 1984.

Carson, D. A., and Douglas J. Moo. *An Introduction to the New Testament*, 2nd ed. Grand Rapids: Zondervan, 2005.

Carson, D. A., et al., eds. *New Bible Commentary: 21st Century Edition*, 4th ed. Leicester, England; Downers Grove, IL: Inter-Varsity Press, 1994.

Chapell, Bryan. *Christ-Centered Preaching: Redeeming the Expository Sermon*. 2nd ed. Grand Rapids: Baker, 2005.

Chartier, Myron. *Preaching as Communication: Interpersonal Perspective*. Nashville: Abingdon, 1981.

Ciampa, Roy E., and Brian S. Rosner. *The First Letter to the Corinthians*. Grand Rapids: Eerdmans, 2010.

Collins, John J. *The Apocalyptic Imagination: An Introduction to Jewish Apocalyptic Literature*. 3rd ed. Grand Rapids: Eerdmans, 2014.

Craddock, Fred B. *As One without Authority*. 4th edition revised and with new sermons. St. Louis: Chalice Press, 2001.

———. *Preaching*. Nashville: Abingdon, 1985.

Craig, A. C. "Five Temptations of the Pulpit." In *Preaching to Convince*, edited by James D. Berkley, 147–56. Waco, TX: Word, 1986.

Cranfield, C. E. B. *The Epistle to the Romans*. International Critical Commentary. 2 vols. Edinburgh: T&T Clark, 1975.

Crenshaw, James L. "Proverbs 1, Book Of." In *The Anchor Yale Bible Dictionary*, edited by David Noel Freedman, 5:513–20. New York: Doubleday, 1992.

Dahan, Gilbert. "Genres, Forms, and Various Methods in Christian Exegesis of the Middle Ages." In *Hebrew Bible, Old Testament: The History of Its Interpretation—Vol. 1, from the Beginnings to the Middle Ages (until 1300); Part 1, Antiquity*, edited by Chris Brekelmans and Magne Saebø, 196–236. Göttingen, Germany: Vandenhoeck and Ruprecht, 1996.

Deppe, Dean. *All Roads Lead to the Text: Eight Methods of Inquiry into the Bible*. Grand Rapids: Eerdmans, 2011.

Dieter, O. A. "Arbor Picta: The Medieval Tree of Preaching." *Quarterly Journal of Speech* 51 (1965): 123–44.

Dodd, C. H. *Parables of the Kingdom.* Rev. ed. London: Nisbet, 1961.

Duvall, J. Scott. *The Heart of Revelation.* Grand Rapids: Baker, 2016.

Duvall, J. Scott, and J. Daniel Hays. *Grasping God's Word.* 3rd ed. Grand Rapids: Zondervan, 2012.

Earley, Dave. *Pastoral Leadership Is . . . : How to Shepherd God's People with Passion and Confidence.* Nashville: B&H, 2012.

Edwards, J. Kent. *Deep Preaching: Creating Sermons That Go Beyond the Superficial.* Nashville: B&H, 2009.

Edwards, O. C. *Elements of Homiletic: A Method for Preparing to Preach.* Collegeville, MN: Liturgical Press, 1990.

———. *A History of Preaching.* Nashville: Abingdon, 2004.

Ellingworth, Paul, and Howard A. Hatton. *A Handbook on Paul's First Letter to the Corinthians.* New York: United Bible Societies, 1995.

Ericson, Jon M. *Rhetoric of the Pulpit: A Preacher's Guide to Effective Sermons.* Eugene, OR: Wipf & Stock, 2016.

Eskanazi, Tamara Cohn. "Torah as Narrative and Narrative as Torah." In *Old Testament Interpretation: Past, Present, and Future*, edited by James Luther Mays, David L. Petersen, and Kent Harold Richards, 11–30. Edinburgh: T&T Clark, 1995.

Estes, Daniel J. "Proverbs." In *Handbook of the Wisdom Books and Psalms*, 213–69. Grand Rapids: Baker, 2005.

Fallon, Derrick T. "The Bible Preaches on the Bible: Transformation in Jesus' Proclamation." *Word & World* 32, no. 3 (Summer 2012): 294–301.

Fant, Gene C. *God as Author: A Biblical Approach to Narrative.* Nashville: B&H, 2010.

Fasol, Al. "What Do You Mean by Sin, and What Do You Mean by the Cross?" In *Preaching Evangelistically: Proclaiming the Saving Message of Jesus,* 108–18. Nashville: Broadman & Holman, 2006.

Fee, Gordon D., and Douglas K. Stuart. *How to Read the Bible Book by Book: A Guided Tour.* Grand Rapids: Zondervan, 2014.

———. *How to Read the Bible for All Its Worth.* 4th ed. Grand Rapids: Zondervan, 2014.

Ferguson, Everett. *Backgrounds of Early Christianity.* 2nd ed. Grand Rapids: Eerdmans, 1993.

Fewell, Danna Nolan, and David M. Gunn. "Narrative, Hebrew." In *The Anchor Yale Bible Dictionary*, edited by David Noel Freedman, 4:1023–1027. New York: Doubleday, 1992.

Fisher, Fred L. *Commentary on 1 and 2 Corinthians*. Waco, TX: Word, 1975.

Fox, Michael V. *Proverbs: A New Translation with Introduction and Commentary*. The Anchor Yale Bible. New Haven, CT: Yale University Press, 2009.

France, R. T. *The Gospel of Matthew*. The New International Commentary on the New Testament. Grand Rapids: Eerdmans, 2007.

Franklin, Ben, and Richard Saunders. *Poor Richard's Almanac: For the Year of Christ 1733*. Reprint ed. Bedford, IN: Applewood Books, 2002.

Friedman, N. "Imagery." In *The Princeton Encyclopedia of Poetry and Poetics*, edited by A. Preminger, 363–69. Princeton, NJ: Princeton University Press, 1965.

Garrett, Duane A. *Proverbs, Ecclesiastes, Song of Songs*. The New American Commentary. Nashville: Broadman & Holman, 1993.

————. "Proverbs 3: History of Interpretation." In *Dictionary of the Old Testament: Wisdom, Poetry, and Writings*, edited by Tremper Longman III and Peter Enns, 566–78. Downers Grove, IL: InterVarsity Press, 2008.

Gentry, Kenneth L. *Before Jerusalem Fell: Dating the Book of Revelation*. Tyler, TX: Institute for Christian Economics, 1989.

Genung, John Franklin. "Proverbs, Book Of." In *The International Standard Bible Encyclopedia*, edited by James Orr et al., 2471–72. Chicago: The Howard-Severance Company, 1915.

Gill, A. L. *God's Promises for Your Every Need*. Dallas: Word, 1995.

Godsey, John D. "Barth and Bonhoeffer: What Did Bonhoeffer Think of This Century's Most Influential Theologian?" *Christian History* 32 (1991). http://www.christianitytoday.com/history/issues/issue-32/barth-and-bonhoeffer.html.

Goldingay, John. *Old Testament Theology, Volume 1: Israel's Gospel*. Downers Grove, IL: InterVarsity Press, 2003.

Gowler, David. *The Parables after Jesus: Their Imaginative Receptions across Two Millennia*. Grand Rapids: Baker, 2017.

————. *What Are They Saying about the Parables?* New York: Paulist Press, 2000.

Greidanus, Sidney. *The Modern Preacher and the Ancient Text: Interpreting and Preaching Biblical Literature*. Grand Rapids: Eerdmans, 1988.

———. *Sola Scriptura: Problems and Principles in Preaching Historical Texts*. Kampen, Netherlands: J. H. Kok, 1970.

———. "Preaching in the Gospels." In *Handbook of Contemporary Preaching*, edited by Michael Duduit, 329–44. Nashville: Broadman Press, 1992.

Hamilton, Donald L. *Homiletical Handbook*. Nashville: Broadman Press, 1992.

Heath, Chip, and Dan Heath. *Switch: How to Change Things When Change Is Hard*. London: Random House, 2011.

Hemer, Colin J. *The Letters to the Seven Churches of Asia in Their Local Setting*. The Biblical Resource Series. Grand Rapids: Eerdmans, 1989.

Hendricks, Howard. "What Makes Christian Education Distinct?" In *Mastering Teaching*, edited by Earl Palmer et al., 13–26. Portland: Multnomah, 1991.

Hendriksen, William. *More Than Conquerors*. Grand Rapids: Baker, 1962.

Hess, Richard S. *The Old Testament: A Historical, Theological, and Critical Introduction*. Grand Rapids: Baker, 2016.

Hirsh, Sandra Krebs, and Jane A. G. Kise. *Looking at Type and Spirituality: Using Psychological Type to Discover Your Unique Spiritual Expression*. Gainesville, FL: Center for Applications of Psychological Type. 1997.

Horn, Stephen Norwood. "The Author's Use of Hymns as Summaries of the Theology of the Book of Revelation." PhD diss., New Orleans Baptist Theological Seminary, 1998.

Howard, David M., Jr. "The Psalms and Current Study." In *Interpreting the Psalms: Issues and Approaches*, edited by David Firth and Philip S. Johnston, 23–40. Downers Grove, IL: InterVarsity Press, 2005.

———. *An Introduction to the Old Testament Historical Books*. Chicago: Moody Press, 1993.

Hultgren, Arland J. *The Parables of Jesus: A Commentary*. Grand Rapids: Eerdmans, 2001.

Hunt, Boyd. *Redeemed! Eschatological Redemption and the Kingdom of God*. Nashville: Broadman & Holman, 1993.

Hunter, A. M. *Interpreting the Parables*. 2nd revised ed. London: SCM, 2012.

Hurtado, Larry W. *At the Origins of Christian Worship: The Context and Character of Earliest Christian Devotion*. Grand Rapids: Eerdmans, 2000.

_____. "Gospel (Genre)." In *Dictionary of Jesus and the Gospels*, edited by Joel B. Green and Scot McKnight, 276–82. Downers Grove, IL: InterVarsity Press, 1992.

Jackman, David. "Preaching That Connects, Part 2: Internal Transformation: Pastoral Patterns and Practice." *Trinity Journal* no. 29 (2008): 189–203.

Jacobs, Alan. *A Theology of Reading: The Hermeneutics of Love*. Boulder, CO: Westview Press, 2001.

Johnson, Alan F. *1 Corinthians*. The IVP New Testament Commentary Series. Downers Grove, IL: InterVarsity Press, 2004.

Jones, Peter Rhea. *Studying the Parables of Jesus*. Macon, GA: Smyth & Helwys, 1999.

Keener, Craig S. *Revelation*. The NIV Application Commentary. Grand Rapids: Zondervan, 2000.

Keller, Timothy. *Preaching: Communicating Faith in an Age of Skepticism*. New York: Viking, 2015.

Kennedy, J. Hardee. "Ruth." In *The Broadman Bible Commentary: Leviticus–Ruth*, edited by Clifton J. Allen, 464–80. Nashville: Broadman Press, 1970.

Kistemaker, Simon J. *Exposition of the Book of Revelation*. New Testament Commentary. Grand Rapids: Baker, 2001.

_____. *The Parables*. 2nd ed. Grand Rapids: Baker, 2002.

Kitchen, Kenneth A. "Proverbs 2: Ancient Near Eastern Background." In *Dictionary of the Old Testament: Wisdom, Poetry, and Writings*, edited by Tremper Longman III and Peter Enns, 552–66. Downers Grove, IL: InterVarsity Press, 2008.

Klein, William W., Craig Blomberg, and Robert L. Hubbard, eds. "Wisdom." In *Introduction to Biblical Interpretation*, 387–98. Nashville: Nelson, 2004.

Knowles, Malcolm S., Elwood F. Holton, and Richard A. Swanson. *The Adult Learner: The Definitive Classic in Adult Education and Human Resource Development*. London: Routledge, 2011.

Koester, Craig R. *Revelation: A New Translation with Introduction and Commentary*. Anchor Yale Bible Commentaries. Garden City, NY: Yale University Press, 2014.

Köstenberger, Andreas J., and Richard D. Patterson. *For the Love of God's Word: An Introduction to Biblical Interpretation*. Grand Rapids: Kregel, 2015.

Kugel, James L. *The Idea of Biblical Poetry: Parallelism and Its History*. New Haven, CT: Yale University Press, 1981.

Lamb, Jonathan. *The Dynamics of Biblical Preaching*. Carlisle, UK: Langham, 2016.

Larsen, David L. *The Anatomy of Preaching: Identifying the Issues in Preaching Today*. Grand Rapids: Kregel, 1999.

_____. *The Company of the Preachers: A History of Biblical Preaching from the Old Testament to the Modern Era*. Grand Rapids: Kregel, 1998.

Latourette, Kenneth S. *A History of Christianity, Volume 1: Beginnings to 1500*. New York: HarperCollins, 1953.

Long, Thomas G. *Preaching and the Literary Forms of the Bible*. Philadelphia: Fortress Press, 1989.

_____. *The Witness of Preaching*. Louisville: Westminster John Knox, 1989.

Long, V. Philips. "The Art of Biblical History." In *Foundations of Contemporary Interpretation*, edited by Moisés Silva, 281–429. Grand Rapids: Zondervan, 1996.

Longman, Tremper, III. "Literary Approaches to Biblical Interpretation." In *Foundations of Contemporary Interpretation: Six Volumes in One*, edited by Moisés Silva, 91–192. Grand Rapids: Zondervan, 1996.

_____. *Proverbs*. Baker Commentary on the Old Testament. Grand Rapids: Baker, 2006.

_____. *How to Read Proverbs*. Downers Grove, IL: InterVarsity Press, 2002.

_____. "Proverbs, Book of." In *Dictionary of the Old Testament: Wisdom, Poetry, and Writings*, edited by Tremper Longman III and Peter Enns, 539–52. Downers Grove, IL: InterVarsity Press, 2008.

Maine, Henry Sumner. *Ancient Law: Its Connection with the Early History of Society and Its Relation to Modern Ideas*. 10th ed. London: John Murray, 1905.

McConville, J. Gordon. *Law and Theology in Deuteronomy*. Journal for the Study of the Old Testament Supplement Series. Sheffield: Sheffield Academic Press, 1984.

McConville J. Gordon, and J. G. Millan. *Time and Place in Deuteronomy*. Journal for the Study of the Old Testament Supplement Series. Sheffield: Sheffield Academic Press, 1994.

McLuhan, Marshall, and W. Terrence Gordon. *Understanding Media: The Extensions of Man*. Berkeley, CA: Gingko Press, 2003.

McLuhan, Marshall, Eric McLuhan, and Frank Zingrone. *Essential McLuhan*. New York: Basic Books, 1995.

Melick, Richard R., and Shera Melick. *Teaching That Transforms: Facilitating Life Change through Adult Bible Teaching*. Nashville: B&H, 2010.

Metaxas, Eric. *Bonhoeffer: Pastor, Martyr, Prophet, Spy*. Nashville: Nelson, 2011.

Meyer, F. B. *Expository Preaching Plans and Methods*. New York: Hodder & Stoughton, 1912.

Michaels, J. Ramsey. *Revelation*. The IVP New Testament. Downers Grove, IL: InterVarsity Press, 1997.

Mohler, R. Albert. "As One with Authority." *The Master's Seminary Journal* (Spring 2001): 89–98.

Moo, Douglas J. *The Letter of James*. The Pillar New Testament Commentary. Grand Rapids: Eerdmans, 2000.

_____. "Romans." In *New Bible Commentary*, 4th ed., edited by D. A. Carson et al., 1150. Leicester, England: Inter-Varsity Press, 1994.

Morris, Leon. *The Epistle to the Romans*, The Pillar New Testament Commentary. Grand Rapids: Eerdmans, 1988.

Mounce, Robert H. *The Book of Revelation*. The New International Commentary on the New Testament. Grand Rapids: Eerdmans, 1997.

_____. *Romans*. The New American Commentary. Nashville: Broadman and Holman, 1995.

Murphy, Roland E. *Proverbs*. Word Biblical Commentary. Nashville: Nelson, 1998.

_____. "Wisdom in the Old Testament." In *The Anchor Yale Bible Dictionary*, edited by David Noel Freedman, 6:920–31. New York: Doubleday, 1992.

Norwak, Maria. *Wills in the Roman Empire: A Documentary Approach.* Journal of Juristic Papyrology Supplements. Warsaw, Poland: University of Warsaw Press, 2015.

Osborne, Grant R. *The Hermeneutical Spiral: A Comprehensive Introduction to Biblical Interpretation.* Downers Grove, IL: InterVarsity Press, 2006.

_____. *Revelation.* Baker Exegetical Commentary on the New Testament. Grand Rapids: Baker, 2002.

Pennington, Jonathan T. *Reading the Gospels Wisely: A Narrative and Theological Introduction.* Grand Rapids: Baker, 2012.

Pickering, Jerry V. *Theatre: A Contemporary Introduction.* Eagan, MN: West Publishing, 1978.

Provan, Iain, V. Philips Long, and Tremper Longman III. *A Biblical History of Israel.* Louisville: Westminster John Knox, 2003.

Robinson, Haddon W. *Biblical Preaching: The Development and Delivery of Expository Messages.* 3rd ed. Grand Rapids: Baker, 2014.

Rowell, Edward K. *Preaching with Spiritual Passion.* Minneapolis: Bethany House, 1998.

Ryken, Leland, James C. Wilhoit, and Tremper Longman III. "Proverbs, Book Of." In *Dictionary of Biblical Imagery*, edited by Leland Ryken, James C. Wilhoit, and Tremper Longman III, 679–83. Downers Grove, IL: InterVarsity Press, 1998.

Sandy, D. Brent. *Plowshares and Pruning Hooks: Rethinking the Language of Biblical Prophecy and Apocalyptic.* Downers Grove, IL: InterVarsity Press, 2002.

Satterthwaite, Philip, and J. Gordon McConville. *Exploring the Old Testament: A Guide to the Historical Books.* Downers Grove, IL: InterVarsity Press, 2016.

Selby, Rosalind M. *The Comical Doctrine: An Epistemology of New Testament Hermeneutics.* Milton Keynes, England: Paternoster, 2006.

Sider, John W. *Interpreting the Parables: A Hermeneutical Guide to Their Meaning.* Grand Rapids: Zondervan, 1995.

Silva, Moisés. "God, Language, and Scripture." In *Foundations of Contemporary Interpretation*, edited by Moisés Silva, 193–280. Grand Rapids: Zondervan, 1996.

Smyth, Charles H. E. *The Art of Preaching: A Practical Survey of Preaching in the Church of England, 747–1939.* London: SPCK, 1940.

Snearly, Michael K. "The Return of the King: An Editorial-Critical Analysis of Psalms 107–150." PhD diss., Golden Gate Baptist Theological Seminary, 2012.

Snodgrass, Klyne. *Stories with Intent: A Comprehensive Guide to the Parables of Jesus.* Grand Rapids: Eerdmans, 2008.

Snyder, Blake. *Save the Cat! The Last Book on Screenwriting You'll Ever Need.* Studio City, CA: Michael Wiese Productions, 2005.

Stanley, Andy, and Lane Jones. *Communicating for a Change.* Sisters, OR: Multnomah, 2006.

Stein, Robert H. *A Basic Guide to Interpreting the Bible: Playing by the Rules.* 2nd ed. Grand Rapids: Baker, 2011.

———. *An Introduction to the Parables of Jesus.* Philadelphia: Westminster, 1981.

———. *The Method and Message of Jesus' Teachings.* Rev. ed. Louisville: Westminster John Knox, 1994.

Stitzinger, James F. "The History of Expository Preaching." In *Rediscovering Expository Preaching*, edited by John MacArthur, 36–62. Dallas: Word, 1992.

Stott, John R. W. *Between Two Worlds: The Art of Preaching in the Twentieth Century.* Grand Rapids: Eerdmans, 1982.

Strauss, Mark. *Four Portraits, One Jesus: An Introduction to Jesus and the Gospels.* Grand Rapids: Zondervan, 2007.

Sunukjian, Donald R. *Invitation to Biblical Preaching: Proclaiming Truth with Clarity and Relevance.* Grand Rapids: Kregel, 2007.

Sweet, Leonard I., Brian D. McLaren, and Jerry Haselmayer. *A is for Abductive: The Language of the Emerging Church.* Grand Rapids: Zondervan, 2003.

Tannehill, Robert C. *The Gospel according to Luke.* Vol. 1 of *The Narrative Unity of Luke-Acts: A Literary Interpretation.* Philadelphia: Fortress Press, 1991.

Taylor, Gardner. "Shaping Sermons by the Shape of Text and Preacher." In *Preaching Biblically: Creating Sermons in the Shape of Scriptures*, edited by Don M. Wardlaw, 60–83. Philadelphia: Westminster Press, 1983.

Thiselton, Anthony C. *The First Epistle to the Corinthians: A Commentary on the Greek Text.* Grand Rapids: Eerdmans, 2000.

Thomas, John Christopher, and Frank Macchia. *Revelation.* Two Horizons Commentary. Grand Rapids: Eerdmans, 2016.

Trail, Ronald L. *An Exegetical Summary of 1 Corinthians 10–16*. 2nd ed. Dallas: SIL International, 2008.

Tucker, Dennis, *Jonah: A Handbook on the Hebrew Text*. Waco, TX: Baylor University Press, 2006.

Tuckett, C. M. "Synoptic Problem." In *The Anchor Yale Bible Dictionary*, edited by David Noel Freedman, 6:263–70. New York: Doubleday, 1992.

Turner, David L. *Matthew*. Baker Exegetical Commentary on the New Testament. Grand Rapids: Baker, 2008.

VanGemeren, Willem A. "Psalms." In *Psalms, Proverbs, Ecclesiastes, Song of Songs*, volume 5 of *The Expositor's Bible Commentary*, edited by Frank E. Gaebelein, 23–28. Grand Rapids: Zondervan, 1991.

Vanhoozer, Kevin J. *The Drama of Doctrine: A Canonical-Linguistic Approach to Christian Theology*. Louisville: Westminster John Knox, 2005.

Van Leeuwen, Raymond C. "Proverbs, Book Of." In *Dictionary for Theological Interpretation of the Bible*, edited by Kevin J. Vanhoozer, 638–41. Grand Rapids: Baker, 2005.

Van Pelt, M. V., and Walter C. Kaiser, "יָרֵא." In *New International Dictionary of Old Testament Theology and Exegesis*, edited by Willem VanGemeren, 2:527–33. Grand Rapids: Zondervan, 1997.

Vogel, Robert. "Biblical Genres and the Text-Driven Sermon." In *Text-Driven Preaching: God's Word at the Heart of Every Sermon*, edited by Daniel L. Akin, David Lewis Allen, and Ned Lee Mathews, 163–92. Nashville: B&H, 2010.

Vorster, Willem S. "Gospel Genre." In *The Anchor Yale Bible Dictionary*, edited by David Noel Freedman, 2:1077–1079. New York: Doubleday, 1992.

Waltke, Bruce K. *The Book of Proverbs*. 2 vols. New International Commentary on the Old Testament. Grand Rapids: Eerdmans, 2004.

Waltke, Bruce K., and Charles Yu. *An Old Testament Theology: An Exegetical, Canonical, and Thematic Approach*. Grand Rapids: Zondervan, 2007.

West, Ralph Douglas. "Selecting the Text for an Evangelistic Sermon." In *Preaching Evangelistically: Proclaiming the Saving Message of*

Jesus, edited by Al Fasol et al., 17–40. Nashville: Broadman & Holman, 2006.

Wiarda, Timothy. *Interpreting Gospel Narratives: Scenes, People, and Theology*. Nashville: B&H, 2010.

Wilder, Terry L., J. Daryl Charles, and Kendell Easley. *Faithful to the End: An Introduction to Hebrews through Revelation*. Nashville: B&H, 2007.

Willimon, William. "How an Audience Becomes a Congregation." In *A Voice in the Wilderness: Clear Preaching in a Complicated World*, 107–20. Sisters, OR: Multnomah, 1993.

———. "Pumping Truth to a Disinclined World." *Leadership: A Practical Journal for Church Leaders* 11, no. 2 (1990): 128–37.

———. "Transforming Word." *Word & World* 32, no. 4 (Fall 2012): 327–33.

Wilson, Jim L. *Fresh Start Devotionals, Volume 2: April–June*. North Charleston, SC: CreateSpace, 2015.

———. *How to Write Narrative Sermons*. Fresno, CA: Willow City Press, 2002.

———. *Pastoral Ministry in the Real World: Loving, Teaching, and Leading God's People*. Bellingham, WA: Lexham Press, 2018.

Wright, Stephen I. *Tales Jesus Told: An Introduction to the Narrative Parables of Jesus*. London: Paternoster, 2002.

———. *Jesus the Storyteller*. Louisville: Westminster John Knox, 2015.

Young, F. E. "Uriah." In *The Zondervan Pictorial Encyclopedia of the Bible*, edited by Merrill Tenney, 5:848–50. Grand Rapids: Zondervan, 1978.

Scripture Index

General Index

single primary, 26
single transformative, 43
transition, 159
transformational, 193
transformative, 33, 52, 56, 58, 59,
60, 63, 64, 79, 80, 92, 93, 104,
110, 145, 151, 164, 169, 197,
211, 233
turning, 157, 174, 180
polemic
white-hot, 196
politician, 47
polysemy, 20n4
pop-psychology, 52
portion, 120, 227
postscript
epistolary, 216
poverty, 146, 148
power(s), 75, 76, 77, 82, 89, 114, 124,
146, 147, 149, 150, 151, 156, 179,
203, 206, 211, 224, 228, 230, 231,
232
supernatural, 219
transformative, 58
pragmatism, 199
prayer(s), 27, 46, 47, 92, 160, 161, 168,
204, 212
answered, 212
of lament, 212
people's, 224
results of, 212
preacher(s), 19, 20, 21, 22, 23, 25,
26n28, 27, 28, 32, 33, 34, 36n4, 37,
40, 43, 44, 49, 50, 52, 53, 54, 55,
56, 57, 63, 133, 134, 135, 137, 138,
151, 158, 161, 162, 171, 175, 187,
195, 196, 197, 198, 206, 209, 210,
212, 217, 222, 223, 232
expositional, 24
expository, 22, 25, 26, 171
faithful, 196
multi-point, 132
sermonic, 32

verse-by-verse, 132
preaching, 24, 28, 32, 33, 47, 52, 53,
54, 55, 56, 58, 64, 104, 129, 144,
151, 158, 159, 169, 180, 186, 192,
195, 202, 215, 217, 232
boring, 196
proper, 144
event, 28
expositional, 197
expository, 20, 21
for information, 197
for transformation, 197
goal of, 58, 206
gospel, 58
how-to, 59
inductive sermons, 92
ministry, 214
moralistic, 58, 152
new approach, 33
propositional, 31
serial, 50
verse-by-verse, 23
predicament, 71
pre-exilic period, 97
pregnant, 105, 110
presence, 45
presentation, 209
simple gospel, 204
president
America's, 222
price, 74
pride, 37
priest(s), 156, 161, 172t, 228, 232
chief, 165
priesthood, 172t
principle(s), 38, 74, 99, 104, 136, 137,
138, 151, 180
first, 199
organizing, 97
of transcendence, 199
underlying, 199
printing press, 29, 30, 31
prison, 84, 97, 205

final, 68
heavenly worship, 227
inexpressible, 220
pivotal, 85
Schechem, 126
Scholasticism, 25
scholars, 102, 106, 154, 171, 174, 176,
178, 195, 222
contemporary, 171
Psalms, 116n7
scoffer, 124
scribes, 186
Scripture(s), 33, 48, 53, 54, 58, 90,
107, 132, 138, 151, 152, 202, 204
exposition of, 53
holy, 53
interpret, 187
passage, 41, 44
passage of, 181
sufficiency of, 52, 53
testimony, 230
whole counsel of, 136, 145
scroll, 227, 229, 231, 232
sea, 45, 70, 72, 228, 232
of indicatives, 200
Mediterranean, 71
storm-tossed, 46
seal(s), 218, 225, 227, 229, 230, 231
seven, 222, 223, 224, 229, 232
wax, 229
second coming, 214n1, 217, 220, 226
secrecy, 190
segments
geographical, 160
semantics, 54
Sennacherib, 98
sensations, 118
sense(s), 117, 136
-impressions, 114
intuitive, 135
logical, 39
macro, 31
micro, 31

multiple, 30
single, 30
visual, 30
sentences
transition, 164
sermon(s), 19, 22, 23, 24, 26, 27, 28,
31, 32, 33, 35, 39, 40, 43, 44, 48,
49, 50, 51, 52, 53, 54, 55, 56, 58,
60, 63, 64, 74, 79, 80, 81, 86, 90,
91, 92, 93, 104, 109, 110, 111, 123,
130, 131, 132, 135, 138, 143, 144,
145, 146, 151, 157, 158, 159, 160,
164, 165, 168, 169, 170, 174, 178,
181, 182, 187, 188, 193, 196, 199,
202, 211, 212, 213, 223, 227, 232,
233
body of, 79
candidates for, 223
chassis, 28
examples, 130
expositional, 194
expository, 20, 28, 32
expository one-point, 182
four-movement, 164
four-point, 36n4
goal, 36
idea-centered, 31
introduction of, 150
manuscript(s), 73, 74n10
medieval structure, 25
modern-day, multi-point, 25n23
moralistic interpretive approach,
80
multiple-point, 200
multi-point, 27, 32, 34, 35, 39, 40,
196, 201, 212, 223, 226
multi-point, topical, self-help, 124
one-point, 32, 33, 34, 40, 41, 43,
44, 49, 182, 188, 202, 213, 223,
224, 225, 227
one-point expository, 26, 33, 35n3,
73, 158, 178, 179, 198, 200,
201, 212